ESSENTIALS OF
ORGANIZATIONAL BEHAVIOR

Fourth Edition

Stephen P. Robbins

San Diego State University

Prentice Hall, Englewood Cliffs, New Jersey 07632

Library of Congress Cataloging-in-Publication Data

Robbins, Stephen P.
    Essentials of organizational behavior/Stephen P. Robbins. —4th ed.
      p.   cm.
    Includes bibliographical references and index.
    ISBN 0-13-300096-6 (paper)
    1. Organizational behavior.   I. Title.
    HD58.7.R6   1994   93–26322
    658.3—dc20   CIP

Acquisitions Editor: *Natalie Anderson*
Assistant Editor: *Lisamarie Brassini*
Production Editor: *Edith Pullman*
Interior Design: *Rosemarie Paccione*
Cover Design: *Pencil Point Studio*
Cover Illustration: *Ken Coffelt*
Manufacturing Buyer: *Herb Klein*
Electronic Page Makeup: *Christy Mahon*

 © 1994, 1992, 1988, 1984 by Prentice-Hall, Inc.
A Paramount Communications Company
Englewood Cliffs, New Jersey 07632

Printed in the United States of America
10 9 8 7 6 5 4 3 2 1

ISBN 0-13-300096-6

Prentice-Hall International (UK) Limited, *London*
Prentice-Hall of Australia Pty. Limited, *Sydney*
Prentice-Hall Canada Inc., *Toronto*
Prentice-Hall Hispanoamericana, S.A., *Mexico*
Prentice-Hall of India Private Limited, *New Delhi*
Prentice-Hall of Japan, Inc., *Tokyo*
Simon & Schuster Asia Pte. Ltd., *Singapore*
Editora Prentice-Hall do Brasil, Ltda., *Rio de Janeiro*

With thanks to my friends in
The Organizational Behavior Teaching Society

OTHER PRENTICE HALL TEXTBOOKS
BY THE SAME AUTHOR

MANAGEMENT, 4th Edition

ORGANIZATION THEORY: Structure, Design,
and Applications, 3rd Edition

ORGANIZATIONAL BEHAVIOR: Concepts,
Controversies, and Applications, 6th Edition

TRAINING IN INTERPERSONAL SKILLS: TIPS for
Managing People at Work

CONTENTS

PREFACE

Bigger isn't *always* better. Less *can* be more. A balanced textbook doesn't *have* to be 700 pages long. Welcome to the world of OB-Lite!

Essentials of Organizational Behavior is designed to provide a distinct alternative to the large selection of 700- or 800-page hardback texts available for courses in organizational behavior (OB). It is ideally suited to short courses, executive programs, and as a companion to experiential, skill development, case, or readings books. Users of past editions of this book tell me they've found it works well in all these ways.

As this book has evolved through its four editions, I have listened carefully to comments from users. I've made changes in each edition in order to fine-tune its content. My goal continues to be to capture the *essentials* of OB and leave out the less relevant topics. Some of the missing content relates to pedagogy. For instance, there are no end-of-chapter discussion questions, exercises, or cases. And though the findings in this book are based on hundreds of research studies, footnoting has been kept to a bare minimum. I footnote only the classic studies and those that support the more controversial findings. But cutting pedagogical aids and footnotes is a "no-brainer." The real challenge is choosing the proper topics and concepts, which is a lot harder than it looks. It's always easier to add material than to delete. Moreover, there is rarely unanimous agreement among users as to what should be added or cut. But we've surveyed many adopters, and many more have written me or pulled me aside at meetings to suggest ways I could improve this book. And I've responded. The result, I think, is a book that continues its tradition of reflecting a current perspective on the essential issues in organizational behavior.

So what's new in this fourth edition? I'm glad you asked! I've updated the content to reflect recent research and applications. There has been some judicious editing to streamline the presentation of many topics. Some nonessential issues have been deleted. And a number of issues have been added or significantly expanded. These include work force diversity, ethics, empowering employees, total quality management and continuous improvement, behavioral decision making, developing effective teams, sexual harassment, negotiation, computers and organization design, and stimulating innovation. And, for the first time, there's an Instructor's Manual with a Test Item File available for instructors.

Let me conclude by thanking all those who suggested improvements in this edition and, of course, all the people at Prentice Hall for continuing to support the concept of an essentials text.

Stephen P. Robbins
Del Mar, California

CHAPTER 1

INTRODUCTION TO ORGANIZATIONAL BEHAVIOR

After reading this chapter, you should be able to:

1. Define organizational behavior (OB)
2. Identify the primary behavioral disciplines contributing to OB
3. Describe the three goals of OB
4. Explain why work force diversity has become an important issue to managers

5. Describe how improving organizational competitiveness has affected employees
6. Define the bimodal work force
7. Explain how managers and organizations are responding to the problem of employee ethical dilemmas

When I ask managers to describe their most frequent or troublesome problems, the answers I get tend to exhibit a common theme. The managers most often describe *people* problems. They talk about their bosses' poor communication skills, subordinates' lack of motivation, conflicts between employees in their department, overcoming employee resistance to a departmental reorganization, and similar concerns.

Since a manager's job is inherently one of working with and through other people—bosses, peers, and subordinates—to solve these problems, good "people skills" become a valuable, even an essential, asset. This book has been written to help managers, and potential managers, develop these people skills.

■ THE FIELD OF ORGANIZATIONAL BEHAVIOR

The study of people at work is generally referred to as the study of organizational behavior. Let's begin, then, by defining the term *organizational behavior* and briefly reviewing its origins.

Definition

Organizational behavior (OB) is the systematic study of the actions and attitudes that people exhibit within organizations. Let's look at the key parts of this definition.

Each of us regularly uses intuition or our "gut feelings" in trying to explain phenomena. For instance, a friend catches a cold and we're quick to remind him that he "didn't take his vitamins," "doesn't dress properly," or that "it happens every year when the seasons change." We're not really sure why he caught cold, but that doesn't stop us from offering our intuitive analysis. The field of OB seeks to replace intuitive explanations with systematic study; that is, the use of scientific evidence gathered under controlled conditions and measured and interpreted in a reasonably rigorous manner to attribute cause and effect. The objective, of course, is to draw more accurate conclusions. So the field of OB—its theories and conclusions—is based upon a large number of systematically designed research studies.

What does OB systematically study? Actions (or behaviors) and attitudes! But not *all* actions and attitudes. Three types of behavior have proven to be important determinants of employee performance: *productivity, absenteeism,* and *turnover.* The importance of productivity is obvious. Managers are clearly concerned with the quantity and quality of output that each employee generates. But absence and turnover—particularly excessively high rates—can adversely affect this output. In terms of absence, it's hard for an employee to be productive if he or she isn't at work. In addition, high rates of employee turnover increase costs and tend to place less experienced people into jobs.

OB is also concerned with employee *job satisfaction,* which is an attitude. The reasons managers should be concerned with their employees' job satisfaction are threefold. First, there may be a link between satisfaction and productivity. Second, satisfaction appears to be negatively related to absenteeism and turnover. Finally, it can be argued that managers have a humanistic responsibility to provide their employees with jobs that are challenging, intrinsically rewarding, and satisfying.

The last part of our OB definition that needs elaboration is the term *organization.* The fields of psychology and sociology are well-known disciplines that study behavior, but they do not concentrate solely on work-related issues. OB, in contrast, is specifically concerned with work-related behavior—and *that* takes place in organizations. An organization is a formal structure of planned coordination, involving two or more people, in order to achieve a common goal. It is characterized by authority relationships and some degree of division of labor. So OB encompasses the behavior of people in such diverse organizations as manufacturing and service firms; schools; hospitals; churches; military units; charitable organizations; and local, state, and federal government agencies.

Contributing Disciplines

Organizational behavior is applied behavioral science, and as a result is built upon contributions from a number of behavioral disciplines. The predominant areas are psychology, sociology, social psychology, anthropology, and political science. As we shall learn, psychology's contributions have been mainly at the individual or micro level of analysis, while the latter disciplines have contributed to our understanding of macro concepts—group processes and organization. Exhibit 1–1 overviews the contributions made toward a distinct field of study: organizational behavior.

Psychology. Psychology is the science that seeks to measure, explain, and sometimes change the behavior of humans and other animals. Psychologists concern themselves with studying and attempting to understand *individual* behavior. Those who have contributed and continue to add to the knowledge of OB are learning theorists, personality theorists, counseling psychologists, and, most important, industrial and organizational psychologists.

Early industrial psychologists concerned themselves with problems of fatigue, boredom, and any other factor relevant to working conditions that could impede efficient work performance. More recently, their contributions have been expanded to include learning, perception, personality, individual decision making, training, leadership effectiveness, needs and motivational forces, job satisfaction, performance appraisals, attitude measurement, job design, and work stress.

Sociology. Whereas psychologists focus their attention on the individual, sociologists study the social system in which individuals fill their roles; that is, sociology studies people in relation to their fellow human beings. Sociologists have made their greatest contribution to OB through their study of group behavior in organizations, particularly formal and complex organizations. Areas within OB that have received valuable input from sociologists include group dynamics, organizational culture, formal organization theory and structure, bureaucracy, communications, status, power, and conflict.

Social Psychology. Social psychology is an area within psychology, blending concepts from both psychology and sociology. It focuses on the influence of people on one another. One of the major areas receiving considerable investigation by social psychologists has been *change*—how to implement it and how to reduce barriers to its acceptance. Additionally, we find social psychologists making significant contributions in measuring, understanding, and changing attitudes, communication patterns, the ways in which group activities can satisfy individual needs, and group decision-making processes.

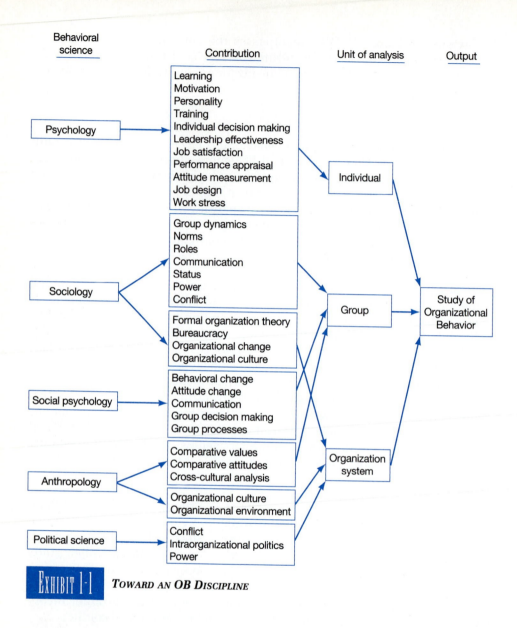

Behavioral science | **Contribution** | **Unit of analysis** | **Output**

Psychology → Learning / Motivation / Personality / Training / Individual decision making / Leadership effectiveness / Job satisfaction / Performance appraisal / Attitude measurement / Job design / Work stress

Sociology → Group dynamics / Norms / Roles / Communication / Status / Power / Conflict

Sociology → Formal organization theory / Bureaucracy / Organizational change / Organizational culture

Social psychology → Behavioral change / Attitude change / Communication / Group decision making / Group processes

Anthropology → Comparative values / Comparative attitudes / Cross-cultural analysis

Anthropology → Organizational culture / Organizational environment

Political science → Conflict / Intraorganizational politics / Power

Individual / Group / Organization system → Study of Organizational Behavior

EXHIBIT 1-1   *TOWARD AN OB DISCIPLINE*

Anthropology. Anthropologists study societies to learn about human beings and their activities. Their work on cultures and environments, for instance, has helped us to understand differences in fundamental values, attitudes, and behavior between people in different countries and within different organizations. Much of our current understanding of organizational culture, organizational environments, and differences between national cultures is the result of the work of anthropologists or those using their methods.

Political Science. Although frequently overlooked, the contributions of political scientists are significant to the understanding of behavior in organizations. Political scientists study the behavior of individuals and groups within a political environment. Specific topics of concern to political scientists include structuring conflict, allocation of power, and how people manipulate power for individual self-interest.

■ GOALS OF ORGANIZATIONAL BEHAVIOR

What does OB seek to do? We know it is concerned with developing people skills, but what precisely are its goals? The goals of OB are to help you to *explain, predict,* and *control* human behavior.

Explanation

When we seek answers to *why* an individual or a group of individuals did something, we are pursuing the explanation objective. It is probably the least important of the three goals, from a management perspective, because it occurs after the fact. Yet if we are to understand a phenomenon, we must begin by trying to explain it. We can then use this understanding to determine a connective cause. For example, if a number of valued employees resign, we undoubtedly want to know why, in order to determine if it was something that could have been prevented. Obviously, employees quit their jobs for many reasons, but if the explanation for a high quit rate is inadequate pay or boring jobs, managers often can take actions that will correct this behavior in the future.

Prediction

The goal of prediction focuses on future events. It seeks to determine what outcomes will result from a given action. When the manager of a small factory attempts to assess how employees will respond to the installation of new robotic equipment, that manager is engaging in a predictive exercise. Based on a knowledge of OB, the manager can predict certain behavioral responses to the change. Of course, there are a number of ways to implement a major change, so the manager is likely to assess employee responses to a number of change interventions. In this way, the manager can anticipate which approaches will generate the least degree of employee resistance and use that information in making his or her decision.

Control

The most controversial goal is using OB knowledge to control behavior. When a manager asks, for instance: "What can I do to make Dave put out more effort on his job?" that manager is concerned with control.

Why is control controversial? A democratic society is built upon the concept of personal freedom. Therefore, the idea that one person should attempt to get others to behave in some premeditated way, when the subjects of that control may be unaware that their behavior is being manipulated, has been viewed in some circles as unethical and/or repugnant. That OB offers technologies that facilitate the control of people is a fact. Whether these technologies should be used in organizations becomes an ethical question. However, you should be aware that the control objective is frequently seen by managers as the most valuable contribution that OB makes toward their effectiveness on the job.

■ CHALLENGES AND OPPORTUNITIES FOR OB: A MANAGERIAL PERSPECTIVE

The ability to explain, predict, and control organizational behavior has never been more important to managers. A quick look at a few of the dramatic changes now taking place in organizations supports this claim. For instance, more and more women and nonwhites are in the workplace, corporate restructuring and cost cutting are severing the bonds of loyalty that historically tied many employees to their employers, and global competition is requiring employees to become more flexible and to learn to cope with rapid change and innovation.

In short, there are currently a number of OB challenges and opportunities for managers. In this section, we briefly introduce a few of the more critical issues confronting managers for which OB offers solutions—or at least some meaningful insights toward solutions.

Responding to Globalization

Management is no longer constrained by national borders. Burger King is owned by a British firm and McDonald's sells hamburgers in Moscow. Exxon, a so-called American company, receives almost 75 percent of its revenues from sales outside the United States. Toyota makes cars in Kentucky; General Motors makes cars in Brazil; and Toyota and General Motors jointly own a plant that makes cars in California. These examples illustrate that the world has become a global market. In turn, managers have to become capable of working with people from different cultures.

Globalization affects a manager's "people skills" in at least two ways. First, you're increasingly likely to find yourself in a foreign assignment. You'll be transferred to your employer's operating division or subsidiary in another country. Once there, you'll have to manage a work force that is likely to be very different in needs, aspirations, and attitudes from the ones you were used to back home. Second, even in your own country, you're going to find yourself working with bosses, peers, and subordinates who were born and raised in different cultures. What motivates you may not motivate them. While your style of communication may be straightforward and open, they may find this style uncomfortable and threatening. This suggests that if you're going to be able to work effectively with these people, you'll need to understand their culture, how it has shaped them, and learn to adapt your management style to these differences.

Adapting to a Diversified Work Force

Globalization addresses national differences. *Work force diversity* is a broader concept that addresses gender, race, ethnicity, and other differences. Work force diversity encompasses *anyone* in an organization who varies from the "norm." In addition to the more obvious groups—women, African Americans, Hispanic Americans, Asian Americans—it also includes the physically disabled, gays and lesbians, and the elderly.

We used to take a melting pot approach to differences in organizations, assuming that people who were different would somehow automatically want to assimilate. But we now recognize that employees don't set aside their values, differences, and lifestyle preferences when they come to work. The challenge for managers, therefore, is to become more accommodating to diverse groups of people by addressing their different lifestyles, family needs, and work styles. The melting pot assumption is being replaced by one that recognizes and values differences.

Haven't organizations always included members of diverse groups? Yes, but they were such a small percentage of the work force that no one paid much attention to them. Moreover, it was assumed that these minorities would seek to blend in and assimilate. The bulk of the pre-1980s work force were male Caucasians working full time to support a nonemployed wife and school-aged children. Now such employees are the true minority! Currently, 45 percent of the U.S. labor force are women. Minorities and immigrants make up 22 percent. Moreover, new worker growth in the United States throughout the rest of the 1990s will be occurring most rapidly among women and Hispanics.

Work force diversity has important implications for management practice. Managers will need to shift their philosophy from treating everyone alike to recognizing differences and responding to those differences in ways that will ensure employee retention and greater productivity, while at the same time not discriminating. Diversity, if properly managed, can increase creativity and innovation in organizations as well as improve decision making by providing different perspectives on problems. When diversity is not managed properly, there is potential for higher turnover, more difficult communication, and more interpersonal conflicts.

Improving Competitiveness

In recent years, managers have taken a number of steps to improve their organizations' competitiveness. For instance, they have invested in automated equipment and computers, modified work processes to improve flexibility and to respond to changes more rapidly, restructured their organizations to reduce costs, and introduced total quality management programs. What you shouldn't overlook is that all of these steps to improve competitiveness directly affect the work of the people in these organizations and provide challenges for managers. We can highlight this point with just a few examples.

Automated equipment, computerization, and changes in work processes are demanding new skills from employees. They're having to learn to work with computers, read complex operating manuals, and make decisions that previously were made by their supervisors.

As organizations have restructured themselves, they have cut out unnecessary jobs and combined others. Large companies like American Express, Boeing, Eastman Kodak, General Dynamics, IBM, Sears, and U.S. West have literally each fired thousands of people. And those employees who remain are being expected to do more work. The historical loyalty bonds that existed between employees and employers have been irrevocably damaged. As companies have shown less loyalty to employees, employees are showing less commitment to their organizations. And to further undermine these bonds, organizations have increasingly turned to the use of contingent employees to fill vacancies—temporary and part-time workers who supplement an organization's permanent work force. These contingent workers have limited legal protection, receive minimal benefits, and express far less commitment to the organization than do regular permanent employees.

One of the fastest moving trends in recent years to help in the competitive battles has been the introduction of quality improvement programs, frequently called total quality management (TQM). TQM is a philosophy of management that seeks constant attainment of customer satisfaction through the continuous improvement of all organizational processes. It is a never-ending commitment to do things better. A major element of TQM is the belief that quality is increased by employee involvement, and that the primary means for increasing that involvement is through empowering employees and using teams. TQM defines new roles for both employees and managers.

Motivating the Bi-Modal Work Force

As recently as 20 years ago plenty of unskilled jobs in the steel, automobile, rubber, and similar manufacturing industries paid solid middle-class wages. A young man in Pittsburgh, for example, could graduate from high school and immediately get a relatively high-paying and secure job in a local steel plant. That job would allow him to buy a home, finance a car or two, support a family, and enjoy other lifestyle choices that come with a middle-class income. But that's ancient history. A good portion of those manufacturing jobs in first-world industrialized countries are gone—either replaced by automated equipment, reconstituted into a job requiring considerably higher technical skills, or taken by workers in other countries who will do this same work for a fraction of the wages. What's left can best be described as a *bi-modal work force*—where employees tend to either perform low-skilled service jobs for near-minimum wage or high-skilled jobs that provide the means to maintain a middle-class or upper-class lifestyle.

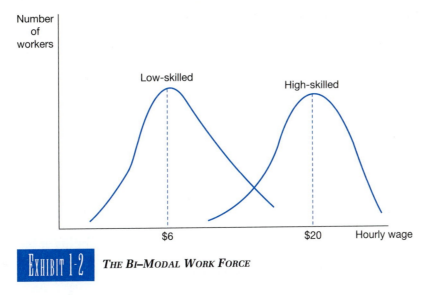

Number
of
workers

Low-skilled   High-skilled

$6 $20   Hourly wage

EXHIBIT 1-2   *THE BI–MODAL WORK FORCE*

Exhibit 1–2 illustrates this bi-modal phenomenon. It has been created by the massive decline of blue-collar manufacturing jobs that pay $25,000 to $35,000 a year in current dollars.

Most organization's employee practices were designed to keep and motivate well-paid manufacturing employees and high-paid skilled workers. They don't, however, seem to be working very well with the low-skilled, low-paid service workers in the left curve of Exhibit 1–2.

At wages of $4.50 to $7.00 an hour, today's low-skilled workers can't come close to moving into the middle class. Moreover, their promotion opportunities are limited. This leads to a major challenge for managers: How do you motivate individuals who are making very low wages and have little opportunity to significantly increase their pay either in their current jobs or through promotions? Can effective leadership fill the void? Can these employees' jobs be redesigned to make them more challenging? Should managers target these jobs for elimination? These are questions that, until 20 years ago, managers didn't have to concern themselves with.

Fostering Ethical Behavior

In an organizational world characterized by cutbacks, expectations of increasing worker productivity, and tough competition in the marketplace, it's not altogether surprising that many employees feel pressured to cut corners, break rules, and engage in other forms of questionable practices.

Employees are increasingly finding themselves facing *ethical dilemmas,* situations where they are required to define right and wrong conduct. Unfortunately, the line differentiating right from wrong has become blurred in recent years. Employees see people all around them engaging in unethical practices—elected officials indicted for padding their expense accounts or taking bribes; high-powered lawyers, who know the rules, are found to be avoiding payment of Social Security taxes for their household help; successful executives who use insider information for personal financial gain; employees in other companies participating in massive cover-ups of defective military weapons. When caught, they hear these people giving excuses like "everyone does it," or "you have to seize every advantage nowadays," or "I never thought I'd get caught!"

Managers and their organizations are responding to this problem from a number of directions. They're writing and distributing codes of ethics to guide employees through ethical dilemmas. They're offering seminars, workshops, and similar training programs to try to improve ethical behaviors. They're providing in-house advisers who can be contacted, in many cases anonymously, for assistance in dealing with ethical issues. And they're creating protection mechanisms for employees who reveal internal unethical practices.

Today's manager needs to create an ethically healthy climate for his or her employees, where they can do their work productively and confront a minimal degree of ambiguity regarding what constitutes right and wrong behaviors.

■ THE PLAN OF THIS BOOK

How is this book going to help you better explain, predict, and control behavior? Our approach uses a building-block process. As pictured in Exhibit 1–3, there are three levels of analysis in OB. As we move from the individual level through to the organization system level, we increase in an additive fashion our understanding of behavior in organizations.

Chapters 3 through 6 deal with the individual in the organization. We begin by looking at the foundations of individual behavior—attitudes, personality, perception, and learning. Then we move to motivation issues and the topic of individual decision making.

The behavior of people in groups is something more than the sum total of each individual acting in his or her own way. People's behavior in groups is different from their behavior when they are alone. Chapters 7 through 11 address group behavior. We introduce a group behavior model, discuss ways to make teams more effective, consider communication issues and group deci-

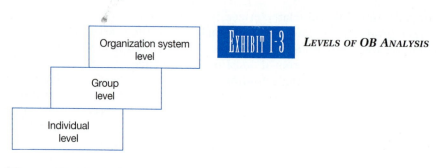

EXHIBIT 1-3   *LEVELS OF OB ANALYSIS*

Organization system level

Group level

Individual level

sion making, and then investigate the important topics of leadership, power, politics, conflict, and negotiation.

Organizational behavior reaches its highest level of sophistication when we add the formal organizational system to our knowledge of individual and group behavior. Just as groups are more than the sum of their individual members, organizations are not necessarily merely the summation of the behavior of a number of groups. In Chapters 12 through 16, we discuss how an organization's structure and design affect behavior, the effect that an organization's formal performance appraisal and reward system has on people, how each organization has its own culture that acts to mold the behavior of its members, and the various organizational change and development techniques that managers can use to affect behavior for the organization's benefit.

However, before we begin our analysis of individual behavior, we must discuss the importance of putting organizational behavior in a global context. Organizational behavior is different in different countries. What motivates employees in the United States doesn't necessarily motivate workers in Mexico or Denmark. The next chapter explores this theme.

SUGGESTIONS FOR FURTHER READING

COATES, J.F., J. JARRAT, and J.B. MAHAFFIE, *Future Work* (San Francisco: Jossey-Bass, 1990).

DUNNETTE, MARVIN D., "Blending the Science and Practice of Industrial and Organizational Psychology: Where Are We and Where Are We Going?" in M.D. Dunnette and L.M. Hough, eds., *Handbook of Industrial & Organizational Psychology,* 2nd ed., Vol. 1 (Palo Alto, CA: Consulting Psychologists Press, 1990), pp. 1–27.

JACKSON, SUSAN E., and ASSOCIATES, *Diversity in the Workplace* (New York: Guilford Press, 1992).

O'REILLY, CHARLES A., III, "Organizational Behavior: Where We've Been, Where We're Going," in M.R. Rosenzweig and L.W. Porter, eds., *Annual Review of Psychology,* Vol. 42 (Palo Alto, CA: Annual Reviews, 1991), pp. 427–58.

PETTIT, JOHN D., JR., B.C. VAUGHT, and R.L. TREWATHA, "Interpersonal Skill Training: A Prerequisite for Success," *Business,* April–June 1990, pp. 8–14.

ROBBINS, STEPHEN P., *Organizational Behavior: Concepts, Controversies, and Applications,* 6th ed. (Englewood Cliffs, NJ: Prentice Hall, 1993).

SIMS, RONALD R., "The Challenge of Ethical Behavior in Organizations," *Journal of Business Ethics,* July 1992, pp. 505–13.

WHETTEN, DAVID A., and KIM S. CAMERON, *Developing Management Skills,* 2nd ed. (New York: HarperCollins, 1991).

CHAPTER 2

ORGANIZATIONAL BEHAVIOR IN A GLOBAL CONTEXT

After reading this chapter, you should be able to:

1. Describe the reason for maquiladoras

2. Explain what NAFTA is and what countries are involved

3. Contrast American and European managers regarding parochialism

4. Identify the six cultural dimensions in the Kluckhohn-Strodtbeck framework

5. Explain the four dimensions of national culture in Hofstede's framework

For anyone who thinks all successful management practices should be transferable from one country to another, consider the case of the Walt Disney Company.

Disney has had unparalleled success with its two theme parks in California and Florida. In April 1992, they opened Euro Disneyland outside Paris. It is a near replica of the company's U.S. theme parks. After its first 18 months, the $4.1 billion project was proving a disappointment for management. Attendance was well below projections and the park had lost more than $300 million. Part of the problem is that French people are not clones of their American counterparts. For example:

- In contrast to Americans, the French have little previous exposure to theme parks. Just the idea of having to pay to merely walk inside the gate is totally alien to them.

- The French reserve one day and only one day a week—Sunday—for family outings. The notion of going out with the family on a Saturday or weekday isn't something they're used to doing.

- The French do their vacationing en masse. In August, everything closes up and everyone goes on holiday. Demand at the theme park is unlikely, therefore, to be ongoing as it is in the United States.
- The French have long had an aversion to meeting strangers. The idea of being welcomed by strangers with buoyant smiles and a lighthearted greeting is not appreciated.
- In the United States, 50 percent of Disney visitors eat fast food at the parks. Most French, however, don't snack. Should Euro Disneyland have all the eating places like the U.S. parks? If they do, will they be empty of customers?
- The French are impatient. They are not comfortable waiting in long lines. Americans seem to accept waiting 30 minutes or more for the more popular rides at Disneyland and Disney World. Will this limit attendance and be the "kiss of death" to the new park?
- The French adore their dogs. They take them everywhere—inside most French resorts and even fine restaurants. Dogs, however, have always been banned from Disney parks.
- The practice of Disney employees wearing badges with only their first names on them is fine in the United States, where informality is well accepted. Such a practice is not the French way of doing business.
- French workers don't like to obey orders. They are not likely to take kindly to management's demands that they not smoke, chew gum, or converse with their co-workers.

The French are obviously different from Americans and managing a theme park in France requires different practices than those in the United States. Unfortunately, Disney's management didn't fully consider all these differences.

This Euro Disneyland example is meant to illustrate a problem that managers are increasingly likely to face as we approach the twenty-first century: What changes, if any, do you need to make in your management style when managing in a different country?

■ WELCOME TO THE GLOBAL VILLAGE

A number of respected observers of world affairs have been arguing for more than a decade that the world has become a global village. Transportation and communication capabilities—for example, supersonic jets, international telephone and computer networks, and worldwide news broadcast via satellites—make it easier to talk with or visit people on other continents than it was for our ancestors of a century ago to do the same with friends in a neighboring village. Distance and national borders are rapidly disappearing as major barriers to business transactions.

The global village theme can be demonstrated by looking at the growing impact of multinational corporations and the rise of regional cooperative arrangements between countries.

Multinational Corporations

Most of the firms currently listed in the *Fortune* 500 are multinational corporations. They are companies that maintain significant operations in two or more countries simultaneously.

While international businesses have been around for centuries, multinationals are a relatively recent phenomenon. They are a natural outcome of a global economy. For instance, Ford focuses on building a "world car"—a standardized vehicle that can be manufactured and sold around the globe. And these multinationals use their worldwide operations to develop global strategies. Rather than confining themselves to their domestic borders, they are scanning the world for competitive advantages. The result? Manufacturing, assembly, sales, and other functions are being strategically located to give firms advantages in the marketplace. A photocopying machine, for instance, might be designed in Toronto, have its microprocessing chips made in Taiwan, its physical case manufactured in Japan, both shipped to South Korea for assembly, then sold out of warehouses located in Melbourne, London, and Los Angeles.

Managers of multinationals confront a wealth of challenges. They face diverse political systems, laws, and customs. But these differences create both problems and opportunities. It's obviously more difficult to manage an operation that spans 15,000 miles and whose employees speak five different languages than one located under a single roof where a common language is spoken. Differences create opportunities and that has been the primary motivation for corporations to expand their worldwide operations.

The European Community

The year 1993 marked the creation of a United States of Europe. There are 335 million people in the 12 nations making up the European Community—France, Denmark, Belgium, Greece, Ireland, Italy, Luxembourg, Portugal, Spain, the Netherlands, the United Kingdom, and Germany. Separated by borders, they used to have border controls, border taxes, border subsidies, nationalistic policies, and protected industries. Now they are a single market. Gone are national barriers to travel, employment, investment, and trade. They are moving toward a free flow of money, workers, goods, and services. A driver hauling cargo from Amsterdam to Lisbon can now clear four border crossings and five countries by showing a single piece of paper. In 1991, that same driver needed about two pounds of documents.

The primary motivation for these 12 nations to unite was to reassert their position against the industrial might of the United States and Japan. As separate countries, creating barriers against one another, European industries were unable to develop the economies of scale enjoyed by the United States and Japan. The new European Community, however, allows European firms to tap into what is now the world's single richest market. This reduction in trade barriers also encourages non-Western European companies to invest in these countries to take advantage of new opportunities. Finally, European multinationals now have new clout in attacking U.S., Japanese, and other worldwide markets.

Maquiladoras

Maquiladoras are domestic Mexican firms that manufacture or assemble products for a company of another nation which are then sent back to the foreign company for sale and distribution. The key to maquiladoras is that they allow non-Mexican firms to take advantage of Mexico's low labor costs with minimal trade restrictions. More than 2,400 foreign companies—including General Motors, General Electric, Zenith, Honeywell, Hitachi, and Sanyo—are currently doing business with maquiladoras along the Mexican side of the border from Texas to California.

The maquiladoras concept was devised by the Mexican and U.S. governments in 1965 to help develop both sides of the impoverished border region. But it was the massive devaluation of the peso, which occurred in 1982, that initiated a virtual explosion of maquiladoras. Since 1982, the number of these plants has nearly tripled. They're in Cuidad Juaréz, Nogales, Tijuana, Mexicali, and similar northern Mexican cities. One estimate indicates that these cross-border plants could employ as many as 3 million workers by the year 2000.

Mexican wages are now equal to, or even less, than many countries in Asia. With a Mexican minimum wage of around 40 cents an hour, at current exchange rates, companies producing for North American markets no longer have to go to the Far East to find low-cost labor.

NAFTA

Maquiladoras may become obsolete if the United States, Mexico, and Canada finally approve the North American Free Trade Agreement (NAFTA). This agreement builds on the recent signing of the U.S.-Canadian Free Trade Agreement that phased out tariffs on most goods trading between the United States and Canada.

Whether NAFTA will become a reality any time soon is anyone's guess. American opponents, for instance, have expressed concern over issues such as the environmental impact of increased manufacturing on the U.S. border with Mexico and the potential shifting of American jobs to Mexico. Nevertheless, the economic interdependence of the United States, Canada, and Mexico is a reality, and it is only a matter of time until an alliance along the lines of NAFTA is approved by all three countries.

The New Eastern Europe

The Cold War is over, communism is on the retreat, and capitalism is spreading throughout the world. In the last several years, Germany has been reunited, countries like Poland and Romania have introduced democratic governments, and the former Soviet Union has become a set of independent states trying to implement market-based reforms.

In terms of the changing global environment, the spread of capitalism makes the world a smaller place. Business has new markets to conquer. Additionally, well-trained and reliable workers in countries like Hungary and Czechoslovakia provide a rich source of low-cost labor. The implementation of free markets in Eastern Europe further underscores the growing interdependence between countries of the world and the potential for goods, labor, and capital to easily move across national borders.

■ CONFRONTING PAROCHIALISM

A global economy presents challenges to managers that they never had to confront when their operations were constrained within national borders. They face different legal and political systems. They confront different economic climates and tax policies. But they also must deal with varying national cultures—the primary values and practices that characterize particular countries—many of which are nothing like the one where they have spent their entire life.

The major dilemma for American managers is that, in contrast to their European counterparts, many suffer from parochialism. That is, they view the world solely through their own eyes and perspective. People with a parochial perspective do not recognize that other people have different ways of living and working. We see this most explicitly in Americans' knowledge of foreign languages. While it is not uncommon for Europeans to speak three or four languages, Americans are almost entirely monolingual. The reasons probably reflect the huge domestic market in the United States, the geographical separation of the United States from Europe and Asia, and the reality that English has become the international business language in many parts of the world.

To add insult to injury, Americans also frequently believe their cultural values and customs are superior to all others. This may also explain why Americans don't learn foreign languages. Many think their language is superior and that it's the rest of the world's responsibility to learn English.

There's no shortage of stories illustrating the problems created when American managers failed to understand cultural differences. Consider the following examples:[1]

A U.S. manager recently transferred to Saudi Arabia successfully obtained a million-dollar contract from a Saudi manufacturer. The manufacturer's representative had arrived at the meeting several hours late, but the U.S. executive considered it unimportant. The American was certainly surprised and frustrated to learn later that the Saudi had no intention of honoring the contract. He had signed it only to be polite after showing up late for the appointment.

---

[1] D. A. Ricks, M. Y. C. Fu, and J. S. Arpas, *International Business Blunders* (Columbus, OH: Grid, 1974); and Charles F. Valentine, "Blunders Abroad," *Nation's Business* (March 1989), p. 54.

A U.S. executive operating in Peru was viewed by Peruvian managers as cold and unworthy of trust because, in face-to-face discussions, the American kept backing up. He did not understand that in Peru the custom is to stand quite close to the person with whom you are speaking.

A U.S. manager in Japan offended a high-ranking Japanese executive by failing to give him the respect his position deserved. The manager was introduced to the Japanese executive in the latter's office. The American assumed that the executive was a low-level manager and paid him little attention because of the small and sparsely furnished office he occupied. The American didn't realize that the offices of top Japanese executives do not flaunt the status symbols their American counterparts do.

■ ASSESSING DIFFERENCES BETWEEN COUNTRIES

American children are taught early the values of individuality and uniqueness. In contrast, Japanese children are indoctrinated to be "team players," to work within the group, and to conform. A significant part of an American student's education is to learn to think, analyze, and question. Their Japanese counterparts are rewarded for recounting facts. These different socialization practices reflect different cultures and, not surprisingly, result in different types of employees. The average U.S. worker is more competitive and self-focused than the Japanese worker. Predictions of employee behavior, based on samples of U.S. workers, are likely to be off target when they are applied to a population of employees—like the Japanese—who prefer and perform better in standardized tasks, as part of a work team, with group-based decisions and rewards.

It's relatively easy to learn about the Japanese culture. Dozens of books and hundreds of articles have been written on the subject. But how do you gain an understanding of Venezuela's or Denmark's national cultures? A popular notion is to talk with people from those countries. Evidence suggests, however, that this rarely works because people born and raised in a country are preprogrammed in the ways of its culture by the time they're adults. They understand how things are done and can work comfortably within their country's unwritten norms, but they *can't* explain their culture to someone else. It is pervasive, but it is hidden. Most people are unaware of just how their culture has shaped them. Culture is like water to fish. It's there all the time but the fish are oblivious to it. So one of the frustrations of moving into a different culture is that the "natives" are often the least capable of explaining its unique characteristics to an outsider.

Although foreign cultures are difficult to fathom from what the "natives" tell you, there is an expanding body of research that can tell us how cultures vary and key differences between, say, the United States and Italy. Let's look at the two best known of these research frameworks.

The Kluckhohn-Strodtbeck Framework

One of the most widely referenced approaches for analyzing variations among cultures is the Kluckhohn-Strodtbeck framework.[2] It identifies six basic cultural dimensions: relationship to the environment, time orientation, nature of people, activity orientation, focus of responsibility, and conception of space.

Relationship to the Environment. Are people *subjugated* to their environment, in *harmony* with it, or able to *dominate* it? In many Middle Eastern countries, people see life as essentially preordained. When things happen, they tend to see it as "God's will." In contrast, Americans and Canadians believe they can control nature. They're willing to spend billions of dollars each year on cancer research, for instance, because they think that cancer's cause can be identified, a cure found, and the disease can eventually be eradicated.

In between these two extreme positions is a more moderate view. This one seeks harmony with nature. In many Far Eastern countries, the way to deal with the environment is to work around it.

You should expect these different perspectives toward the environment to influence organizational practices. Take the setting of goals as an example. In a subjugation society, goal setting is not likely to be very popular. Why set goals if you believe people can't do much toward achieving them? In a harmony society, goals are likely to be used but deviations are expected and penalties for failing to reach the goals are likely to be minimal. In a domination society, goals are widely applied. People are expected to achieve their goals and the penalties for failure tend to be quite high.

Time Orientation. Does the culture focus on the *past, present,* or *future?* Societies differ on the value placed on time. For instance, Western cultures perceive time as a scarce resource. "Time is money" and must be used efficiently. Americans focus on the present and the near future. You see evidence of this in the short-term orientation in performance appraisals. In the typical North American organization, people are evaluated every six months or a year. The Japanese, in contrast, take a longer-term view and this is reflected in their performance appraisal methods. Japanese workers are often given ten years or more to prove their worth.

Some cultures have still another approach to time: They focus on the past. Italians, for instance, follow traditions and seek to preserve historical practices.

Knowledge of a culture's time orientation can provide you with insights into the importance of deadlines, whether long-term planning is widely practiced, the length of job assignments, or what constitutes lateness. It can explain, for example, the fascination Americans have with making and keeping appointments.

---

[2] Florence Kluckhohn and F. L. Strodtbeck, *Variations in Value Orientations* (Evanston, IL: Row, Peterson, 1961).

Nature of People. Does a culture view people as *good, evil,* or some *mix* of these two? In many Third World countries, people see themselves as basically honest and trustworthy. North Korea, on the other hand, takes a rather evil view of human nature. North Americans tend to be somewhere in between. They see people as basically good but stay on guard so as not to be taken advantage of.

You can readily see how a culture's view on the nature of people might influence the dominant leadership style of managers in a given society. A more autocratic style is likely to rule in countries that focus on the evil aspects of people. Participation or even a laissez-faire style should appeal to countries that emphasize trusting values. In mixed cultures, leadership is likely to emphasize participation but provide close controls that can quickly identify deviations.

Activity Orientation. Some cultures emphasize *doing* or action. They stress accomplishments. Some cultures emphasize *being* or living for the moment. These cultures stress experiencing life and seeking immediate gratification of desires. Still other cultures focus on *controlling,* where people restrain their desires by detaching themselves from objects.

North Americans live in doing-oriented societies. They work hard and expect to be rewarded with promotions, raises, and other forms of recognition for their accomplishments. Mexico, in contrast, is being-oriented. The afternoon siesta is consistent with a slower pace and enjoying the moment. The French represent a controlling orientation. The emphasis is on rationality and logic.

An understanding of a culture's activity orientation can give you insights into how people approach work and leisure, how they make decisions, or the criteria they use for allocating rewards. For instance, in cultures with a dominant being orientation, decisions are likely to be emotional. In contrast, doing and controlling cultures are likely to emphasize pragmatism and rationality in decision making, respectively.

Focus of Responsibility. Cultures can be classified according to where responsibility lies for the welfare of others. Americans, for instance, are highly *individualistic.* They use personal characteristics and achievements to define themselves. They believe a person's responsibility is to take care of himself or herself. Countries like Malaysia and Israel focus more on the *group.* In an Israeli kibbutz, for example, people share chores and rewards. Emphasis is on group harmony, unity, and loyalty. The British and French follow another orientation by relying on *hierarchical* relationships. Groups in these countries are hierarchically ranked and a group's position remains essentially stable over time. Hierarchical societies tend to be aristocratic.

This dimension of culture has implications for the design of jobs, approaches to decision making, communication patterns, reward systems, and selection practices in organizations. For instance, selection in individualistic societies emphasizes personal accomplishments. In group societies, working

VALUE DIMENSION	VARIATIONS		
Relationship to the environment	Domination	Harmony	Subjugation
Time orientation	Past	Present	Future
Nature of people	Good	Mixed	Evil
Activity orientation	Being	Controlling	Doing
Focus of responsibility	Individualistic	Group	Hierarchical
Conception of space	Private	Mixed	Public

EXHIBIT 2-1 *VARIATIONS IN KLUCKHOHN-STRODTBECK'S VALUE DIMENSIONS*

well with others is likely to be of primary importance. In hierarchical societies, selection decisions are made on the basis of a candidate's social ranking.

Conception of Space. The final dimension in the Kluckhohn-Strodtbeck framework relates to ownership of space. Some cultures are very open and conduct business in *public.* At the other extreme are cultures that place a great deal of emphasis on keeping things *private.* Many societies *mix* the two and fall somewhere in between.

Japanese organizations reflect the public nature of their society. There are, for instance, few private offices. Managers and operative employees work in the same room and no partitions separate the desks. North American firms also reflect their cultural values. They use offices and privacy to reflect status. Important meetings are held behind closed doors. Space is frequently given over for the exclusive use of specific individuals. In societies that have a mixed orientation, there is a blend of the private and public. For instance, there might be a large office where walls are only 5 or 6 feet high, thus creating "limited privacy." These differences in the conception of space have obvious implications for organizational concerns such as job design and communication.

Summary. Exhibit 2–1 summarizes the six cultural dimensions in the Kluckhohn-Strodtbeck framework and the possible variations for each. As a point of reference, the jagged line in the exhibit identifies where the United States tends to fall along these dimensions.

The Hofstede Framework

A more comprehensive analysis of cultural diversity has been done by Geert Hofstede.[3] In contrast to most of the previous organizational studies, which

---

[3] Geert Hofstede, *Culture's Consequences: International Differences in Work-Related Values* (Beverly Hills, CA: Sage, 1980); and Geert Hofstede, "The Cultural Relativity of Organizational Practices and Theories," *Journal of International Business Studies* (Fall 1983), pp. 75–89.

either included a limited number of countries or analyzed different companies in different countries, Hofstede surveyed over 116,000 employees in 40 countries who all worked for a single multinational corporation. This data base eliminated any differences that might be attributable to varying practices and policies in different companies. So any variations that he found between countries could reliably be attributed to national culture.

What did Hofstede find? His huge data base confirmed that national culture had a major impact on employees' work-related values and attitudes. In fact, it explained more of the differences than did age, sex, profession, or position in the organization. More important, Hofstede found that managers and employees vary on four dimensions of national culture: (1) individualism versus collectivism; (2) power distance; (3) uncertainty avoidance; and (4) masculinity versus femininity.

Individualism versus Collectivism. *Individualism* refers to a loosely knit social framework in which people are supposed to look after their own interests and those of their immediate family. This is made possible because of the large amount of freedom that such a society allows individuals. Its opposite is *collectivism,* which is characterized by a tight social framework where people expect others in groups of which they are a part (such as an organization) to look after them and protect them when they are in trouble. In exchange for this, they feel they owe absolute loyalty to the group.

Hofstede found that the degree of individualism in a country is closely related to that country's wealth. Rich countries like the United States, Great Britain, and the Netherlands are very individualistic. Poor countries like Colombia and Pakistan are very collectivist.

Power Distance. People naturally vary in terms of physical and intellectual abilities. This, in turn, creates differences in wealth and power. How does a society deal with these inequalities? Hofstede used the term *power distance* as a measure of the extent to which a society accepts the fact that power in institutions and organizations is distributed unequally. A high power distance society accepts wide differences in power in organizations. Employees show a great deal of respect for those in authority. Titles, rank, and status carry a lot of weight. When negotiating in high power distance countries, companies find it helps to send representatives with titles at least as high as those with whom they're bargaining. Countries high in power distance include the Philippines, Venezuela, and India. In contrast, a low power distance society plays down inequalities as much as possible. Superiors still have authority, but employees are not fearful or in awe of the boss. Denmark, Israel, and Austria are examples of countries with low power distance scores.

Uncertainty Avoidance. We live in a world of uncertainty. The future is largely unknown and always will be. Societies respond to this uncertainty in different ways. Some socialize their members into accepting it with equanimity. People in such societies are more or less comfortable with risks. They're also relatively tolerant of behavior and opinions that differ from their own because they don't feel threatened by them. Hofstede describes such societies as having low *uncertainty avoidance.* That is, people feel relatively secure. Countries that fall into this category include Singapore and Denmark.

A society high in uncertainty avoidance is characterized by an increased level of anxiety among its people, which manifests itself in greater nervousness, stress, and aggressiveness. Because people feel threatened by uncertainty and ambiguity in these societies, mechanisms are created to provide security and reduce risk. Their organizations are likely to have more formal rules, there will be less tolerance for deviant ideas and behaviors, and members will strive to believe in absolute truths. Not surprisingly, in organizations in countries with high uncertainty avoidance, employees demonstrate relatively low job mobility, and lifetime employment is a widely practiced policy. Countries in this category include Japan, Portugal, and Greece.

Masculinity versus Femininity. The fourth dimension, like individualism and collectivism, represents a dichotomy. Hofstede called it *masculinity* versus *femininity.* Though his choice of terms is unfortunate (as you'll see, he gives them a strong sexist connotation), to maintain the integrity of his work we'll use his labels.

According to Hofstede, some societies allow both men and women to take many different roles. Others insist that people behave according to rigid sex roles. When societies make a sharp division between male and female activities, Hofstede claims "the distribution is always such that men take more assertive and dominant roles and women the more service-oriented and caring roles."[4] Under the category masculinity he puts societies that emphasize assertiveness and the acquisition of money and material things, while deemphasizing caring for others. In contrast, under the category femininity he puts societies that emphasize relationships, concern for others, and the overall quality of life. Where femininity dominates, members put human relationships before money and are concerned with the quality of life, preserving the environment, and helping others.

Hofstede found Japan to be the most masculine country. In Japan, almost all women are expected to stay home and take care of children. At the other extreme, he found the Nordic countries and the Netherlands to be the most feminine. There it's common to see men staying home as househusbands while their wives work; and working men are offered paternity leave to take care of newborn children.

The United States and Other Countries on Hofstede's Dimensions. Comparing the 40 countries on the four dimensions, Hofstede found U.S. culture to rank as follows:

- Individualism/collectivism = Highest among all countries on individualism
- Power distance = Below average

---

4 Geert Hofstede, "The Cultural Relativity of Organizational Practices and Theories," p. 85.

EXHIBIT 2-2   EXAMPLES OF HOFSTEDE'S CULTURAL DIMENSIONS

Country	Individualism/ Collectivism	Power Distance	Uncertainty Avoidance	Masculinity/ Femininity*
Australia	Individual	Small	Moderate	Strong Masculinity
Canada	Individual	Moderate	Low	Moderate
England	Individual	Small	Moderate	Strong
France	Individual	Large	High	Weak
Greece	Collective	Large	High	Moderate
Italy	Individual	Moderate	High	Strong
Japan	Collective	Moderate	High	Strong
Mexico	Collective	Large	High	Strong
Singapore	Collective	Large	Low	Moderate
Sweden	Individual	Small	Low	Weak
United States	Individual	Small	Low	Strong
Venezuela	Collective	Large	High	Strong

*A weak masculinity score is equivalent to high femininity.
Source: Based on G. Hofstede, Cultures and Organizations: Software of the Mind (London: McGraw-Hill, 1991), pp. 23-138.

- Uncertainty avoidance = Well below average
- Masculinity/femininity = Well above average on masculinity

The results are not inconsistent with the world image of the United States. The below-average score on power distance aligns with what one might expect from a representative type of government with democratic ideals. In this category, the United States would rate below nations with a small ruling class and a large, powerless set of subjects, and above those nations with very strong commitments to egalitarian values. The well-below-average ranking on uncertainty avoidance is also consistent with a representative type of government having democratic ideals. Americans perceive themselves as being relatively free from threats of uncertainty. The individualistic ethic is one of the most frequently used stereotypes to describe Americans, and, based on Hofstede's research, the stereotype seems well founded. The United States was ranked as the single most individualistic country in his entire set. Finally, the well-above-average score on masculinity is no surprise. Capitalism—which values aggressiveness and materialism—is consistent with Hofstede's masculine characteristics.

We haven't the space to review the results Hofstede obtained for each of the 40 countries, although a dozen examples are presented in Exhibit 2–2. Since our concern is essentially with identifying similarities and differences among cultures, let's briefly identify those countries that are most like and least like the United States on the four dimensions.

The United States is strongly individualistic but low on power distance. This same pattern was exhibited by Great Britain, Australia, Canada, the Netherlands, and New Zealand. Those least similar to the United States on these dimensions were Venezuela, Colombia, Pakistan, Singapore, and the Philippines.

The United States scored low on uncertainty avoidance and high on masculinity. The same pattern was shown by Ireland, Great Britain, the Philippines, Canada, New Zealand, Australia, India, and South Africa. Those least similar to the United States on these dimensions were Chile, Yugoslavia, and Portugal.

■ KEEPING OB IN A GLOBAL CONTEXT

Most of the concepts that currently make up the body of knowledge we call *organizational behavior* have been developed by Americans, using American subjects, within domestic contexts. A comprehensive study, for instance, of more than 11,000 articles published in 24 management and organizational behavior journals over a ten-year period revealed that approximately 80 percent of the studies were of the United States and had been conducted by Americans.[5] What this means is that not all the concepts you'll read about in future chapters may be universally applicable to managing people around the world.

As you review concepts in this book, ask yourself: *Is this concept culture bound?* If it was developed and tested in the United States, for instance, do you think it is generalizable to Mexico, or France, or India? If not, *why?*

The more that a country's culture deviates from that of the United States—as depicted by the jagged line in Exhibit 2–1 or the ratings of the United States on Hofstede's four cultural dimensions—the more you need to consider how cultural differences might modify the application of OB concepts.

■ IMPLICATIONS FOR MANAGERS

The findings and conclusions presented in this book are, for the most part, based on research studies conducted in the United States. As long as managers are concerned with trying to understand the behavior of employees born

---

[5] Nancy J. Adler, "Cross-Cultural Management Research: The Ostrich and the Trend," *Academy of Management Review* (April 1983), pp. 226–32. These findings have also been confirmed in Lynn Godkin, C. E. Braye and C.L. Caunch, "U.S.-Based Cross Cultural Management Research in the Eighties," *Journal of Business and Economic Perspectives* (Fall 1989), pp. 37–45; and T.K. Peng, M. F. Peterson, and Y.P. Shyi, "Quantitative Methods in Cross-National Management Research: Trends and Equivalence Issues," *Journal of Organizational Behavior* (Vol. 12, No. 2, 1991), pp. 87–107.

and raised in the United States or in countries with similar cultural values, such as Canada, Great Britain, or Australia, they should find it unnecessary to consider national culture as a confounding variable. It's not that national culture doesn't affect these employees; it's just that the concepts we discuss in this text already reflect this influence.

An understanding of differences between cultures should be particularly valuable for managers who were born and raised in non-Anglo-American countries, those who plan on living and working in another country, or who manage people whose cultural backgrounds are different from his or her own.

As a manager, if you fall into one of these groups, how should you use the information provided in this chapter? First, determine from what country the person comes whose behavior you are trying to understand. Second, evaluate the country of that person's origin using one or both of the cultural differences frameworks presented in this chapter. Third, compare the national culture in question against the data for the United States and identify relevant differences. This is necessary because this text's frame of reference is essentially the United States. Finally, modify the application of concepts to reflect these differences.

SUGGESTIONS FOR FURTHER READING

ADLER, NANCY J., *International Dimensions of Organizational Behavior,* 2nd ed. (Boston: PWS-Kent, 1991).

AXTELL, ROGER E., *Do's and Taboos Around the World* (New York: Wiley, 1990).

CAUDRON, SHARI, "Surviving Cross-Cultural Shock," *Industry Week,* July 6, 1992, pp. 35–38.

HALL, EDWARD T., and MILDRED REED HALL, *Understanding Cultural Differences* (New York: Intercultural Press, 1989).

HARRIS, P.R., and R.T. MORAN, *Managing Cultural Differences,* 3rd ed. (Houston: Gulf, 1991).

HOFSTEDE, GEERT, "Cultural Constraints in Management Theories," *Academy of Management Executive,* February 1993, pp. 81–94.

HOFSTEDE, GEERT, *Cultures and Organizations: Software of the Mind* (London: McGraw-Hill, 1991).

JOHNSTON, W.B., "Global Work Force 2000: The New World Labor Market," *Harvard Business Review,* March–April 1991, pp. 115–27.

CHAPTER 3

FOUNDATIONS OF INDIVIDUAL BEHAVIOR

After reading this chapter, you should be able to:

1. Explain the theory of cognitive dissonance
2. Describe the moderating factors that lessen the tension to reduce dissonance
3. Summarize the relationship between attitudes and behavior
4. List and define five personality attributes that are relevant to behavior in organizations
5. Describe the impact of job typology on the personality-job performance relationship
6. Explain how two people can see the same thing and interpret it differently
7. Summarize attribution theory
8. Outline the learning process

An understanding of individual behavior begins with a review of the major psychological contributions to OB. These contributions are subdivided into the following four concepts: attitudes, personality, perception, and learning.

■ ATTITUDES

Attitudes are evaluative statements—either favorable or unfavorable—concerning objects, people, or events. They reflect how one feels about something. When I say "I like my job," I am expressing my attitude about work.

A person can have thousands of attitudes, but OB focuses on a very limited number of job-related attitudes. These include job satisfaction, job involvement (the degree to which a person identifies with his or her job and actively participates in it), and organizational commitment (an indicator of loyalty to, and identification with, the organization). Without question, however, job satisfaction has received the bulk of attention.

Job satisfaction refers to an individual's general attitude toward his or her job. A person with a high level of job satisfaction holds positive attitudes toward the job; a person who is dissatisfied with his or her job holds negative attitudes about the job. When people speak of employee attitudes, more often than not they mean job satisfaction. In fact, the two terms are frequently used interchangeably.

People Seek to Reduce Dissonance

One of the most relevant findings pertaining to attitudes is the fact that individuals seek consistency. The theory of *cognitive dissonance* suggests that people seek to minimize dissonance.[1] Individuals attempt to reduce dissonance and hence the discomfort that occurs when there are inconsistencies between two or more of their attitudes, or between their behavior and their attitudes.

Of course, no individual can avoid dissonance completely. You know "honesty is the best policy" but say nothing when a store clerk gives you back too much change. Or you tell your children to brush after every meal, but *you* don't. So how do people cope? A person's desire to reduce dissonance is determined by the importance of the elements creating the dissonance, the degree of influence the individual believes he or she has over the elements, and the rewards that may be involved in dissonance.

If the elements creating the dissonance are relatively unimportant, the pressure to correct this imbalance will be low. However, say a corporate manager—Mrs. Smith, who has a husband and several children—believes strongly that no company should pollute the air or water. Unfortunately, because of the requirements of her job, Mrs. Smith is placed in the position of having to make decisions that would trade off her company's profitability against her attitudes on pollution. She knows that dumping the company's sewage into the local river (which we shall assume is legal) is in the best economic interest of her firm. What will she do? Clearly, Mrs. Smith is experiencing a high degree of cognitive dissonance. Because of the importance of the elements in this example, we cannot expect Mrs. Smith to ignore the inconsistency. There are several paths that she can follow to deal with her dilemma. She can change her behavior (stop polluting the river). Or she can reduce dissonance by concluding that the dissonant behavior is not so important after all ("I've got to make a living and, in my role as a corporate decision maker, I often have to place the good of my company above that of the environment or society"). A third alternative would be for Mrs. Smith to change her attitude ("There is nothing wrong in polluting the river"). Still another choice would be to seek out more consonant elements to outweigh the dissonant ones ("The

---

[1] Leon Festinger, *A Theory of Cognitive Dissonance* (Stanford, CA: Stanford University Press, 1957).

benefits to society from manufacturing our products more than offset the cost to society of the resulting water pollution").

The degree of influence that individuals believe they have over the elements will have an impact on how they will react to the dissonance. If they perceive the dissonance to be an uncontrollable result—something over which they have no choice—they are less likely to be receptive to attitude change. If, for example, the dissonance-producing behavior was required as a result of the boss's directive, the pressure to reduce dissonance would be less than if the behavior was performed voluntarily. Although dissonance exists, it can be rationalized and justified.

Rewards also influence the degree to which individuals are motivated to reduce dissonance. The tension inherent in high dissonance may be reduced when accompanied by a high reward. The reward acts to reduce dissonance by increasing the consistency side of the individual's balance sheet. Since people in organizations are given some form of reward or remuneration for their services, employees often can deal with greater dissonance on their jobs than off their jobs.

These moderating factors suggest that just because individuals experience dissonance, they will not necessarily move directly toward consistency, that is, toward reduction of this dissonance. If the issues underlying the dissonance are of minimal importance, if an individual perceives that the dissonance is externally imposed and is substantially uncontrollable by him or her, or if rewards are significant enough to offset the dissonance, the individual will not be under great tension to reduce the dissonance.

What are the organizational implications of the theory of cognitive dissonance? It can help to predict the propensity to engage in both attitude and behavioral change. For example, if individuals are required, by the demands of their job, to say or to do things that contradict their personal attitude, they will tend to modify their attitude in order to make it compatible with the cognition of what they have said or done. Additionally, the greater the dissonance—after it has been moderated by importance, choice, and reward factors—the greater the pressures to reduce the dissonance.

The Attitude-Behavior Relationship

The early research on the relationship between attitudes and behavior assumed them to be causally related; that is, the attitudes people hold determine what they do. Common sense, too, suggests a relationship. Isn't it logical that people watch television programs they say they like or that employees try to avoid assignments they find distasteful?

However, in the late 1960s, this assumed relationship between attitudes and behavior (A-B) was challenged by a review of the research.[2] Based on an evaluation of a number of studies which investigated the A-B relationship, the reviewer concluded that attitudes were unrelated to behavior or, at best,

---

[2] A. W. Wicker, "Attitude versus Action: The Relationship of Verbal and Overt Behavioral Responses to Attitude Objects," *Journal of Social Issues* (Autumn 1969), pp. 41–78.

only slightly related. More recent research has demonstrated that there is indeed a measurable relationship if moderating contingency variables are taken into consideration.

One thing that improves our chances of finding significant A-B relationships is the use of both specific attitudes and specific behaviors. It is one thing to talk about a person's attitude toward "being socially responsible" and another to speak of her attitude toward "donating $25 to the National Multiple Sclerosis Society." The more specific the attitude we are measuring and the more specific we are in identifying a related behavior, the greater the probability that we can show a relationship between A and B.

Another moderator is social constraints on behavior. Discrepancies between attitudes and behavior may occur because the social pressures on the individual to behave in a certain way may hold exceptional power. Group pressures, for instance, may explain why an employee who holds strong anti-union attitudes attends pro-union organizing meetings.

Of course, A and B may be at odds for other reasons. Individuals can and do hold contradictory attitudes at a given time, though, as we have noted, there are pressures toward consistency. Additionally, other things besides attitudes influence behavior. But it is fair to say that, in spite of some attacks, most A-B studies yield positive results—in other words, attitudes *do* influence behavior.

■ PERSONALITY

Some people are quiet and passive; others are loud and aggressive. When we describe people in terms of characteristics such as quiet, passive, loud, aggressive, ambitious, loyal, or sociable, we are categorizing them in terms of personality traits. An individual's *personality,* therefore, is the combination of psychological traits we use to classify that person.

Psychologists have studied personality traits extensively, resulting in the identification of 16 primary personality traits.[3] They are shown in Exhibit 3–1. Notice that each trait is bipolar; that is, each has two extremes (e.g., reserved-outgoing). These 16 traits have been found to be generally steady and constant sources of behavior, allowing prediction of an individual's behavior in specific situations by weighing the characteristics for their situational relevance. Unfortunately, the relevance of these traits for understanding behavior in organizations is far from clear.

Key Personality Attributes

Five personality attributes have been identified that appear to have more direct relevance for explaining and predicting behavior in organizations. These are: locus of control, authoritarianism, Machiavellianism, self-monitoring, and risk propensity.

---

3 Raymond B. Cattell, "Personality Pinned Down," *Psychology Today* (July 1973), pp. 40–46.

1. Reserved.............................Outgoing
2. Less intelligent..................More intelligent
3. Affected by feelings..........Emotionally stable
4. Submissive........................Dominant
5. Serious..............................Happy-go-lucky
6. Expedient..........................Conscientious
7. Timid.................................Venturesome
8. Tough-minded...................Sensitive
9. Trusting.............................Suspicious
10. Practical............................Imaginative
11. Forthright..........................Shrewd
12. Self-assured.......................Apprehensive
13. Conservative......................Experimenting
14. Group-dependent..............Self-sufficient
15. Uncontrolled......................Controlled
16. Relaxed..............................Tense

 16 PRIMARY TRAITS

Some people believe they are masters of their own fate. Other people see themselves as pawns of fate, believing that what happens to them in their lives is due to luck or chance. *Locus of control* in the first case is internal; these people believe they control their destiny. Those who see their life controlled by outsiders are externals. The evidence shows that employees who rate high in externality are less satisfied with their jobs, more alienated from the work setting, and less involved in their jobs than are internals. A manager might also expect to find that externals blame a poor performance evaluation on their boss's prejudice, their co-workers, or other events outside their control. Internals would probably explain the same evaluation in terms of their own actions.

Authoritarianism is the belief that there should be status and power differences among people in organizations. The extremely high authoritarian personality is intellectually rigid, judgmental of others, deferential to those above and exploitative of those below, distrustful, and resistant to change. Of course, few people are extreme authoritarians, so conclusions must be guarded. It seems reasonable to postulate, however, that possessing a high authoritarian personality would be related negatively to performance where the job demands sensitivity to the feelings of others, tact, and the ability to adapt to complex and changing situations. On the other hand, where jobs are highly structured and success depends on close conformity to rules and regulations, the high authoritarian employee should perform quite well.

Closely related to authoritarianism is *Machiavellianism* (Mach), named after Niccolo Machiavelli, who wrote in the sixteenth century on how to gain and manipulate power. An individual exhibiting strong Machiavellian tendencies is pragmatic, maintains emotional distance, and believes that ends can justify means. "If it works, use it" is consistent with a high-Mach perspective. Do high-Machs make good employees? That answer depends on the type of job and whether you consider ethical implications in evaluating performance. In jobs that require bargaining skills (such as labor negotiator) or where there are substantial rewards for winning (as in commissioned sales), high-Machs will be productive. But if the ends can't justify the means or if there are no absolute standards of performance, our ability to predict a high-Mach's performance will be severely curtailed.

Did you ever notice that some people are much better than others at adjusting their behavior to changing situations? This is because they score high in *self-monitoring*. High self-monitors are sensitive to external cues and can behave differently in different situations. They're chameleons—able to change to fit the situation and to hide their true selves. On the other hand, low self-monitors are consistent. They display their true dispositions and attitudes in every situation. The evidence suggests that high self-monitors tend to pay closer attention to the behavior of others and are more capable of conforming than low self-monitors. High self-monitors also tend to be better at playing organizational politics because they're sensitive to cues and can put on different "faces" for different audiences.

People differ in their willingness to take chances. Individuals with a high *risk propensity* make more rapid decisions and use less information in making their choices than low-risk propensity individuals. Managers might use this information to align employee risk-taking propensity with specific job demands. For instance, a high-risk taking propensity may lead to more effective performance for a stock trader in a brokerage firm. This type of job demands rapid decision making. On the other hand, this personality characteristic might prove a major obstacle to an accountant who performs auditing activities. This latter job might be better filled by someone with a low risk-taking propensity.

Matching Personalities and Jobs

Obviously, individual personalities differ. So, too, do jobs. Following this logic, efforts have been made to match the proper personalities with the proper jobs. The most researched personality job-fit theory is the six personality types model. This model states that an employee's satisfaction with and propensity to leave his or her job depends on the degree to which the individual's personality matches his or her occupational environment.[4] Six major personality types have been identified. They are listed in Exhibit 3–2, along with their compatible occupations.

A Vocational Preference Inventory questionnaire has been developed that contains 160 occupational titles. Respondents indicate which of these

---

[4]Arnold R. Spokane, "A Review of Research on Person-Environment Congruence in Holland's Theory of Careers," *Journal of Vocational Behavior* (June 1985), pp. 306–43.

EXHIBIT 3-2 *HOLLAND'S TYPOLOGY OF PERSONALITY AND SAMPLE OCCUPATIONS*

Type	Personality Characteristics	Sample Occupations
Realistic: Prefers physical activities that require skill, strength, and coordination	Shy, genuine, persistent, stable, conforming, practical	Mechanic, drill press operator, assembly line worker, farmer
Investigative: Prefers activities involving thinking, organizing, and understanding	Analytical, original, curious, independent	Biologist, economist, mathematician, news reporter
Social: Prefers activities that involve helping and developing others	Sociable, friendly, cooperative,understanding	Social worker, teacher, counselor, clinical psychologist
Conventional: Prefers rule-regulated, orderly, and unambiguous activities	Conforming, efficient, practical, unimaginative, inflexible	Accountant, corporate manager, bank teller, file clerk
Enterprising: Prefers verbal activities where there are opportunities to influence others and attain power	Self-confident, ambitious, energetic, domineering	Lawyer, real estate agent, public relations specialist, small business manager
Artistic: Prefers ambiguous and unsystematic activities that allow creative expression	Imaginative, disorderly, idealistic, emotional, impractical	Painter, musician, writer, interior decorator

occupations they like or dislike and their answers are used to form personality profiles. Utilizing this procedure, research strongly supports the hexagonal diagram in Exhibit 3–3. This figure shows that the closer two fields or orientations are in the hexagon, the more compatible they are. Adjacent categories are quite similar, while those diagonally opposite are highly dissimilar.

What does all this mean? The theory argues that satisfaction is highest and turnover lowest where personality and occupation are in agreement. Social individuals should be in social jobs, conventional people in conventional jobs, and so forth. A realistic person in a realistic job is in a more congruent situation than a realistic person in an investigative job. A realistic person in a social job is in the most incongruent situation possible. The key points of this model are that (1) there do appear to be intrinsic personality differences among individuals; (2) there are different types of jobs; and (3) people in job environments congruent with their personality type should be more satisfied and less likely to resign voluntarily than people in incongruent jobs.

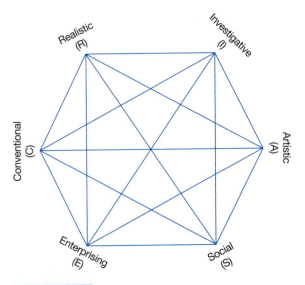

■ PERCEPTION

Perception is a process by which individuals organize and interpret their sensory impressions in order to give meaning to their environment. Research on perception consistently demonstrates that different individuals may look at the same thing, yet perceive it differently. The fact is that none of us sees reality. What we do is interpret what we see and call it reality.

Factors Influencing Perception

How do we explain the fact that people perceive the same thing differently? A number of factors operate to shape and sometimes distort perception. These factors can reside in the *perceiver,* in the object or *target* being perceived, or in the context of the *situation* in which the perception is made.

When an individual looks at a target and attempts to interpret what he or she sees, that interpretation is heavily influenced by personal characteristics of the individual perceiver. Personal characteristics affecting perception include attitudes, personality, motives, interests, past experiences, and expectations.

Characteristics of the target being observed can affect what is perceived. Loud people are more likely to be noticed in a group than quiet ones. So, too, are extremely attractive or unattractive individuals. Because targets are not looked at in isolation, the relationship of a target to its background influences perception, as does our tendency to group close things and similar things together.

The context in which we see objects or events is also important. The time at which an object or event is seen can influence attention, as can location, light, heat, or any number of situational factors.

Attribution Theory

Much of the research on perception is directed at inanimate objects. But OB is concerned with human beings, so our discussion of perception should focus on person perception.

Our perceptions of people differ from our perceptions of inanimate objects like desks, machines, or buildings because we make inferences about the actions of people that we don't make about inanimate objects. Nonliving objects are subject to the laws of nature, but they have no beliefs, motives, or intentions. People do. The result is that when we observe people, we attempt to develop explanations of why they behave in certain ways. Our perception and judgment of a person's actions, therefore, will be significantly influenced by the assumptions we make about the person's internal state.

Attribution theory has been proposed to develop explanations of how we judge people differently depending on what meaning we attribute to a given behavior. Basically, the theory suggests that when we observe an individual's behavior, we attempt to determine whether it was internally or externally caused. That determination, however, depends on three factors: (1) distinctiveness, (2) consensus, and (3) consistency. First, let's clarify the differences between internal and external causation, then elaborate on each of the three determining factors.

Internally caused behaviors are those that are believed to be under the personal control of the individual. Externally caused behavior results from outside causes; that is, the person is seen as forced into the behavior by the situation. If one of your employees was late for work, you might attribute his lateness to his partying into the wee hours of the morning and then oversleeping. This would be an internal interpretation. But if you attributed his arriving late to a major automobile accident that tied up traffic on the road your employee regularly uses, then you would be making an external attribution. As observers, we have a tendency to assume that others' behavior is internally controlled, while we tend to exaggerate the degree to which our own behavior is externally determined. But this is a broad generalization. There still exists a considerable amount of deviation in attribution, depending on how we interpret the distinctiveness, consensus, and consistency of the actions.

Distinctiveness refers to whether or not an individual displays different behaviors in different situations. Is the employee who arrives late today also the source of complaints by co-workers for being a "goof off"? What we want to know is if this behavior is unusual or not. If it is, the observer is likely to give the behavior an external attribution. If this action is not unique, it will probably be judged as internal.

If everyone who is faced with a similar situation responds in the same way, we can say the behavior shows *consensus*. Our tardy employee's behavior would meet this criterion if all employees who took the same route to work were also late. From an attribution perspective, if consensus is high you would be expected to give an external attribution to the employee's tardiness; whereas if other employees who took the same route made it to work on time, your conclusion for causation would be internal.

Finally, an observer looks for *consistency* in a person's actions. Does the person respond the same way over time? Coming in ten minutes late for work is not perceived in the same way if for one employee it represents an unusual case (she hasn't been late for several months), while for another it is part of a routine pattern (she is regularly late two or three times a week). The more consistent the behavior, the more the observer is inclined to attribute it to internal causes.

The preceding explains what you have seen operating for years. All similar behaviors are not perceived similarly. We look at actions and judge them within their situational context. If you have a reputation as a good student yet blow one test in a course, the instructor is more likely to disregard the poor exam. Why? He or she will attribute the cause of this unusual performance to external conditions. It may not be your fault! But for the student who has a consistent record of being a poor performer, it is unlikely the teacher will ignore the low test score. Similarly, if everyone in class blew the test, the instructor might attribute the outcome to external causes rather than to causes under the students' own control. (He or she might conclude that the questions were poorly written, the room was too warm, or that the students didn't have the necessary prerequisites.)

Shortcuts to Judging Others

Making judgments about others is done all the time by people in organizations. For example, managers regularly evaluate the performance of their employees, and operatives assess whether their co-workers are putting forth their full effort or not. But making judgments about others is difficult. To make the task easier, individuals take shortcuts. Some of these shortcuts are valuable—they allow us to make accurate perceptions rapidly and provide valid data for making predictions. However, they can also result in significant distortions.

Individuals cannot assimilate all they observe, so they engage in *selectivity*. They take in bits and pieces. But these bits and pieces are not chosen randomly; rather, they are selectively chosen depending on the interests, background, experience, and attitudes of the observer. Selective perception allows us to "speed read" others, but not without the risk of drawing an inaccurate picture.

It is easy to judge others if we assume they are similar to us. *Assumed similarity,* or the "like me" effect, results in an individual's perception of others being influenced more by what the observer is like than by what the person being observed is like. If you want challenge and responsibility in your job, you may assume others want the same. People who assume others are like them will be right some of the time, but only in those cases when they judge someone who is actually like them. The rest of the time, they're wrong.

When we judge someone on the basis of our perception of the group to which he or she belongs, we are using the shortcut called *stereotyping.* "Married people are more stable employees than singles" or "union people expect something for nothing" are examples of stereotypes. To the degree that a stereotype is a factual generalization, it helps in making accurate judgments. But many stereotypes have no foundation in fact. In these latter cases, stereotypes distort judgments.

When we draw a general impression about an individual based on a single characteristic such as intelligence, sociability, or appearance, a *halo effect* is operating. It is not unusual for the halo effect to occur during selection interviews. A sloppily dressed candidate for a marketing research position may be perceived by an interviewer as an irresponsible person with an unprofessional attitude and marginal abilities, when in fact the candidate may be highly responsible, professional, and competent. What has happened is that a single trait—appearance—has overridden other characteristics in the interviewer's general perception about the individual.

■ LEARNING

The final concept introduced in this chapter is learning. It is included for the obvious reason that almost all complex human behavior is learned. If we want to explain, predict, or control behavior, we need to understand how people learn.

The psychologist's definition of learning is considerably broader than the layperson's view that "it's what we did when we went to school." In actuality, each of us is continuously going "to school." Learning is going on all the time. A more correct definition of *learning,* therefore, is any relatively permanent change in behavior that occurs as a result of experience.

How do we learn? Exhibit 3–4 summarizes the learning process. First, learning helps us to adapt to, and master, our environment. By changing our behavior to accommodate changing conditions, we become responsible citizens and productive employees. But learning is built upon the *law of effect,* which says that behavior is a function of its consequences.[5] Behavior that is

---

[5] Edward L. Thorndike, *Educational Psychology: The Psychology of Learning* (New York: Columbia University Press, 1913), and B. F. Skinner, *Beyond Freedom and Dignity* (New York: Knopf, 1971).

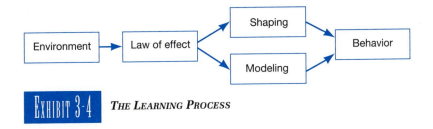

EXHIBIT 3-4   *THE LEARNING PROCESS*

followed by a favorable consequence tends to be repeated; behavior followed by an unfavorable consequence tends not to be repeated. Consequence, in this terminology, refers to anything a person considers rewarding (i.e., money, praise, promotions, a smile). If your boss compliments you on your sales approach, you're likely to repeat that behavior. Conversely, if you're reprimanded for your sales approach, you're less likely to repeat it. But the keys to the learning process are the two theories, or explanations, of how we learn. One is *shaping* and the other is *modeling.*

When learning takes place in graduated steps, it is shaped. Managers shape employee behavior by systematically reinforcing, through rewards, each successive step that moves the employee closer to the desired behavior. Much of our learning has been done by shaping. When we speak of "learning by mistakes," we are referring to shaping. We try, we fail, and we try again. Through such series of trial and error, most of us have mastered such skills as riding a bicycle, performing basic mathematical computations, taking classroom notes, and answering multiple-choice tests.

In addition to shaping, much of what we have learned is the result of observing others and modeling our behavior after them. While trial and error is usually a slow learning process, modeling can produce complex behavioral changes quite rapidly. For instance, most of us, at one time or another, when having trouble in school or in a particular class, look around to find someone who seems to have the system down pat. Then we observe that person to see what he or she is doing that is different from our approach. If we find some differences, we then incorporate them into our behavior repertoire. If our performance improves (a favorable consequence), we're likely to make a permanent change in our behavior to reflect what we've seen work for others. The process is the same at work as it is in school. A new employee, who wants to be successful on her job, is likely to look for someone in the organization who is well respected and successful, and then try to imitate that person's behavior.

■ IMPLICATIONS FOR MANAGERS

This chapter has introduced a number of psychological concepts. Let's now turn toward putting them together and demonstrating their importance for the manager who is trying to understand organizational behavior.

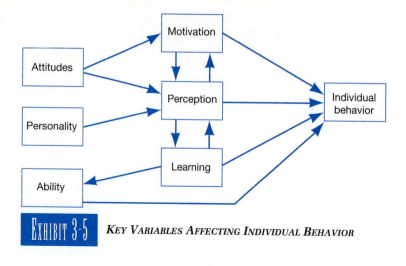

EXHIBIT 3-5 *KEY VARIABLES AFFECTING INDIVIDUAL BEHAVIOR*

Exhibit 3–5 summarizes our discussion of individual behavior. In very simplified terms, we can say that an individual enters an organization with a relatively entrenched set of attitudes and a substantially established personality. While not permanently fixed, an employee's attitudes and personality are essentially "givens" at the time he or she enters an organization. How employees interpret their work environment (perception) will influence their level of motivation (the topic of the next chapter), what they learn on the job, and, eventually, their individual work behavior. We've also added *ability* to our model to acknowledge that an individual's behavior is influenced by the talents and skills that person holds when he or she joins the organization. Learning, of course, will alter this variable over time.

Attitudes

Managers should be interested in their employees' attitudes because attitudes influence behavior. Satisfied employees, for instance, have lower rates of turnover and absenteeism. Given that managers want to keep resignations and absences down—especially among their more productive employees—they will want to do those things that will generate positive job attitudes.

Managers should also be aware that employees will try to reduce cognitive dissonance. More importantly, dissonance can be managed. If employees are required to engage in activities that appear inconsistent to them or that are at odds with their attitudes, the pressures to reduce the resulting dissonance are lessened when the employee perceives the dissonance is externally imposed and is beyond his or her control, or if the rewards are significant enough to offset the dissonance.

Personality

The major value of a manager's understanding personality differences probably lies in selection. You are likely to have higher performing and more satisfied employees if consideration is given to matching personality types with compatible jobs. In addition, there may be other benefits. For instance, managers can expect that individuals with an external locus of control may be less satisfied with their jobs than internals and also that they may be less willing to accept responsibility for their actions.

Perception

Managers need to recognize that their employees react to perceptions, not reality. So whether a manager's appraisal of an employee is *actually* objective and unbiased or whether the organization's wage levels are *actually* among the highest in the industry is less relevant than what employees perceive. If individuals perceive appraisals to be biased or wage levels as low, they will behave as if these conditions actually exist. Employees organize and interpret what they see; this creates the potential for perceptual distortion.

The message to managers should be clear: They need to pay close attention to how employees perceive both their jobs and management practices. Remember, the competent employee who quits for an invalid reason is just as "gone" as one who quits for a valid reason.

Learning

The issue isn't whether employees continually learn on the job or not. They do! The only issue is whether managers are going to let employee learning occur randomly or whether they are going to manage learning—through the rewards they allocate and the examples they set. If marginal employees are rewarded with pay raises and promotions, they will have little reason to change their behavior. If managers want behavior A, but reward behavior B, it shouldn't surprise them to find employees learning to engage in behavior B. Similarly, managers should expect that employees will look to them as models. Managers who are constantly late to work, or take two hours for lunch, or help themselves to company office supplies for personal use, should expect employees to read the message they're sending and model their behavior accordingly.

SUGGESTIONS FOR FURTHER READING

Buss, Arnold H., "Personality as Traits," *American Psychologist,* November 1989, pp. 1378–88.

Cranny, C.J., Patricia Cain Smith, and Eugene F. Stone, *Job Satisfaction* (New York: Lexington, 1992).

Day, David V., and Stanley B. Silverman, "Personality and Job Performance: Evidence of Incremental Validity," *Personnel Psychology,* Spring 1989, pp. 25–36.

Falkenberg, Loren, "Improving the Accuracy of Stereotypes within the Workplace," *Journal of Management,* March 1990, pp. 107–18.

George, Jennifer M., "The Role of Personality in Organizational Life: Issues and Evidence," *Journal of Management,* June 1992, pp. 185–213.

OSTROFF, CHERI, "The Relationship between Satisfaction, Attitudes, and Performance: An Organizational Level Analysis," *Journal of Applied Psychology,* December 1992, pp. 963–74.

PREDIGER, DALE J., AND TIMOTHY R. VANSICKLE, "Locating Occupations on Holland's Hexagon: Beyond RIASEC," *Journal of Vocational Behavior,* April 1992, pp. 111–28.

WEISS, HOWARD M., "Learning Theory and Industrial and Organizational Psychology," in M.D. Dunnette and L.M. Hough, eds., *Handbook of Industrial and Organizational Psychology,* 2nd ed., Vol. 1 (Palo Alto, CA: Consulting Psychologists Press, 1990), pp. 171–221.

CHAPTER 4

UNDERSTANDING MOTIVATION

After reading this chapter, you should be able to:

1. Outline the basic motivation process

2. Describe Maslow's hierarchy of needs theory

3. Contrast Theory X and Theory Y

4. Differentiate motivators from hygiene factors

5. List the characteristics that high achievers prefer in a job

6. Summarize the types of goals that increase performance

7. Contrast reinforcement and goal-setting theories

8. Explain equity theory

9. Clarify the key relationships in expectancy theory

Referring to their son or daughter, parents have said it for so many years that it has achieved cliché status: "He/she has the ability but just won't apply him/herself." Few of us work to, or even near, our potential, and most of us will admit to that. Einstein underscored his belief in the importance of hard work for achieving success when he said that "genius is 10 percent inspiration and 90 percent perspiration." The fact is that some people work harder or exert more effort than others. The result is that individuals of lesser ability can, and do, outperform their more gifted counterparts. For this reason, an individual's performance at work or otherwise depends not only on ability but on motivation as well. This chapter considers various explanations of why some people exert more effort on their jobs than others. We also extract from these explanations a set of general guidelines to help you motivate others more effectively.

■ WHAT IS MOTIVATION?

We might define motivation in terms of some outward behavior. People who are motivated exert a greater effort to perform than those who are not motivat-

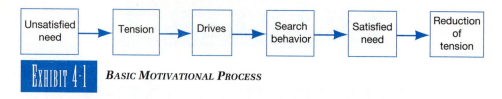

EXHIBIT 4-1 **BASIC MOTIVATIONAL PROCESS**

ed. However, such a definition is relative and tells us little. A more descriptive but less substantive definition would say that motivation is the willingness to do something, and is conditioned by this action's ability to satisfy some need for the individual. A need, in our terminology, means a physiological or psychological deficiency that makes certain outcomes appear attractive. This motivation process can be seen in Exhibit 4–1.

An unsatisfied need creates tension, which stimulates drives within the individual. These drives generate a search to find particular goals that, if attained, will satisfy the need and lead to the reduction of tension.

Motivated employees are in a state of tension. In order to relieve this tension, they engage in activity. The greater the tension, the more activity will be needed to bring about relief. Therefore, when we see employees working hard at some activity, we can conclude they are driven by a desire to achieve some goal they value.

EARLY THEORIES OF MOTIVATION

The decade of the 1950s was a fruitful period in the development of motivation concepts. Three specific theories were formulated during this period, which, though now heavily attacked and their validity called into question, are probably still the best-known explanations for employee motivation: the hierarchy of needs theory, Theory X and Y, and the motivation-hygiene theory. As you'll see later in this chapter, we have since developed more valid explanations of motivation, but you should know these early theories for at least two reasons: (1) they represent a foundation from which contemporary theories have grown, and (2) practicing managers regularly use these theories and their terminologies in explaining employee motivation.

Hierarchy of Needs Theory

It's probably safe to say that the best-known theory of motivation is Abraham Maslow's *hierarchy of needs*.[1] He hypothesized that within every human being there exists a hierarchy of five needs. These needs are:

1. **Physiological**—includes hunger, thirst, shelter, sex, and other bodily needs
2. **Safety**—includes security and protection from physical and emotional harm

---

[1] Abraham Maslow, *Motivation and Personality* (New York: Harper & Row, 1954).

3. **Social**—includes affection, a sense of belonging, acceptance, and friendship
4. **Esteem**—includes internal factors such as self-respect, autonomy, and achievement, and external factors such as status, recognition, and attention
5. **Self-actualization**—the drive to become what one is capable of becoming; includes growth, achieving one's potential, and self-fulfillment

As each of these needs becomes substantially satisfied, the next need becomes dominant. In terms of Exhibit 4–2, the individual moves up the hierarchy. From the standpoint of motivation, Maslow's theory would say that although no need is ever fully gratified, a substantially satisfied need no longer motivates.

Maslow separated the five needs into higher and lower orders. Physiological and safety needs were described as lower order; social, esteem, and self-actualization were categorized as higher-order needs. The differentiation between the two orders was made on the premise that higher-order needs are satisfied internally, whereas lower-order needs are predominantly satisfied externally (by such things as wages, union contracts, and tenure). In fact, the natural conclusion to be drawn from Maslow's classification is that, in times of economic plenty, almost all permanently employed workers will have their lower-order needs substantially met.

Maslow's need theory has received wide recognition, particularly among practicing managers. This can be attributed to the logic and ease with which the theory is intuitively understood. Unfortunately, however, research does not generally validate the theory. For instance, little support is found for the

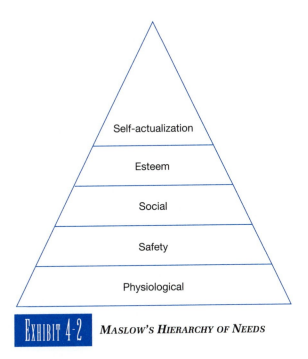

EXHIBIT 4-2 **MASLOW'S HIERARCHY OF NEEDS**

prediction that need structures are organized along the dimensions proposed by Maslow or the prediction that the substantial satisfaction of a given need leads to the activation of the next higher need. So, although the need hierarchy is well known and undoubtedly used by many managers as a guide toward motivating their employees, little substantive evidence exists to indicate that following the theory will lead to a more motivated work force.

Theory X and Y

Douglas McGregor proposed two distinct views of human beings: one basically negative, labeled *Theory X,* and the other basically positive, labeled *Theory Y.*[2] After viewing the way managers dealt with employees, McGregor concluded that a manager's view of the nature of human beings is based on a certain grouping of assumptions, and that he or she tends to mold his or her behavior toward subordinates according to these assumptions.

Under Theory X, four assumptions are held by the manager:

1. Employees inherently dislike work and, whenever possible, will attempt to avoid it.
2. Since employees dislike work, they must be coerced, controlled, or threatened with punishment to achieve desired goals.
3. Employees will shirk responsibilities and seek formal direction whenever possible.
4. Most workers place security above all other factors associated with work, and will display little ambition.

In contrast to these negative views toward the nature of human beings, McGregor listed four other assumptions that he called Theory Y:

1. Employees can view work as being as natural as rest or play.
2. A person will exercise self-direction and self-control if he is committed to the objectives.
3. The average person can learn to accept, even seek, responsibility.
4. Creativity—that is, the ability to make good decisions—is widely dispersed throughout the population, and not necessarily the sole province of those in management functions.

What are the motivational implications if you accept McGregor's analysis? The answer is best expressed in the framework presented by Maslow. Theory X assumes that lower-order needs dominate individuals. Theory Y assumes that higher-order needs dominate individuals. McGregor, himself, held to the belief that Theory Y assumptions were more valid than Theory X. Therefore, he proposed ideas like participation in decision making, responsible and challenging jobs, and good group relations as approaches that would maximize an employee's job motivation.

---

[2] Douglas McGregor, *The Human Side of Enterprise* (New York: McGraw-Hill, 1960).

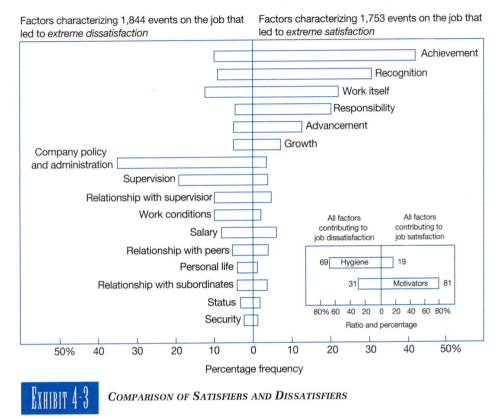

Factors characterizing 1,844 events on the job that led to *extreme dissatisfaction*

Factors characterizing 1,753 events on the job that led to *extreme satisfaction*

Achievement
Recognition
Work itself
Responsibility
Advancement
Growth
Company policy and administration
Supervision
Relationship with supervisior
Work conditions
Salary
Relationship with peers
Personal life
Relationship with subordinates
Status
Security

All factors contributing to job dissatisfaction

All factors contributing to job satisfaction

69 Hygiene 19
31 Motivators 81

80% 60 40 20 0 20 40 60 80%
Ratio and percentage

50% 40 30 20 10 0 10 20 30 40 50%
Percentage frequency

EXHIBIT 4-3 *COMPARISON OF SATISFIERS AND DISSATISFIERS*

Source: Frederick Herzberg, "One More Time, How Do You Motivate Employees?" *Harvard Business Review,* January–February 1968, p. 57. With permission. Copyright © 1968 by the President and Fellows of Harvard College; all rights reserved.

Unfortunately, there is no evidence to confirm that either set of assumptions is valid, or that acceptance of Theory Y assumptions and altering one's actions accordingly will lead to more motivated workers. As will become evident later in this chapter, either Theory X or Theory Y assumptions may be appropriate in a particular situation.

Motivation-Hygiene Theory

The motivation-hygiene theory was proposed by psychologist Frederick Herzberg.[3] In the belief that an individual's relation to his work is a basic one and that his attitude to his work can very well determine his success or failure, Herzberg investigated the question, "What do people want from their jobs?" He asked people to describe, in detail, situations in which they felt

---

[3] Frederick Herzberg, B. Mausner, and B. Snyderman, *The Motivation to Work* (New York: Wiley, 1959).

exceptionally good or bad about their jobs. These responses were tabulated and categorized. Factors affecting job attitudes, as reported in 12 investigations conducted by Herzberg, are illustrated in Exhibit 4–3.

From the categorized responses, Herzberg concluded that the replies people gave when they felt good about their jobs were significantly different from the replies given when they felt bad. As seen in Exhibit 4–3, certain characteristics tend to be consistently related to job satisfaction, and others to job dissatisfaction. Intrinsic factors, such as achievement, recognition, the work itself, responsibility, and advancement seem to be related to job satisfaction. When those questioned felt good about their work, they tended to attribute these characteristics to themselves. On the other hand, when they were dissatisfied, they tended to cite extrinsic factors, such as company policy and administration, supervision, interpersonal relations, and working conditions.

The data suggest, says Herzberg, that the opposite of satisfaction is not dissatisfaction, as was traditionally believed. Removing dissatisfying characteristics from a job does not necessarily make the job satisfying. Herzberg proposes that his findings indicate the existence of a dual continuum: The opposite of "Satisfaction" is "No Satisfaction," and the opposite of "Dissatisfaction" is "No Dissatisfaction."

According to Herzberg, the factors leading to job satisfaction are separate and distinct from those that lead to job dissatisfaction. Therefore, managers who seek to eliminate factors that can create job dissatisfaction may bring about peace, but not necessarily motivation. They will be placating their work force rather than motivating them. As a result, such characteristics as company policy and administration, supervision, interpersonal relations, working conditions, and salary have been characterized by Herzberg as hygiene factors. When they are adequate, people will not be dissatisfied; however, neither will they be satisfied. If we want to motivate people on their jobs, Herzberg suggests emphasizing achievement, recognition, the work itself, responsibility, and growth. These are the characteristics that people find intrinsically rewarding.

The motivation-hygiene theory is not without its detractors. The criticisms of the theory include the following:

1. The procedure that Herzberg used is limited by its methodology. When things are going well, people tend to take credit themselves. Contrarily, they blame failure on the extrinsic environment.

2. The reliability of Herzberg's methodology is questioned. Since raters have to make interpretations, it is possible they may contaminate the findings by interpreting one response in one manner while treating a similar response differently.

3. No overall measure of satisfaction was utilized. A person may dislike part of his or her job, yet still think the job is acceptable.

4. The theory is inconsistent with previous research. The motivation-hygiene theory ignores situational variables.

5. Herzberg assumes a relationship between satisfaction and productivity, but the research methodology he used looked only at satisfaction, not at productivity. To make such research relevant, one must assume a strong relationship between satisfaction and productivity.

Regardless of criticisms, Herzberg's theory has been widely popularized and few managers are unfamiliar with his recommendations. As a case in point, much of the initial enthusiasm for vertically expanding jobs to allow workers greater responsibility in planning and controlling their work (which we discuss in Chapter 5) can probably be attributed largely to Herzberg's findings and recommendations.

■ CONTEMPORARY THEORIES OF MOTIVATION

The previous theories are well known but, unfortunately, have not held up well under close examination. However, all is not lost. We have a number of contemporary theories that have one thing in common—each has a reasonable degree of valid supporting documentation. The following theories represent the current state of the art in explaining employee motivation.

Three-Needs Theory

David McClelland and others have proposed three major relevant motives or needs in the workplace:[4]

1. The need for achievement (*nAch*)—the drive to excel, to achieve in relation to a set of standards, to strive to succeed.
2. The need for power (*nPow*)—the need to make others behave in a way they would not have behaved otherwise.
3. The need for affiliation (*nAff*)—the desire for friendly and close interpersonal relationships.

Some people have a compelling drive to succeed, but they are striving for personal achievement rather than the rewards of success. They have a desire to do something better or more efficiently than it has been done before. This drive is the need for achievement. From research into the need for achievement, McClelland found that high achievers differentiate themselves from others by their desire to do things better. They seek situations where they can attain personal responsibility for finding solutions to problems, where they can receive rapid and unambiguous feedback on their performance so they can tell easily whether they are improving or not, and where

---

[4] David C. McClelland, *The Achieving Society* (New York: Van Nostrand Reinhold, 1961); John W. Atkinson and Joel O. Raynor, *Motivation and Achievement* (Washington, DC: Winston, 1974); and David C. McClelland, *Power: The Inner Experience* (New York: Irvington, 1975).

they can set moderately challenging goals. High achievers are not gamblers; they dislike succeeding by chance. They prefer the challenge of working at a problem and accepting the personal responsibility for success or failure, rather than leaving the outcome to chance or the actions of others. They avoid what they perceive to be very easy or very difficult tasks.

High achievers perform best when they perceive their probability of success as being 0.5, that is, when they estimate they have a 50-50 chance of success. They dislike gambling with high odds because they get no achievement satisfaction from happenstance success. Similarly, they dislike low odds (high probability of success) because then there is no challenge to their skills. They like to set goals that require stretching themselves a little. When there is an approximately equal chance of success or failure, there is the optimum opportunity to experience feelings of accomplishment and satisfaction from their efforts.

The need for power is the desire to have impact, to be influential, and to control others. Individuals high in *nPow* enjoy being in charge, strive for influence over others, prefer to be placed in competitive and status-oriented situations, and tend to be more concerned with gaining influence over others and prestige than with effective performance.

The third need isolated by McClelland is affiliation. This need has received the least attention of researchers. Affiliation can be likened to Dale Carnegie's goals—the desire to be liked and accepted by others. Individuals with a high *nAff* strive for friendship, prefer cooperative situations rather than competitive ones, and desire relationships involving a high degree of mutual understanding.

How do you find out if someone is, for instance, a high achiever? All three motives are typically measured through a projective test in which subjects respond to a set of pictures. Each picture is briefly shown to the subject and then he or she writes a story based on the picture. As an example, the picture may show a male sitting at a desk in a pensive position, looking at a picture of a woman and two children that sits at the corner of the desk. The subject will then be asked to write a story describing what is going on, what preceded this situation, what will happen in the future, and the like. The stories become, in effect, projective tests that measure unconscious motives. Each story is scored and a subject's rating on each of the three motives is obtained.

Based on an extensive amount of research, some reasonably well-supported predictions can be made based on the relationship between achievement need and job performance. Though less research has been done on power and affiliation needs, there are consistent findings here too. First, individuals with a high need to achieve prefer job situations with personal responsibility, feedback, and an intermediate degree of risk. When these characteristics are prevalent, high achievers will be strongly motivated. The evidence consistently demonstrates, for instance, that high achievers are successful in entrepreneurial activities such as running their own business, managing a self-contained unit within a large organization, and many sales positions. Second, a high need to achieve does not necessarily lead to being a good manager, especially in large organizations. High *nAch* salespeople do not necessarily make good sales managers, and the good manager in a large organization does not typically have a high need to achieve. Third, the needs for affiliation and power tend to be closely related to managerial success. The best managers are high in the need for power and low in their need for affiliation. Lastly, employees have been successfully trained to stimulate their achievement need. If the job calls for a high achiever, management can select a person with a high *nAch* or develop its own candidate through achievement training.

Goal-Setting Theory

Considerable evidence supports the theory that intentions—expressed as goals—can be a major source of work motivation. We can say, with a considerable degree of confidence, that specific goals lead to increased performance and that difficult goals, when accepted, result in higher performance than easy goals.[5]

Specific, difficult-to-achieve goals produce a higher level of output than a generalized goal of "do your best." The specificity of the goal itself acts as an internal stimulus. For instance, when a trucker commits to making 18 round-trip hauls between Baltimore and Washington, D.C. each week, this intention gives him a specific objective to reach for. We can say that, all things being equal, the trucker with a specific goal will outperform his counterpart who operates either with no goals or with the generalized goal of "do your best."

If factors such as ability and acceptance of the goals are held constant, we can also state that the more difficult the goals, the higher the level of performance. However, it's logical to assume that easier goals are more likely to be accepted. But once an employee accepts a hard task, he or she will exert a high level of effort until the goal is achieved, lowered, or abandoned.

If employees have the opportunity to participate in the setting of their own goals, will they try harder? The evidence is mixed regarding the superiority of participation over assigned goals. In some cases, goals that have been set participatively have elicited superior performance, while in other cases individuals have performed best when assigned goals by their boss. A major advantage of participation may be in increasing acceptance of the goal, itself, as a desirable one to work toward. As we noted earlier, resistance is greater when goals are difficult. If people participate in goal setting, they are more likely to accept even a difficult goal than if it is arbitrarily assigned to them by their boss. The reason is that individuals are more committed to choices in which they have a voice. Thus, although participative goals may have no superiority over assigned goals when acceptance is taken as a given, participation does increase the probability that more difficult goals will be agreed to and acted upon.

---

[5] Mark E. Tubbs, "Goal-Setting: A Meta-Analysis Examination of the Empirical Evidence," *Journal of Applied Psychology* (August 1986), pp. 474–83.

Studies on goal setting have demonstrated the superiority of specific and challenging goals as motivating forces. While we can't conclude that having employees participate in the goal-setting process is *always* desirable, participation is probably preferable to assignment when you expect resistance to more difficult challenges. As an overall conclusion, therefore, we have significant evidence that intentions—as articulated in terms of goals—are a potent motivating force.

The observant reader may have noted what appears to be a contradiction between the findings on achievement motivation and goal setting. Is it a contradiction that achievement motivation is stimulated by moderately challenging goals, while goal-setting theory says motivation is maximized by difficult goals? The answer is "No!" The explanation is twofold. First, goal-setting theory deals with people in general. The conclusions on achievement motivation are based only on people who have a high *nAch*. Given that probably not more than 10 to 20 percent of North Americans are naturally high achievers, difficult goals are still recommended for the majority of workers. Second, goal setting's conclusions apply to those who accept, and are committed to, the goals. Difficult goals will only lead to higher performance if they are accepted.

Reinforcement Theory

A counterpoint to goal-setting theory is reinforcement theory. The former is a cognitive approach, proposing that an individual's purposes direct his or her actions. In reinforcement theory we have a behavioristic approach, which argues that reinforcement conditions behavior. The two theories are clearly at odds philosophically. Reinforcement theorists see behavior as environmentally caused; internal cognitive events are not matters for concern. What controls behavior are reinforcers—any consequences which, when immediately following a response, increase the probability that the behavior will be repeated.

Reinforcement theory ignores the inner state of the individual and concentrates solely on what happens to a person when he or she takes some action. Because it does not concern itself with what initiates behavior, it is not, strictly speaking, a theory of motivation. However, it does provide a powerful means of analysis of what controls behavior, and it is for this reason that it is typically considered in discussions of motivation.

The last chapter introduced the law of effect as it relates to learning and showed that reinforcers condition behavior and help to explain how people learn. But the law of effect and the concept of reinforcement also have a wide following as an explanation of motivation. A large amount of supportive research indicates that people will exert higher levels of effort in tasks that are reinforced.[6] Reinforcement *is* undoubtedly an important influence on work behavior. What people do on their jobs and the amount of effort they allocate

---

[6] Fred Luthans and Robert Kreitner, *Organizational Behavior Modification and Beyond: An Operant and Social Learning Approach* (Glenview, IL: Scott, Foresman, 1984).

to various tasks is affected by the consequences that follow their behavior. But reinforcement is not the single explanation for differences in employee motivation. Goals, for instance, have an impact on motivation; so, too, do levels of achievement motivation, inequities in rewards, and expectations.

Equity Theory

Employees don't work in a vacuum. They make comparisons. If someone offered you $40,000 a year for your first job upon graduation from college, you'd probably grab at the offer and report to work enthused and certainly satisfied with your pay. How would you react, however, if you found out a month or so into the job that a co-worker—another recent graduate, your age, with comparable grades from a comparable college—was getting $45,000 a year? You'd probably be upset! Even though, in absolute terms, $40,000 is a lot of money for a new graduate to make (and you know it!), that suddenly isn't the issue. The issue now centers around relative rewards and what you believe is fair. There is considerable evidence for us to conclude that employees make comparisons of their job inputs and outcomes relative to others and that inequities can influence the degree of effort that employees exert.[7]

Equity theory says that employees perceive what they get from a job situation (outcomes) in relation to what they put into it (inputs), and then compare their input-outcome ratio with the input-outcome ratio of relevant others. If they perceive their ratio to be equal to the relevant others with whom they compare themselves, a state of equity is said to exist. They feel their situation is fair, that justice prevails. If the ratios are unequal, inequity exists; that is, the employees tend to view themselves as underrewarded or overrewarded. When inequities occur, employees will attempt to correct them.

The referent that employees choose to compare themselves against is an important variable in equity theory. The three referent categories have been classified as "other," "system," and "self." The "other" category includes other individuals with similar jobs in the same organization, and also includes friends, neighbors, or professional associates. Based on information that employees receive through word of mouth, newspapers, and magazines, on such issues as executive salaries or a recent union contract, employees can compare their pay to that of others.

The "system" category considers organizational pay policies and procedures, as well as the administration of this system. It considers organization-wide pay policies, both implied and explicit. Precedents set by the organization in terms of allocation of pay would be a major determinant in this category.

The "self" category refers to input-outcome ratios that are unique to the individual. This category is influenced by such criteria as past jobs or family commitments.

---

[7] Robert P. Vecchio, "Models of Psychological Inequity," *Organizational Behavior and Human Performance* (October 1984), pp. 266–82.

The choice of a particular set of referents is related to the information available about referents as well as to their perceived relevance. Based on equity theory, when employees envision an inequity, they may make one or more of five choices:

1. Distort either their own or others' inputs or outcomes
2. Behave in some way so as to induce others to change their inputs or outcomes
3. Behave in some way so as to change their own inputs or outcomes
4. Choose a different comparison referent
5. Quit their job

Equity theory recognizes that individuals are concerned not only with the absolute amount of rewards they receive for their efforts, but also with the relationship of this amount to what others receive. They make judgments based on the relationship between their inputs and outcomes and the inputs and outcomes of others. Inputs, such as effort, experience, education, and competence, can be compared to outcomes such as salary levels, raises, recognition, and other factors. When people perceive an imbalance in their input-outcome ratio relative to others, tension is created. This tension provides the basis for motivation, as people strive for what they perceive as equity and fairness.

Specifically, the theory establishes four propositions relating to inequitable pay:

1. **Given payment by time, overrewarded employees will produce more than equitably paid employees.** Hourly and salaried employees will generate a high quantity or quality of production in order to increase the input side of the ratio and bring about equity.
2. **Given payment by quantity of production, overrewarded employees will produce fewer but higher-quality units than equitably paid employees.** Individuals paid on a piece-rate basis will increase their effort to achieve equity, which can result in greater quality or quantity. However, increases in quantity will only increase inequity, since every unit produced results in further overpayment. Therefore, effort is directed toward increasing quality rather than quantity.
3. **Given payment by time, underrewarded employees will produce less or a poorer quality of output.** Effort will be decreased, which will bring about lower productivity or poorer quality of output than equitably paid subjects.
4. **Given payment by quantity of production, underrewarded employees will produce a large number of low-quality units in comparison with equitably paid employees.** Employees on piece-rate pay plans can bring about equity because trading off quality of output for quantity will result in an increase in rewards with little or no increase in contributions.

A review of the recent research tends to consistently confirm the equity thesis: Employee motivation is influenced significantly by relative rewards as well as absolute rewards. When employees perceive inequity, they will act to correct the situation. The result might be lower or higher productivity, improved or reduced quality of output, increased absenteeism, or voluntary resignation.

The preceding does not mean that equity theory is without problems. The theory leaves some key issues unclear. For instance, how do employees select who is included in the "other" referent category? How do they define inputs and outcomes? How do they combine and weight their inputs and outcomes to arrive at totals? When and how do the factors change over time? However, regardless of these problems, equity theory has an impressive amount of research support and offers us some important insights into employee motivation.

Expectancy Theory

The most comprehensive explanation of motivation is expectancy theory.[8] Though it, too, has its critics, most of the research evidence is supportive of the theory.

Essentially, *expectancy theory* argues that the strength of a tendency to act in a certain way depends on the strength of an expectation that the act will be followed by a given outcome, and on the attractiveness of that outcome to the individual. Therefore, it includes these three variables:

1. **Attractiveness**—the importance the individual places on the potential outcome or reward that can be achieved on the job. This considers the unsatisfied needs of the individual.
2. **Performance-reward linkage**—the degree to which the individual believes performing at a particular level will lead to the attainment of a desired outcome.
3. **Effort-performance linkage**—the probability perceived by the individual that exerting a given amount of effort will lead to performance.

While this may sound pretty complex, it really is not that difficult to visualize. Whether or not one has the desire to produce at any given time depends on one's particular goals and one's perception of the relative worth of performance as a path to the attainment of these goals.

Exhibit 4–4 is a considerable simplification of expectancy theory, but expresses its major contentions. The strength of a person's motivation to perform (effort) depends on how strongly she believes she can achieve what she attempts. If she achieves this goal (performance), will she be adequately rewarded and, if she is rewarded by the organization, will the reward satisfy her individual goals? Let us consider the four steps inherent in the theory.

First, what perceived outcomes does the job offer the employee? Outcomes may be positive: pay, security, companionship, trust, fringe benefits, a chance to use talent or skills, congenial relationships. On the other hand, employees may view the outcomes as negative: fatigue, boredom, frustration, anxiety, harsh supervision, threat of dismissal. Importantly, reality is

---

[8] Victor H. Vroom, *Work and Motivation* (New York: Wiley, 1964).

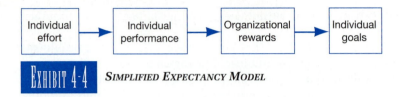

| Individual effort | → | Individual performance | → | Organizational rewards | → | Individual goals |

EXHIBIT 4-4 **SIMPLIFIED EXPECTANCY MODEL**

not relevant here; the critical issue is what the individual employee *perceives* the outcome to be, regardless of whether or not her perceptions are accurate.

Second, how attractive do employees consider these outcomes? Are they valued positively, negatively, or neutrally? This is obviously an internal issue to the individual and considers her personal attitudes, personality, and needs. The individual who finds a particular outcome attractive—that is, positively valued—will prefer attaining it to not attaining it. Others may find it negative and, therefore, prefer not to attain it. Still others may be neutral.

Third, what kind of behavior must the employee exhibit in order to achieve these outcomes? The outcomes are not likely to have any effect on the individual employee's performance unless the employee knows, clearly and unambiguously, what she must do in order to achieve them. For example, what is "doing well" in terms of performance appraisal? On what criteria will the employee's performance be judged?

Fourth and last, how does the employee view her chances of doing what is asked of her? After the employee has considered her own competencies and her ability to control those variables that will determine her success, what probability does she place on successful attainment?

Let's highlight some of the issues that expectancy theory has brought forward. First, it emphasizes payoffs or rewards. As a result, we have to believe the rewards the organization is offering align with what the employee wants. It is a theory based on self-interest, wherein each individual seeks to maximize his or her expected satisfaction. We have to be concerned with the attractiveness of rewards; this requires an understanding and knowledge of what value the individual puts on organizational payoffs. We want to reward individuals with those things they value positively. Second, expectancy theory emphasizes expected behaviors. Does the person know what is expected of her and how she will be appraised? Finally, the theory is concerned with the individual's expectations. What is realistic is irrelevant. An employee's own expectations of performance, reward, and goal satisfaction outcomes, not the objective outcomes themselves, will determine her level of effort.

■ CURRENT ISSUES IN MOTIVATION

Are the theories we've presented in this chapter generalizable across national boundaries? For instance, is goal setting as effective in Portugal as it is in the United States? And what, if any, guidance can we draw from our discussion of motivation that can help us motivate a diverse work force? We try to answer these questions in this section.

Motivation Theories in a Global Context

Most current motivation theories were developed in the United States by Americans and about Americans. Maybe the most blatant pro-American characteristics inherent in these theories is the strong emphasis on individualism and masculinity. For instance, both goal-setting and expectancy theories emphasize goal accomplishment as well as rational and individual thought. Let's take a look at how this bias has affected a few of the motivation theories introduced in this chapter.

Maslow's need hierarchy argues that people start at the physiological level and then move progressively up the hierarchy in this order: physiological, safety, social, esteem, and self-actualization. This hierarchy, if it has any application at all, aligns with American culture. In countries like Japan, Greece, or Mexico, where uncertainty avoidance characteristics are strong, security needs would be on top of the need hierarchy. Countries that score high on femininity characteristics—Denmark, Sweden, Norway, the Netherlands, and Finland—would have social needs on top. We would predict, for instance, that group work will motivate employees more when the country's culture scores high on the femininity criterion.

Another motivation concept that clearly has a U.S. bias is the achievement need. The view that a high achievement need acts as an internal motivator presupposes two cultural characteristics—a willingness to accept a moderate degree of risk (which excludes countries with strong uncertainty avoidance characteristics) and a concern with performance (which applies almost singularly to countries with strong masculinity characteristics). This combination is found in Anglo-American countries like the United States, Canada, and Great Britain. On the other hand, these characteristics are relatively absent in countries such as Chile and Portugal.

Goal setting is also certainly culture bound. It is well adapted to the United States because its key components align reasonably well with U.S. culture. It assumes subordinates will be reasonably independent (not too high a score on power distance), managers and subordinates will seek challenging goals (low in uncertainty avoidance), and performance is considered important by both (high in masculinity). Goal setting's recommendations are not likely to increase motivation in countries in which the opposite conditions exist, such as in France, Portugal, and Chile.

Motivating a Diversified Work Force

Not *everyone* is motivated by money. Not *everyone* wants a challenging job. The needs of women, singles, immigrants, the physically disabled, senior citizens, and others from diverse groups are not the same as a white American male with three dependents. A couple of examples can make this point clearer. Senior citizens, college-age employees, and single mothers typically place a high value on flexible work schedules. A married employee, whose spouse's employer provides a fully paid medical plan for all family members, is not likely to care whether your organization has great medical benefits.

If you're going to maximize your employees' motivation, you've got to understand and respond to this diversity. How? The key word to guide you should be *flexibility*. Be ready to design work schedules, compensation plans, benefits, physical work settings, and the like to reflect your employees' varied needs. This might include offering child care, flexible work hours, and job sharing for employees with family responsibilities. Or flexible leave policies for immigrants who want to return occasionally to their homelands. Or work teams for employees who come from countries with a strong collectivist orientation. Or allowing employees who are going to school to vary their work schedule from semester to semester.

■ IMPLICATIONS FOR MANAGERS

We've presented a number of theories in this chapter, many of which have demonstrated reasonably strong predictive value. If you're a manager, concerned with motivating your employees, how do you apply these theories? While there is no simple, all-encompassing set of guidelines, the essence of what we know about motivating employees in organizations is distilled in the following suggestions.

Recognize Individual Differences. Almost every contemporary motivation theory recognizes that employees are not homogeneous. People have different needs. They also differ in terms of attitudes, personalities, and other important individual variables. For instance, expectancy predictions tend to be more accurate with individuals who have an internal rather than external locus of control. Why? Such individuals believe events in their lives are influenced by themselves, consistent with expectancy theory's assumptions that people rationally pursue their individual goals.

Match People to Jobs. Abundant evidence supports the idea that motivational benefits accrue from carefully matching people to jobs. For example, if the job involves running a small business or an autonomous unit within a larger business, high achievers should be sought. However, if the job to be filled is a managerial slot in a large bureaucratic organization, a candidate high in *nPow* and low in *nAff* should be selected. Along these same lines, don't put a high achiever into a job that is inconsistent with his or her needs. Achievers will do best where the job provides opportunities to set goals participatively, and where there is autonomy and feedback. But keep in mind that not everybody will be motivated by jobs with increased autonomy, variety, and responsibility.

Use Goals. The goal-setting literature gives us considerable confidence in suggesting managers should ensure that employees have hard and specific goals, as well as feedback on how well they are doing in pursuit of those goals. For those with high achievement needs—typically a minority in any organization—the existence of external goals is of less importance because these people are already internally motivated.

Should the goals be assigned by a manager or should they be participatively set in conjunction with the employee? The answer to that question depends on your perception of goal acceptance and the organization's culture. If you expect resistance to goals, the use of participation should increase acceptance. If participation is inconsistent with the culture—that is, if the organization is formal and strongly authority oriented—use assigned goals. Where participation and the culture are incongruous, employees are likely to perceive the participative process as manipulative and distrust it.

Ensure That Goals Are Perceived as Attainable. Regardless of whether goals are actually attainable and well within management's perceptions of the employees' ability, if employees see them as unattainable, they will reduce their effort. Managers must be sure, therefore, that employees feel confident their effort *can* lead to performance goals. For managers, this means employees must have the capability to do the job and employees must perceive the appraisal process by which their performance will be evaluated as both reliable and valid.

Individualize Rewards. Since employees have different needs, what acts as a reinforcer for one may not work for another. Managers should use their knowledge of individual differences to individualize the rewards over which they have control. Some of the more obvious rewards that managers allocate include pay, promotions, autonomy, and the opportunity to participate in goal setting and decision making.

Link Rewards to Performance. In both reinforcement theory and expectancy theory, managers need to make rewards contingent on performance. To reward factors other than performance will only act to reinforce those other factors. Key rewards such as pay increases and promotions should be allocated for the attainment of the employee's specific goals. To maximize the impact of the reward contingency, managers should look for ways to increase the visibility of rewards. Eliminating the secrecy surrounding pay by openly communicating everyone's compensation, publicizing performance bonuses, and allocating annual salary increases in a lump sum rather than spreading them out over the entire year are examples of actions that will make rewards more visible and potentially more motivating.

Check the System for Equity. Rewards or outcomes should be perceived by employees as equaling the inputs they give. At a simplistic level, this means experience, abilities, effort, and other obvious inputs should explain differences in pay, responsibility, and the other obvious outcomes. The problem, however, is complicated by the dozens of inputs and outcomes, and because employee groups place different degrees of importance on them. This suggests that one person's equity is another's inequity, so an ideal reward system should probably weight inputs differently in order to arrive at the proper rewards for each job.

Don't Ignore Money! It's easy to get so caught up in setting goals or providing opportunities for participation that one can forget money is a major reason why most people work. So the allocation of performance-based wage increases, piecework bonuses, and other pay incentives are important in determining employee motivation. Maybe the best case for "money as a motivator" is a review of 80 studies evaluating motivational methods and their impacts on employee productivity.[9] Goal setting alone produced, on average, a 16 percent increase in productivity; efforts to redesign jobs in order to make them more interesting and challenging yielded 8 to 16 percent increases; employee participation in decision making produced a median increase of less than 1 percent; while monetary incentives led to an average increase of 30 percent.

$\mathcal{S}$UGGESTIONS FOR FURTHER READING

DOYLE, KENNETH O., "Money and the Behavioral Sciences," *American Behavioral Scientist,* July-August 1992, pp. 641–57.

HARDER, JOSEPH W., "Play for Pay: Effects of Inequity in a Pay-for-Performance Context," *Administrative Science Quarterly,* June 1992, pp. 321–35.

KANFER, RUTH, "Motivation Theory and Industrial and Organizational Psychology," in M.D. Dunnette and L.M. Hough, eds., *Handbook of Industrial and Organizational Psychology,* 2nd ed., Vol. 1 (Palo Alto, CA: Consulting Psychologists Press, 1990).

KATZELL, RAYMOND A., AND DONNA E. THOMPSON, "Work Motivation: Theory and Practice," *American Psychologist,* February 1990, pp. 144–53.

STEERS, RICHARD M., AND LYMAN W. PORTER, eds., *Motivation and Work Behavior,* 5th ed. (New York: McGraw-Hill, 1991).

WOFFORD, J.C., VICKI L. GOODWIN, AND STEVEN PREMACK, "Meta-Analysis of the Antecedents of Personal Goal Level and of the Antecedents and Consequences of Goal Commitment," *Journal of Management,* September 1992, pp. 595–615.

WRIGHT, PATRICK M., "Operationalization of Goal Difficulty as a Moderator of the Goal Difficulty-Performance Relationship," *Journal of Applied Psychology,* June 1990, pp. 227–34.

WRIGHT, PATRICK M., "An Examination of the Relationships among Monetary Incentives, Goal Level, Goal Commitment, and Performance," *Journal of Management,* December 1992, pp. 677–93.

---

9 Edwin A. Locke, D. V. Feren, V. M. McCaleb, K. N. Shaw, and A. T. Denny, "The Relative Effectiveness of Four Methods of Motivating Employee Performance," in *Changes in Working Life,* eds. K. D. Duncan, M. M. Gruneberg, and D. Wallis (London: Wiley, 1980), pp. 363–83.

CHAPTER 5

DESIGNING MOTIVATING JOBS

After reading this chapter, you should be able to:

1. Contrast the terms *job design, quality of work life,* and *job redesign*

2. Differentiate job *enrichment* from job *enlargement*

3. Explain why autonomous work teams can increase employee motivation

4. Describe problem-solving teams

5. Explain the job characteristics model

6. Identify specific actions that managers can take to make jobs more motivating

One of the more important factors that influence an employee's motivational level is the structure of his or her work. Is there a lot of variety or is the job repetitive? Is the work closely supervised? Does the job allow the employee discretion? The answers to questions like these have a major impact on the motivational properties inherent in the job and hence the level of productivity an employee can expect to achieve. In this chapter, we demonstrate how a job's content and structure affect the level of effort exerted. In addition, we offer options for redesigning jobs to make them more attractive and motivational to employees.

■ DESIGNING JOBS AND MOTIVATING EMPLOYEES

The previous chapter demonstrated the central role that needs play in motivation. Employees have needs, which they seek to satisfy. Obviously, some of these needs can be, and should be, satisfied *off* the job. Since the time a person puts into his job represents about 35 percent of his waking hours, there are ample opportunities for finding fulfillment and satisfaction from non-job-related activities. It can be argued that if jobs are a bore, there are sufficient opportunities for finding excitement off the job. On the other hand, it can also be argued that intrinsically rewarding jobs—those that offer challenge and greater freedom, and that employees find interesting—provide motivation in themselves, and require substantially less reliance on externally initiated motivators.

The key role that job design plays in motivation can be seen in the results from a study where a thousand employees were asked to rank-order, by importance, ten work-related factors. Interesting work was consistently rated near the top of the list—ahead of factors like pay, job security, promotion opportunities, and sympathetic help with personal problems.[1] So, if management can design jobs that employees find interesting, the jobs themselves can provide a major source of motivation.

■ CLARIFYING TERMINOLOGY

The term *job design* is closely associated with "quality of work life" programs and "job *re*design." In this section, we define each of these concepts.

Job Design

The term *job design* refers to the way tasks are combined to form complete jobs. Some jobs are routine because the tasks are standardized and repetitive; others are nonroutine. Some require a large number of varied and diverse skills; others are narrow in scope. Some jobs constrain the employee by requiring him or her to follow very precise procedures; others allow employees substantial freedom in how they do their work. Some jobs are most effectively accomplished by groups of employees working as a team; other jobs are best done by individuals essentially acting independently. The point is that jobs differ in the way tasks are combined and these different combinations create a variety of job designs.

Quality of Work Life

The content and design of jobs have interested engineers and economists for centuries. Adam Smith, for instance, wrote on the economies of specialization—dividing jobs into smaller and smaller pieces—over two hundred years ago. At the turn of this century, Frederick Taylor introduced scientific management that strongly advocated the systematizing and proceduring of jobs. In fact, up until the 1950s, job design was substantially synonymous with job specialization.

---

[1] Kenneth A. Kovach, "What Motivates Employees? Workers and Supervisors Give Different Answers," *Business Horizons* (September–October 1987), pp. 58–65.

However, during the last 40 years or so, psychologists, sociologists, and other social scientists have begun to shift their attention to consider the human needs of employees, which has led to the consideration of human issues in job content and alternative methods, besides specialization, of job design. Today we describe these alternatives as part of *quality of work life* (QWL) programs. QWL has become a label to describe systemwide change programs that improve the work environment and satisfy the needs of individual employees. Job design changes that humanize the workplace and respond to employees' personal needs are central elements in most QWL programs.

Job Redesign

Job redesign is concerned with change. For the most part, *job redesign* programs seek to make jobs more interesting, diverse, and challenging.

We start with the assumption that designing jobs around high specialization offers many economic advantages for managers. The wide popularity of specialization attests to the validity of this assumption. Yet specialization has created jobs that, to many workers, are repetitive, boring, stressful, and generally lacking in meaningfulness. Job redesign, therefore, refers to the alteration of specific jobs or interdependent groups of jobs for the purpose of increasing both the quality of an employee's work experience and on-the-job productivity. The following pages consider the major job redesign options available to managers.

■ INDIVIDUAL REDESIGN OPTIONS

The first set of options is concerned with redesigning individual tasks. Among the individual redesign options that managers may want to consider are job rotation, work modules, job enlargement, and job enrichment.

Job Rotation

Job rotation allows workers to diversify their activities to offset boredom. There are actually two types of rotation: vertical and horizontal. Vertical rotation relates to promotions and demotions. When we talk about job rotation, however, we are referring to the horizontal variety, or what may be more accurately called a lateral transfer.

Horizontal job transfers can be instituted on a planned basis—that is, by means of a training program whereby the employee spends, say, two or three months in an activity and is then moved on. This approach, for example, is common among large Wall Street law firms where new associates work for many different partners before choosing an area of specialization. Horizontal transfers can also be made based on individual situations—moving someone to another activity when the first is no longer challenging or when the needs of the work schedule dictate it. Historically, lateral moves were popular as a means of developing managerial talent. However, in the 1990s, with promotions becoming scarcer, a number of companies, including American Greetings, RJR Nabisco, Corning, and Eastman Kodak, are using lateral transfers as a way to keep and motivate valuable employees.

The advantages of job rotation are clear. It broadens employees and gives them a range of experiences. Boredom and monotony, which develop after a person has acquired the skills to perform his or her task effectively, are reduced when transfers are made frequently. Additionally, since a broad experience permits a greater understanding of other activities within the organization, people are prepared more rapidly to assume greater responsibility, especially at the upper echelons. In other words, as one moves up the organization, it becomes increasingly necessary to understand the intricacies and interrelationships of activities; and these skills can be more quickly acquired by moving about within the organization.

On the other hand, job rotation is not without its drawbacks. Training costs are increased and productivity is reduced by moving a worker into a new position just when his or her efficiency at the prior job created organizational economies. An extensive rotation program can result in having a vast number of employees situated in positions where their experience is very limited. And even though there may be significant long-term benefits from the program, the organization must be equipped to deal with the day-to-day problems that result when inexperienced personnel perform new tasks, and when rotated managers make decisions based on little experience in the activity at hand. Job rotation can also demotivate intelligent and aggressive trainees who seek specific responsibility in their chosen specialty. Finally, rotation that is imposed involuntarily on employees can reduce job satisfaction and increase absenteeism rates.

Work Modules

If you can conceive of extremely rapid job rotation, in which a worker assumes new activities every few hours, you can comprehend the option of *work modules.* This approach has been suggested as a solution to meet the problem of fractionated, boring, and standardized work. It can often be accomplished at an acceptable price, with undiminished quality and quantity of output.

A work module is defined as a time task unit equal to approximately two hours of work at a given task. A normal 40-hour-a-week job would then be defined in terms of four modules a day, five days a week, for between 48 and 50 weeks per year.

Modules can increase work diversity and give employees a greater opportunity to determine the nature of their jobs. Employees could request a set of modules which, together, would constitute a day's work. Additionally, those tasks that are characteristically seen as undesirable could be spread about, for example, by having everyone take a module or two each day. The result would be that people would change activities by changing work modules. Or, as we noted previously, it could be viewed as a very rapid job rotation system.

There are benefits to work modules: letting employees pick their work tasks, thus taking into account individual job preferences; providing a way for the more boring and undesirable tasks to be completed without seriously demoralizing those people who must do them; and allowing employees some say in the choice of modules, thus constructing the job to meet the needs of the individual rather than forcing people to fit a job.

However, work modules would present the same cost and disruption obstacles as job rotation. Considerable time and money are involved in planning and executing the changeover. Bookkeeping and payroll-computation costs increase. Conflicts can also develop over the question of equity and allocation of modules.

Job Enlargement

Job enlargement expands jobs horizontally. It increases *job scope;* that is, it increases the number of different operations required in a job and the frequency with which the job cycle is repeated. By increasing the number of tasks an individual performs, job enlargement increases diversity. Instead of only sorting the incoming mail by department, for instance, a mail sorter's job could be enlarged to include physically delivering the mail to the various departments or running outgoing letters through the postage meter.

Efforts at job enlargement have met with less than enthusiastic results. As one employee who experienced such a redesign on his job remarked, "Before, I had one lousy job. Now, through enlargement, I have three!" So, while job enlargement attacks the problem of lack of diversity in overspecialized jobs, it has done little to instill challenge or a sense of meaningfulness to a worker's activities. Job enrichment has proven effective at dealing with the shortcomings of enlargement.

Job Enrichment

Job enrichment expands jobs vertically. While job enlargement increases job scope, job enrichment increases *job depth.* What this means is that job enrichment allows employees to have greater control over their work. They are allowed to assume some of the tasks typically done by a supervisor—they have greater influence over the planning, executing, and evaluating of the job. The tasks in an enriched job should allow workers to complete an activity with increased freedom, independence, and responsibility; this type of job should also provide feedback so individuals can assess and correct their own performance.

How jobs can be enriched is illustrated by a Citibank program designed for its back office personnel who processed all the firm's financial transactions.[2] These jobs had been split up so each person performed a single routine task over and over again. Employees had become dissatisfied with these mun-

---

2 R. W. Walters, "The Citibank Project: Improving Productivity through Work Design," in *How to Manage Change Effectively,* ed. D. L. Kirkpatrick (San Francisco: Jossey-Bass, 1985), pp. 195–208.

dane jobs and it showed in their work. Severe backlogs had developed and error rates were unacceptably high. Citibank's management redesigned the work around types of customers. Tasks were combined and individual employees were given complete processing and customer-service responsibility for a small group of customers in a defined product area. In the newly designed jobs, employees dealt directly with customers and handled entire transactions from the time they came into the bank until they left. Citibank found this enrichment program improved the quality of work as well as employee motivation and satisfaction.

Where jobs have been enriched, employee satisfaction tends to increase and there is usually lower absenteeism and reduced turnover. But the impact of job enrichment on productivity is unclear. In some situations, job enrichment has increased productivity; in others, productivity has decreased. However, when it decreases, there does appear to be more consistent, conscientious use of resources and a higher quality of product or service. In other words, in terms of efficiency, for the same input a higher quality of output is obtained.

■ GROUP REDESIGN OPTIONS

During the last 15 years, the main focus of attention on redesign options has shifted from the individual to the group. The following approaches—integrated work teams, autonomous work teams, and problem-solving teams—are each designed around group tasks.

Integrated Work Teams

If job enlargement is practiced at the group level rather than the individual level, you have *integrated work teams.* For jobs that require teamwork and cooperation, this approach can increase diversity for team members.

What would an integrated work team look like? Basically, instead of performing a single task, a large number of tasks would be assigned to a group. The group would then decide the specific assignments for members, and be responsible for rotating jobs among the members as the tasks required. The team would still have a supervisor who would oversee the group's activities. You see the frequent use of integrated work teams in such activities as building maintenance and construction. In the cleaning of a sizable office building, it is not unusual for the foreman to identify the tasks to be completed and then let the maintenance workers, as a group, choose how the tasks will be allocated. Similarly, a road construction crew frequently decides, as a group, how its various tasks are to be completed.

Autonomous Work Teams

Autonomous work teams represent job enrichment at the group level. The work the team does is deepened through vertical integration. The team is given a goal to achieve and then is free to determine work assignments, rest breaks, inspection procedures, and the like. Fully autonomous work teams even select their own members and have the members evaluate each other's performance. As a result, supervisory positions take on decreased importance and may even be eliminated. The autonomous work team concept is a reality at the Oklahoma plant of Shaklee Corporation, where nutritional products, vitamins, and other pills are made.

About 190 of the Oklahoma plant's production employees were organized into teams with 3 to 15 members. The team members set their own production schedules, decided what hours to work, selected new team members from a pool approved by the personnel department, and even initiated discharges if necessary. The results were impressive. The company reported that units produced per hour of labor went up nearly 200 percent over levels at other plants. Two-thirds of this increase was attributed to the autonomous work team concept (the rest was explained by better equipment). Management stated that the Oklahoma plant could produce the same volume as the more traditional facilities at 40 percent of the labor costs.

The improvement at Shaklee is not isolated. There are other reports of favorable improvements in worker attitudes and performance when autonomous work teams have been implemented. For instance, a three-year study of coal mining crews found that creation of autonomous teams resulted in more positive attitudes toward work and a slight positive increase in performance.

Problem-Solving Teams

A *problem-solving team* is a work group of four to ten employees and supervisors who have a shared area of responsibility. They meet regularly—typically once a week, on company time and on company premises—to discuss their quality problems, investigate causes, recommend solutions, and take corrective actions. They take over the responsibility for solving quality problems, and they generate and evaluate their own feedback. Of course, it is not presumed that employees inherently have this ability. Therefore, part of the problem-solving team concept includes teaching participating employees group communication skills, various quality strategies, and measurement and problem-analysis techniques.

As total quality management programs have spread in popularity, so too have problem-solving teams. Some companies, like General Electric, have more than a thousand of them in their plants and offices across North America. And employees seem to welcome the idea of participating in, and generating solutions for, product-quality and production problems. Pragmatically, this enthusiasm and cooperation by workers goes beyond the mere opportunity to collaborate with management on production decisions. It can also mean increased job security. Workers recognize that by improving quality and productivity, their organization's products will be more competitive, the product's market share will expand, and their jobs will be more secure.

■ THE JOB CHARACTERISTICS MODEL

If you want to redesign a job or set of jobs, are any guidelines available to help you? The answer is "Yes!" The most complete framework available for analyzing a job's design is the *job characteristics model* (JCM).[3] It identifies five key job characteristics, their interrelationships, and their predicted impact on employee productivity, motivation, and satisfaction. Let's review the model and show you how you can use it in analyzing and designing jobs.

Core Dimensions

According to the JCM, any job can be described in terms of the following five core job dimensions:

Skill variety—the degree to which a job requires a variety of different activities so the worker can use a number of different skills and talents.

Task identity—the degree to which the job requires completion of a whole and identifiable piece of work.

Task significance—the degree to which the job has a substantial impact on the lives or work of other people.

Autonomy—the degree to which the job provides substantial freedom, independence, and discretion to the individuals in scheduling the work and in determining the procedures to be used in carrying it out.

Feedback—the degree to which carrying out the work activities required by the job results in the individual obtaining direct and clear information about the effectiveness of his or her performance.

Interrelationships and Predictions

Exhibit 5–1 presents the model. Notice how the first three dimensions—skill variety, task identity, and task significance—combine to create meaningful work. That is, if these three characteristics exist in a job, we can predict the person will view that job as being important, valuable, and worthwhile. Notice, too, that a job allowing autonomy gives the worker a feeling of personal responsibility for the results; and that if a job provides feedback, the employee will know how effectively he or she is performing. From a motivational standpoint, the model says internal rewards are obtained by an employee when that person *learns* (knowledge of results) he or she *personally* (experienced responsibility) has performed well on a task he or she

---

[3] J. Richard Hackman and Greg R. Oldham, "Motivation through the Design of Work: Test of a Theory," *Organizational Behavior and Human Performance* (August 1976), pp. 250–79.

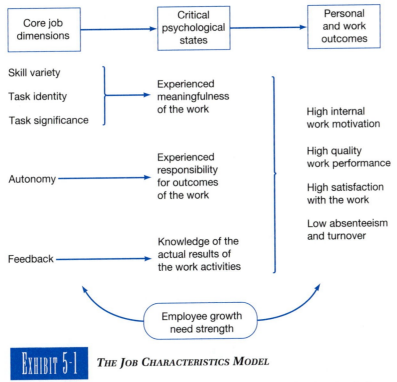

EXHIBIT 5-1   *THE JOB CHARACTERISTICS MODEL*

Source: J. Richard Hackman, "Work Design," in *Improv-ing Life at Work,* eds. J. Richard Hackman and J. Lloyd Suttle (Santa Monica, CA.: Goodyear, 1977), p. 129.

cares about (experienced significance). The more these three psychological states are present, the greater will be the employee's motivation, performance, and satisfaction, and the lower his absenteeism and likelihood of leaving the job. As the model shows, the links between the job dimensions and the outcomes are moderated by the strength of the individual's growth need, that is, the employee's desire for self-esteem and self-actualization. This means individuals with a high growth need are more likely to experience the three psychological states when their jobs are enriched than are their low-growth-need counterparts; that is, they will respond more positively to the psychological states, when they are present, than will low-growth-need individuals.

The core job dimensions can be combined into a single predictive index, called the motivating potential score (MPS). Its computation is shown in Exhibit 5–2.

Jobs high in motivating potential must be high in at least one of the three factors leading to experiencing meaningfulness, plus they must be high on both autonomy and feedback. If jobs score high on motivating potential, the model predicts that motivation, performance, and satisfaction will be positively affected, while the likelihood of absence and turnover is lessened.

$$\text{Motivating Potential Score(MPS)} = \left[\frac{\text{Skill variety} + \text{Task identity} + \text{Task significance}}{3} \right] \times \text{Autonomy} \times \text{Feedback}$$

EXHIBIT 5-2   *COMPUTING A MOTIVATING POTENTIAL SCORE*

Source: J. Richard Hackman, "Work Design," in *Improving Life at Work,* eds. J. Richard Hackman and J. Lloyd Suttle (Santa Monica, CA.: Goodyear, 1977), p. 130.

Tests of the job characteristics model have generally produced encouraging results. At this point in time, we can draw the following conclusions with relative confidence:

1. People who work on jobs with high core job dimensions are more motivated, satisfied, and productive than those who do not.
2. People with strong growth needs respond more positively to jobs that are high in motivating potential than do those with weak growth needs.
3. Job dimensions operate through the psychological states in influencing personal and work outcome variables, rather than influencing them directly.

■ IMPLICATIONS FOR MANAGERS

The JCM offers specific suggestions to managers for job redesign. The following suggestions specify what types of changes in jobs are most likely to lead to improvements in each of the five core dimensions:

1. **Combine tasks.** Managers should seek to take existing fractionalized tasks and put them back together to form a new, larger module of work. This will increase skill variety and task identity.
2. **Create natural work units.** The creation of natural work units means the tasks an employee does form an identifiable and meaningful whole. This increases employee "ownership" of the work and improves the likelihood that employees will view their work as meaningful and important rather than as irrelevant and boring.
3. **Establish client relationships.** The client is the user of the product or service the employee works on. Wherever possible, managers should try to establish direct relationships between workers and their clients. This will increase skill variety, autonomy, and feedback for the employee.
4. **Expand jobs vertically.** Vertical expansion gives employees responsibilities and controls that were formerly reserved for management. It seeks to partially close the gap between the "doing" and the "controlling" aspects of the job and increases employee autonomy.
5. **Open feedback channels.** By increasing feedback, employees not only learn how well they are performing their jobs but also whether their performance is improving, deteriorating, or remaining at a constant level. Ideally, this feedback about performance should be received directly as the employee does the job, rather than from management on an occasional basis.

EXHIBIT 5-3 *JOB REDESIGN OPTIONS ASSESSED IN TERMS OF JOB CHARACTERISTICS*

	JOB CHARACTERISTICS				
Options	**Skill Variety**	**Task Identity**	**Task Significance**	**Autonomy**	**Feedback**
Job rotation	X		?		
Work modules	X		?	X	
Job enlargement	X		?		
Job enrichment	X	X	?	X	X
Integrated work teams	X		?		
Autonomous work teams	X	X	?	X	X
Problem-solving teams	X	X	?	X	X

Exhibit 5–3 summarizes the redesign options we have discussed in terms of their ability to meet the criteria identified in the JCM. All of the options increase skill variety. However, whether or not each increases task significance is often difficult to assess without knowing more about the work content in question. Beyond these two criteria, the various options begin to differ.

A review of Exhibit 5–3 indicates that three options—job enrichment, autonomous work teams, and problem-solving teams—are superior to the other options *in terms of the job characteristics model.* Of course, we have said nothing about the cost of implementing these changes. The benefits each offers must be analyzed in relation to the cost of each approach. For example, common sense tells us the more complex changes—such as autonomous work teams—would have to generate significantly more benefits than a simple change—such as job rotation—to justify the greater time and effort required for implementation by management. Nevertheless, the JCM tells us that for employees who possess a high growth need, their motivation, performance, and satisfaction should be high when working in enriched jobs, on autonomous work teams, or participating in problem-solving teams.

$\mathcal{S}$UGGESTIONS FOR FURTHER READING

CAMPION, MICHAEL A., "Interdisciplinary Approaches to Job Design: A Constructive Replication with Extension," *Journal of Applied Psychology,* August 1988, pp. 467–81.

CAMPION, MICHAEL A., AND CAROL L. MCCLELLAND, "Interdisciplinary Examination of the Costs and Benefits of Enlarged Jobs: A Job Design Quasi-Experiment," *Journal of Applied Psychology,* April 1991, pp. 186–98.

DUMAINE, BRIAN, "Who Needs a Boss?" *Fortune,* May 7, 1990, pp. 52–58.

HACKMAN, J. RICHARD, AND GREG R. OLDHAM, *Work Redesign* (Reading, MA: Addison-Wesley, 1980).

JOHNS, GARY, JIA LIN XIE, AND YONGQING FANG, "Mediating and Moderating Effects in Job Design," *Journal of Management,* December 1992, pp. 657–76.

SPECTOR, PAUL E., AND STEVE M. JEX, "Relations of Job Characteristics from Multiple Data Sources with Employee Affect, Absence, Turnover Intentions, and Health," *Journal of Applied Psychology,* February 1991, pp. 46–53.

SUNDSTROM, ERIC, KENNETH P. DE MEUSE, AND DAVID FUTRELL, "Work Teams," *American Psychologist,* February 1990, pp. 120–33.

ZACCARO, S.J., AND EUGENE F. STONE, "Incremental Validity of an Empirical Based Measure of Job Characteristics," *Journal of Applied Psychology,* May 1988, pp. 245–52.

CHAPTER 6

INDIVIDUAL DECISION MAKING

After reading this chapter, you should be able to:

1. Outline the six steps in the optimizing decision process
2. List the assumptions of the optimizing model
3. Explain how individuals satisfice
4. Describe the implicit favorite model
5. Identify when intuition may enhance decision quality
6. Differentiate among the three ethical decision criteria
7. Explain what influences an individual's ethical decision-making behavior

Individuals in organizations make decisions. Top managers, for instance, determine their organization's goals, what products or services to offer, how best to organize corporate headquarters, or where to locate a new manufacturing plant. Middle- and lower-level managers determine production schedules, select new employees, and decide how pay raises are to be allocated. However, the making of decisions is not the sole province of managers. Nonmanagerial employees also make decisions that affect their jobs and the organizations they work for. The more obvious of these decisions might include whether to come to work or not on any given day, how much effort to put forward once at work, and whether to comply with a request made by the boss.

So every individual in every organization regularly engages in *decision making;* that is, they make choices from among two or more alternatives. Undoubtedly, many of these choices are almost reflex actions, undertaken with little conscious thought. The boss asks you to complete a certain report by the end of the day and you comply, assuming the request is reasonable. In such instances, choices are still being made though they don't require much contemplation. But when individuals confront new or important decisions, they can be expected to reason them out thoughtfully. Alternatives will be developed. Pros and cons will be weighed. The result is that what people do on their jobs is influenced by their decision processes. This chapter reviews how individuals make decisions and considers how this has an impact on their work behavior.

■ THE OPTIMIZING MODEL

Let's begin by describing how individuals should behave in order to maximize a certain outcome. We will call this the *optimizing model* of decision making.

Steps in the Optimizing Model

Exhibit 6–1 outlines the six steps an individual should follow, either explicitly or implicitly, when making a decision.

Step 1: Ascertain the Need for a Decision. The first step requires recognition that a decision needs to be made. What brings about this recognition? The existence of a problem or, more specifically, a disparity between some desired state and the actual condition. If you calculate your monthly expenses and find you're spending $50 more than you allocated in your budget, you have ascertained the need for a decision. There is a disparity between your desired expenditure level and what you're actually spending.

Step 2: Identify the Decision Criteria. Once an individual has determined the need for a decision, the criteria that will be important in making the decision must be identified. For illustration purposes, let's consider the case of a high school senior confronting the problem of choosing a college. The concepts derived from this example may be generalized to any decision a person might confront.

For the sake of simplicity, let's assume our high school senior has already chosen to attend college (versus other noncollege options). We know the need for a decision is precipitated by graduation. Once she has recognized this need for a decision, the student should begin to list the criteria or factors that will be relevant to her decision. For our example, let's assume she has identified the

---

1. Ascertain the need for a decision.
2. Identify the decision criteria.
3. Allocate weights to the criteria.
4. Develop the alternatives.
5. Evaluate the alternatives.
6. Select the best alternative.

 EXHIBIT 6-1 ***STEPS IN THE OPTIMIZING DECISION MODEL***

following criteria about the school: annual cost, availability of financial aid, admission requirements, status or reputation, size, geographic location, curricula offering, male:female ratio, quality of social life, and the physical attractiveness of the campus. These criteria represent what the decision maker thinks is relevant to her decision. Note that, in this step, what is *not* listed is as important as what *is*. For example, our high school senior did not consider factors such as where her friends were going to school, availability of part-time employment, or whether freshmen are required to reside on campus. To someone else making a college selection decision, the criteria used might be considerably different.

This second step is important because it identifies only those criteria that the decision maker considers relevant. If a criterion is omitted from this list, we treat it as irrelevant to the decision maker.

Step 3: Allocate Weights to the Criteria. The criteria listed in the previous step are not all equally important. It's necessary, therefore, to weight the factors listed in Step 2 in order to prioritize their importance in the decision. All the criteria are relevant, but some are more relevant than others.

How does the decision maker weight criteria? A simple approach would merely be to give *the* most important criterion a number—say 10—and then assign weights to the rest of the criteria against this standard. So the result of Steps 2 and 3 is to allow decision makers to use their personal preferences both to prioritize the relevant criteria and to indicate their relative degree of importance by assigning a weight to each. Exhibit 6–2 lists the criteria and weights our high school senior is using in her college decision.

Step 4: Develop the Alternatives. The fourth step requires the decision maker to list all the viable alternatives that could possibly succeed in resolving the problem. No attempt is made in this step to appraise the alternatives, only to list them. To return to our example, let us assume our high schooler has identified eight potential colleges—Alpha, Beta, Delta, Gamma, Iota, Omega, Phi, and Sigma.

Criteria	Weights
• Availability of financial aid	10
• School's reputation	10
• Annual cost	8
• Curricula offering	7
• Geographic location	6
• Admission requirements	5
• Quality of social life	4
• School size	3
• Male:female ratio	2
• Physical attractiveness of the campus	2

 EXHIBIT 6-2 *CRITERIA AND WEIGHTS IN SELECTION OF A COLLEGE*

Step 5: Evaluate the Alternatives. Once the alternatives have been identified, the decision maker must critically evaluate each one. The strengths and weaknesses of each alternative will become evident when they are compared against the criteria and weights established in Steps 2 and 3.

The evaluation of each alternative is done by appraising it against the weighted criteria. In our example, the high school senior would evaluate each college using every one of the criteria. To keep our example simple, we'll assume a 10 means the college is rated as "most favorable" on that criterion. The results from evaluating the various alternative colleges are shown in Exhibit 6–3.

Keep in mind that the ratings given the eight colleges shown in Exhibit 6–3 are based on the assessment made by the decision maker. Some assessments can be made in a relatively objective fashion. If our decision maker prefers a small school, one with an enrollment of 1,000 is obviously superior to one with 10,000 students. Similarly, if a high male:female ratio is sought, 3:1 is clearly higher than 1.2:1. But the assessment of criteria such as reputation, quality of social life, or the physical attractiveness of the campus reflects the decision maker's values. The point is that most decisions contain judgments. They are reflected in the criteria chosen in Step 2, the weights given to these criteria, and the evaluation of alternatives. This explains why two people faced with a similar problem—such as selecting a college—may look at two totally different sets of alternatives or even look at the same alternatives but rate them very differently.

Exhibit 6–3 only represents an evaluation of the eight alternatives against the decision criteria. It does not reflect the weighting done in Step 3. If one choice had scored 10 on every criterion, there would be no need to consider the weights. Similarly, if the weights were all equal, you could evaluate each alternative merely by summing up the appropriate column in Exhibit 6–3. For instance, Omega College would be highest, with a total score of 84. But our high school senior needs to multiply each alternative against its weight. The result of this process is shown in Exhibit 6–4. The summation of these scores represents an evaluation of each college against the previously established criteria and weights.

Step 6: Select the Best Alternative. The final step in the optimizing decision model is the selection of the best alternative from among those enumerated and evaluated. Since best is defined in terms of highest total score, the selection is quite simple. The decision maker merely chooses the alternative that generated the largest total score in Step 5. For our high school senior, that means Delta College. Based on the criteria identified, the weights given to the criteria, and the decision maker's evaluation of each college on each of the criteria, Delta College scored highest and thus becomes the best.

Assumptions of the Optimizing Model

The steps in the optimizing model contain a number of assumptions. It is important to understand these assumptions if we are to determine how accurately the optimizing model describes actual individual decision making.

EXHIBIT 6-3 *EVALUATION OF EIGHT ALTERNATIVES AGAINST THE DECISION CRITERIA**

ALTERNATIVES

Criteria	Alpha College	Beta College	Delta College	Gamma College	Iota College	Omega College	Phi College	Sigma College
Availability of financial aid	5	4	10	7	7	8	3	7
School's reputation	10	6	6	6	9	5	9	6
Annual cost (low cost preferred)	5	7	8	8	5	10	5	8
Curricula offering	6	10	8	9	8	8	9	8
Geographic location	6	7	10	10	6	9	10	7
Admission requirements (in terms of likelihood of acceptance)	7	10	10	10	8	10	8	10
Quality of social life	10	5	7	7	3	7	10	8
School size	10	7	7	7	9	7	9	4
Male:female ratio	2	2	8	8	8	10	2	8
Physical attractiveness of the campus	8	10	6	3	4	10	5	9

*The colleges that achieved the highest rating for a criterion are given 10 points.

EXHIBIT 6-4   *EVALUATION OF COLLEGE ALTERNATIVES*

ALTERNATIVES

Criteria (and Weight)	Alpha College	Beta College	Delta College	Gamma College	Iota College	Omega College	Phi College	Sigma College
Availability of financial aid (10)	50	40	100	70	70	80	30	70
School's reputation (10)	100	60	60	60	90	50	90	60
Annual cost (8)	40	56	64	64	40	80	40	64
Curricula offering (7)	42	70	56	63	56	56	63	56
Geographic location (6)	36	42	60	60	36	54	60	42
Admission requirements (5)	35	50	50	50	40	50	40	50
Quality of social life (4)	40	20	28	28	12	28	40	32
School size (3)	30	21	21	21	27	21	27	12
Male:female ratio (2)	4	4	16	16	16	20	4	16
Physical attractiveness of the campus (2)	16	20	12	6	8	20	10	18
Totals	393	373	467	438	395	459	404	420

The assumptions of the optimizing model are the same as those that underlie the concept of *rationality*. Rationality refers to choices that are consistent and value maximizing. Rational decision making, therefore, implies that the decision maker can be fully objective and logical. The individual is assumed to have a clear goal, and all of the six steps in the optimizing model are assumed to lead toward the selection of the alternative that will maximize that goal. Let's take a closer look at the assumptions inherent in rationality and, hence, the optimizing model.

Goal Oriented. The optimizing model assumes there is no conflict over the goal. Whether the decision involves selecting a college to attend, determining whether or not to go to work today, or choosing the right applicant to fill a job vacancy, it is assumed the decision maker has a single well-defined goal he or she is trying to maximize.

All Options Are Known. It is assumed the decision maker can identify *all* the relevant criteria and can list *all* viable alternatives. The optimizing model portrays the decision maker as fully comprehensive in his or her ability to assess criteria and alternatives.

Preferences Are Clear. Rationality assumes the criteria and alternatives can be assigned numerical values and ranked in a preferential order.

Preferences Are Constant. The same criteria and alternatives should be obtained every time because, in addition to the goal and preferences being clear, it is assumed the specific decision criteria are constant and the weights assigned to them are stable over time.

Final Choice Will Maximize the Outcome. The rational decision maker following the optimizing model will choose the alternative that rates highest. This most preferred solution will, based on Step 5 of the process, give the maximum benefits.

Predictions from the Optimizing Model

Using the preceding assumptions, we would predict the individual decision maker would have a clear and specific goal; a fully comprehensive set of criteria that determine the relevant factors in the decision; a precise ranking of the criteria, which will be stable over time; and the decision maker will select the alternative that scores highest after all options have been evaluated.

In terms of the college selection decision introduced earlier, the optimizing model would predict the high school student could identify every factor that might be important in her decision. Each of these factors would be weighted in terms of importance. All of the colleges that could possibly be viable options would be identified and evaluated against the criteria. Remember, because all alternatives are assumed to be considered, our decision maker might be looking at hundreds of colleges. Also, even if this activity took six months to complete, the criteria and weights would not vary over time. If the college's reputation was most important in September, it would still be so in March. Further, if Beta College was given a score of 6 on this criterion in September, six months later the assessment would be the same. Finally, since every factor that is important in the decision has been considered and given its proper weight, and since every alternative has been identified and evaluated against the criteria, the decision maker can be assured the college that scores highest in the evaluation is the best choice. There are no regrets because all information has been obtained and evaluated in a logical and consistent manner.

■ ALTERNATIVE DECISION-MAKING MODELS

Do individuals actually make their decisions the way the optimizing model predicts? Sometimes. When decision makers are faced with a simple problem having few alternative courses of action, and when the cost of searching out and evaluating alternatives is low, the optimizing model provides a fairly accurate description of the decision process. Buying a pair of shoes or a new personal computer might be examples of decisions where the optimizing model would apply. But many decisions, particularly important and difficult ones—the kind a person hasn't encountered before and for which there are no standardized or programmed rules to provide guidance—don't involve simple and well-structured problems. Rather, they're characterized by complexity, relatively high uncertainty (all the alternatives, for example, are unlikely to be known), and goals and preferences that are neither clear nor consistent. This category of decision would include choosing a spouse, considering whether to accept a new job offer in a different city, selecting among job applicants for a vacancy in your department, developing a marketing strategy for a new product, deciding where to build an additional manufacturing plant, and determining the proper time to take your small company public by selling stock in it. In this section, we review three alternatives to the optimizing model: the satisficing or bounded rationality model, the implicit favorite model, and the intuitive model.

The Satisficing Model

The essence of the satisficing model is that, when faced with complex problems, decision makers respond by reducing the problems to a level at which they can be readily understood. This is because the information-processing capability of human beings makes it impossible to assimilate and understand all the information necessary to optimize. Since the capacity of the human mind for formulating and solving complex problems is far too small to meet all the requirements for full rationality, individuals operate within the confines of bounded rationality. They construct simplified models that extract the essential features from problems without capturing all their complexity.[1] Individuals can then behave rationally within the limits of the simple model.

How does bounded rationality work for the typical individual? Once a problem is identified, the search for criteria and alternatives begins. But the list of criteria is likely to be far from exhaustive. The decision maker will identify a limited list made up of the more conspicuous choices. These are the choices that are easy to find and tend to be highly visible. In most cases, they will represent familiar criteria and the tried-and-true solutions. Once this limited set of alternatives is identified, the decision maker will begin reviewing them. But the review will not be comprehensive. That is, not all the alternatives will be carefully evaluated. Instead, the decision maker will begin with alternatives that differ only in a relatively small degree from the choice currently in effect. Following along familiar and well-worn paths, the decision maker proceeds to review alternatives only until he or she identifies an alternative that satisfices—one that is satisfactory and sufficient. So the satisficer settles for the first solution that is "good enough," rather than continuing to search for the optimum. The first alternative to meet the "good enough" criterion ends the search, and the decision maker can then proceed toward implementing this acceptable course of action.

One of the more interesting aspects of the satisficing model is that the order in which alternatives are considered is critical in determining which alternative is selected. If the decision maker were optimizing, all alternatives would eventually be listed in a hierarchy of preferred order. Since all the alternatives would be considered, the initial order in which they were evaluated would be irrelevant. Every potential solution would get a full and complete evaluation. But this is not the case with satisficing. Assuming a problem has more than one potential solution, the satisficing choice will be the first acceptable one the decision maker encounters. Since decision makers use simple and limited models, they typically begin by identifying alternatives that are obvious, ones with which they are familiar, and those not too far from the status quo. Those solutions that depart least from the status quo and meet the decision criteria are most likely to be selected. This may help to explain why many decisions that people make don't result in the selection of solutions radically different from those they have made before. A unique alternative may present an optimizing solution to the problem; however, it will rarely be chosen. An acceptable solution will be identified well before the decision maker is required to search very far beyond the status quo.

Using the satisficing model, how might we predict that the high school senior introduced earlier would make her college choice? Obviously, she will not consider all of the more than two thousand colleges in the United States or the multitude of others in foreign countries. Based on schools she's heard about from friends and relatives, plus possibly a quick look through a guide to colleges, she will typically select a half-a-dozen or a dozen colleges to which

---

[1] Herbert A. Simon, *Administrative Behavior*, 3rd ed. (New York: Free Press, 1976).

she will send for catalogs, brochures, and applications. Based on a cursory appraisal of the materials she receives from the colleges, and using her rough decision criteria, she will look for a school that meets her minimal requirements. When she finds one, the decision search will be over. If none of the colleges in this initial set meet the "good enough" standards, she will expand her search to include more diverse colleges. But even following this extended search, the first college she uncovers that meets her minimal requirements will become the alternative of choice.

The Implicit Favorite Model

Another model designed to deal with complex and nonroutine decisions is the implicit favorite model.[2] Like the satisficing model, it argues that individuals solve complex problems by simplifying the process. However, simplification in the implicit favorite model means not entering into the difficult "evaluation of alternatives" stage of decision making until one of the alternatives can be identified as an implicit "favorite." In other words, the decision maker is neither rational nor objective. Instead, early in the decision process, he or she implicitly selects a preferred alternative. Then the rest of the decision process is essentially a decision confirmation exercise, where the decision maker makes sure his or her implicit favorite is indeed the "right" choice.

The implicit favorite model evolved from research on job decisions by graduate management students at the Massachusetts Institute of Technology. Clearly, these students knew and understood the optimizing model. They had spent several years repeatedly using it for solving problems and analyzing cases in accounting, finance, management, marketing, and quantitative methods courses. Moreover, the job choice decision was an important one. If there was a decision where the optimizing model should be used, and a group experienced in using it, this should be it. But the researcher found the optimizing model was not followed. Rather, the implicit favorite model provided an accurate description of the actual decision process.

Following the implicit favorite model, once a problem is identified, the decision maker implicitly identifies an early favorite alternative. But the decision maker doesn't end the search at this point. In fact, the decision maker is often unaware that he or she has already identified an implicit favorite and that the rest of the process is really an exercise in prejudice. So more alternatives will be generated. This is important, for it gives the appearance of objectivity. Then the confirmation process begins. The alternative set will be reduced to two—the choice candidate and a confirmation candidate. If the choice candidate is the only viable option, the decision maker will try to obtain another acceptable alternative to become the confirmation candidate, so he or she will have something to compare against. At this point, the decision maker establishes the decision criteria and weights. A great deal of per-

---

[2] P.O. Soelberg, "Unprogrammed Decision Making," *Industrial Management Review* (Spring 1967), pp. 19–29.

ceptual and interpretational distortion is taking place, with the selection of criteria and their weight being "shaped" to ensure victory for the favored choice. And, of course, that's exactly what transpires. The evaluation demonstrates unequivocally the superiority of the choice candidate over the confirmation candidate.

If the implicit favorite model is at work, the search for new alternatives ends well before the decision maker is willing to admit having made his or her decision. In the job search with MIT students, the researcher found that he was able to accurately predict 87 percent of the career jobs taken two to eight weeks before the students would admit that they had reached a decision. This points to a decision process that is influenced a lot more by intuitive feelings than by rational objectivity.

Using the implicit favorite model, let's look at how our high school senior might go about choosing which college to attend. Early on in the process, she will find that one of the colleges seems intuitively right for her. However, she may not reveal this to others, nor be aware of it herself. She'll review catalogs and brochures on a number of schools, but eventually reduce the set to two. One of these two, of course, will be her implied favorite. She'll then focus in on the relevant factors in her decision. Which college has the best reputation? Where will she have the better social life? Which campus is more attractive? Her evaluation of criteria such as these are subjective judgments. Her assessment, though, won't be fair and impartial. Rather, she'll distort her judgments to align with her intuitive preference. Since "the race is fixed," the winner is a foregone conclusion. Our high school student won't necessarily choose the optimum alternative, nor can we say that her choice will satisfice. Remember, she distorted her evaluations to get the results she wanted, so there is no guarantee that her final selection will reflect the assumptions of bounded rationality. What we can say is that, if she follows the implicit favorite model, she'll choose the college that was her early preference, regardless of any relevant facts that may have surfaced later in the decision process.

The Intuitive Model

Joe Garcia has just committed his corporation to spend in excess of $40 million to build a new plant in Atlanta to manufacture electronic components for satellite communication equipment. A vice president of operations for his firm, Joe had before him a comprehensive analysis of five possible plant locations developed by a site location consulting firm he had hired. This report ranked the Atlanta location third among the five alternatives. After carefully reading the report and its conclusions, Joe decided against the consultant's recommendation. When asked to explain his decision, Joe said, "I looked the report over very carefully. But in spite of its recommendation, I felt the numbers didn't tell the whole story. *Intuitively,* I just sensed Atlanta would prove to be the best bet over the long run."

Intuitive decision making, like that used by Joe Garcia, has recently come out of the closet and into some respectability. Experts no longer automatically assume that using intuition to make decisions is irrational or ineffective. There is growing recognition that rational analysis has been overemphasized and that, in certain instances, relying on intuition can improve decision making.[3]

What do we mean by intuitive decision making? There are a number of ways to conceptualize intuition. For instance, some consider it a form of extrasensory power or sixth sense, and some believe it is a personality trait that a limited number of people are born with. For our purposes, we define intuitive decision making as an unconscious process created out of distilled experience. It doesn't necessarily operate independently of rational analysis; rather, the two complement each other.

Research on chess playing provides an excellent example of how intuition works.[4] Novice chess players and grandmasters were shown an actual, but unfamiliar, chess game with about 25 pieces on the board. After five or ten seconds, the pieces were removed and each was asked to reconstruct the pieces by position. On average, the grandmaster could put 23 or 24 pieces in their correct squares, while the novice was able to replace only six. Then the exercise was changed. This time the pieces were placed randomly on the board. Again, the novice got only about six correct, but so did the grandmaster! The second exercise demonstrated that the grandmaster didn't have any better memory than the novice. What he did have was the ability, based on the experience of having played thousands of chess games, to recognize patterns and clusters of pieces that occur on chessboards in the course of games. Studies further show that chess professionals can play 50 or more games simultaneously, where decisions often must be made in only seconds, and exhibit only a moderately lower level of skill than when playing one game under tournament conditions, where decisions take half an hour or longer. The expert's experience allows him or her to recognize a situation and draw upon previously learned information associated with that situation to quickly arrive at a decision choice. The result is that the intuitive decision maker can decide rapidly with what appears to be very limited information.

When are people most likely to use intuitive decision making? Eight conditions have been identified: (1) when a high level of uncertainty exists; (2) when there is little precedent to draw on; (3) when variables are less scientifically predictable; (4) when "facts" are limited; (5) when facts don't clearly point the way to go; (6) when analytical data are of little use; (7) when there are several plausible alternative solutions to choose from, with good arguments for each; and (8) when time is limited and there is pressure to come up with the right decision.

---

[3] Weston H. Agor, "The Logic of Intuition: How Top Executives Make Important Decisions," *Organizational Dynamics* (Winter 1986), pp. 5–18.

[4] Described in Herbert A. Simon, "Making Management Decisions: The Role of Intuition and Emotion," *Academy of Management Executive* (February 1987), pp. 59–60.

Is there a standard model that people follow when using intuition? Individuals seem to follow one of two approaches. They apply intuition to either the front end or the back end of the decision-making process.

When intuition is used at the front end, the decision maker tries to avoid systematically analyzing the problem, but instead gives intuition a free rein. The idea is to try to generate unusual possibilities and new options that might not normally emerge from an analysis of past data or traditional ways of doing things. A back-end approach to using intuition relies on rational analysis to identify and allocate weights to decision criteria, as well as to develop and evaluate alternatives. Once this is done, the decision maker stops the analytical process in order to "sleep on the decision" for a day or two before making the final choice.

Although intuitive decision making has gained in respectability since the early 1980s, don't expect people who use it—especially in North America, Great Britain, and other cultures where rational analysis is the approved way of making decisions—to acknowledge they are doing so. People with strong intuitive abilities don't usually tell their colleagues how they reached their conclusions. Since rational analysis is considered more socially desirable, intuitive ability is often disguised or hidden. As one top executive commented, "Sometimes one must dress up a gut decision in 'data clothes' to make it acceptable or palatable, but this fine-tuning is usually after the fact of the decision."[5]

▪ ETHICS IN DECISION MAKING

No contemporary discussion of decision making would be complete without inclusion of ethics. Why? Because ethical considerations should be an important criterion in organizational decision making. In this section we present three different ways to frame decisions and look at the factors that shape an individual's ethical decision-making behavior.

Three Ethical Decision Criteria

An individual can use three different criteria in making ethical choices. The first is the *utilitarian* criterion, in which decisions are made solely on the basis of their outcomes or consequences. The goal of utilitarianism is to provide the greatest good for the greatest number. This view tends to dominate business decision making. It is consistent with goals like efficiency, productivity, and high profits. By maximizing profits, for instance, a business executive can argue he is securing the greatest good for the greatest number—as he hands out dismissal notices to 15 percent of his employees.

Another ethical criterion is to focus on *rights*. This calls on individuals to make decisions consistent with fundamental liberties and privileges as set

---

5 Weston H. Agor, "The Logic of Intuition," p. 15.

forth in documents like the Bill of Rights. An emphasis on rights in decision making means respecting and protecting the basic rights of individuals, such as the right to privacy, to free speech, and to due process. For instance, use of this criterion would protect employees who report unethical or illegal practices by their organization to the press or government agencies on the grounds of their right to free speech.

A third criterion is to focus on *justice.* This requires individuals to impose and enforce rules fairly and impartially so there is an equitable distribution of benefits and costs. Union members typically favor this view. It justifies paying people the same wage for a given job, regardless of performance differences, and it uses seniority as the primary determinant in making layoff decisions.

Each of these three criteria has advantages and liabilities. A focus on utilitarianism promotes efficiency and productivity, but it can result in ignoring the rights of some individuals, particularly those with minority representation in the organization. The use of rights as a criterion protects individuals from injury and is consistent with freedom and privacy, but it can create an overly legalistic work environment that hinders productivity and efficiency. A focus on justice protects the interests of the underrepresented and less powerful, but it can encourage a sense of entitlement that reduces risk taking, innovation, and productivity.

Decision makers, particularly in for-profit organizations, tend to feel safe and comfortable when they use utilitarianism. A lot of questionable actions can be justified when framed as being in the best interests of "the organization" and stockholders. But many critics of business decision makers argue that this perspective needs to change. Increased concerns in society about individual rights and social justice suggest the need for managers to develop ethical standards based on nonutilitarian criteria. This presents a solid challenge to today's managers because making decisions using criteria such as individual rights and social justice involves far more ambiguities than using utilitarian criteria such as effects on efficiency and profits. This helps explain why managers are increasingly finding themselves criticized for their actions. Raising prices, selling products with questionable effects on consumer health, closing down plants, laying off large numbers of employees, moving production overseas to cut costs, and similar decisions can be justified in utilitarian terms. But that may no longer be the single criterion by which good decisions should be judged.

Factors Influencing Ethical Decision-Making Behavior

What accounts for unethical behavior? Is it immoral individuals or a work environment that promotes unethical activity? The answer is *both!* The evidence indicates that ethical or unethical actions are largely a function of both the individual's characteristics and the environment in which he or she works.[6]

6 Linda Klebe Trevino, "Ethical Decision Making in Organizations: A Person-Situation Interactionist Model," *Academy of Management Review* (July 1986), pp. 601–17; and Linda Klebe Trevino and Stuart A. Youngblood, "Bad Apples in Bad Barrels: A Causal Analysis of Ethical Decision-Making Behavior," *Journal of Applied Psychology* (August 1990), pp. 378–85.

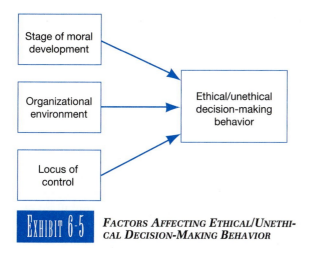

EXHIBIT 6-5 *FACTORS AFFECTING ETHICAL/UNETHI-CAL DECISION-MAKING BEHAVIOR*

Exhibit 6–5 presents a model for explaining ethical or unethical behavior. *Stage of moral development* is an assessment of a person's capacity to judge what is morally right. The higher one's moral development, the less dependent he or she is on outside influences and, hence, the more he or she will be predisposed to behave ethically. For instance, most adults are at a mid-level of moral development—they're strongly influenced by peers and will follow an organization's rules and procedures. Those individuals who have progressed to the higher stages place increased value on the rights of others, regardless of the majority's opinion, and are likely to challenge organizational practices they believe are personally wrong.

We discussed *locus of control* in Chapter 3. It is a personality characteristic that taps the extent to which people believe they are responsible for the events in their lives. Research indicates that people with an external locus of control (i.e., what happens to them in life is due to luck or chance) are less likely to take responsibility for the consequences of their behavior and are more likely to rely on external influences. Internals, on the other hand, are more likely to rely on their own internal standards of right or wrong to guide their behavior.

The *organizational environment* refers to an employee's perception of organizational expectations. Does the organization encourage and support ethical behavior by rewarding it or discourage unethical behavior by punishing it? Written codes of ethics, high moral behavior by senior management, realistic performance expectations, performance appraisals that evaluate means as well as ends, visible recognition and promotions for individuals who display high moral behavior, and visible punishment for those who act unethically are some examples of an organizational environment that is likely to foster high ethical decision making.

In summary, people who lack a strong moral sense are much less likely to make unethical decisions if they are constrained by an organizational environment that frowns on such behaviors. Conversely, very righteous individuals can be corrupted by an organizational environment that permits or encourages unethical practices.

■ IMPLICATIONS FOR MANAGERS

As stated at the beginning of this chapter, individuals think and reason before they act. Thus an understanding of how people make decisions can be helpful if we are to explain and predict their behavior.

Under some decision situations, people follow the optimizing model. But for most people, and most nonroutine decisions, this is probably more the exception than the rule. Few important decisions are simple or unambiguous enough for the optimizing model's assumptions to apply. So we find individuals looking for solutions that satisfice rather than optimize, injecting biases and prejudices into the decision process, and relying on intuition.

The alternative decision models we presented can help us explain and predict behaviors that would appear irrational or arbitrary if viewed under optimizing assumptions. Let's look at a couple of examples.

Employment interviews are complex decision activities. The interviewer finds himself or herself inundated with information. Research indicates that interviewers respond by simplifying the process. Most interviewers' decisions change very little after the first four or five minutes of the interview. In a half-hour interview, the decision maker tends to make a decision about the suitability of the candidate in the first few minutes and then uses the rest of the interview time to select information that supports the early decision. In so doing, interviewers reduce the probability of identifying the highest performing candidate. They bias their decision toward individuals who make favorable first impressions.

Evaluating an employee's performance is a complex activity. Decision makers simplify the process by focusing on visible and easy-to-measure criteria. This may explain why factors such as neatness, promptness, enthusiasm, and a positive attitude are often related to good evaluations. It also explains why quantity measures typically override quality measures. The former category is easier to appraise. This effort at satisficing encourages individuals to take on visible problems rather than important ones.

What can we say regarding ethics? For individuals already employed, managers can influence only the employee's work environment. So managers should overtly seek to convey high ethical standards to employees through the actions the managers take. By what managers say, do, reward, punish, and overlook, they set the ethical tone for their employees. When hiring new employees, managers have an opportunity to weed out ethically undesirable applicants. The selection process—for instance, interviews, tests, and background checks—should be viewed as an opportunity to learn about an individual's level of moral development and locus of control. This then can be used to identify individuals whose ethical standards might be in conflict with those of the organization or who are particularly vulnerable to negative external influences.

$\mathcal{S}$UGGESTIONS FOR FURTHER READING

AGOR, WESTON H. (ed.), *Intuition in Organizations* (Newbury Park, CA: Sage, 1989).

BAZERMAN, MAX H., *Judgement in Managerial Decision Making,* 3rd ed. (New York: Wiley, 1994).

BEHLING, ORLANDO, AND NORMAN L. ECKEL, "Making Sense Out of Intuition," *Academy of Management Executive,* February 1991, pp. 46–54.

KAUFMAN, BRUCE E., "A New Theory of Satisficing," *Journal of Behavioral Economics,* Spring 1990, pp. 35–51.

KNOUSE, STEPHEN B., AND ROBERT A. GIACALONE, "Ethical Decision-Making in Business: Behavioral Issues and Concerns," *Journal of Business Ethics,* May 1992, pp. 369–77.

LANGLEY, ANN, "In Search of Rationality: The Purposes behind the Use of Formal Analysis in Organizations," *Administrative Science Quarterly,* December 1989, pp. 598–631.

SKIDD, DAVID R., "Revisiting Bounded Rationality," *Journal of Management Inquiry,* December 1992, pp. 343–47.

ZEY, MARY (ed.), *Decision Making: Alternatives to Rational Choice* (Newbury Park, CA: Sage, 1992).

CHAPTER 7

FOUNDATIONS OF GROUP BEHAVIOR

After reading this chapter, you should be able to:

1. Differentiate between formal and informal groups
2. Explain why people join groups
3. Describe how role requirements change in different situations
4. Explain the importance of the Hawthorne studies
5. Describe why status is an important factor in understanding behavior
6. Identify the implications of social loafing
7. Outline the benefits and disadvantages of cohesive groups
8. List the characteristics of effective teams

The behavior of individuals in groups is something more than the sum total of each acting in his or her own way. When individuals are in groups they act differently from when they are alone. This chapter introduces basic concepts about groups and demonstrates how an understanding of groups can help to explain the larger phenomenon of organizational behavior.

■ DEFINING AND CLASSIFYING GROUPS

A group is defined as two or more individuals, interacting and interdependent, who come together to achieve particular objectives. Groups can be either formal or informal. By formal, we mean defined by the organization's structure, with designated work assignments establishing tasks and work groups. In formal groups, the behaviors that one should engage in are stipulated by and directed toward organizational goals. In contrast, informal groups are alliances that are neither structured nor organizationally determined. In the work environment, these groups form naturally as responses to the need for social contact.

It is possible to further subclassify groups into command, task, interest, or friendship categories. Command and task groups are dictated by the formal organization, whereas interest and friendship groups are informal alliances.

The *command group* is determined by the organization chart. It is composed of the subordinates who report directly to a given manager. An elementary school principal and her twelve teachers form a command group, as do the director of postal audits and his five inspectors.

Task groups, also organizationally determined, represent those working together to complete a job. However, a task group's boundaries are not limited to its immediate hierarchical superior. It can cross command relationships. For instance, if a college student is accused of a campus crime, it may require communication and coordination among the dean of academic affairs, the dean of students, the registrar, the director of security, and the student's adviser. Such a formation would constitute a task group. It should be noted that all command groups are also task groups, but because task groups can cut across the organization, the reverse need not be true.

People who may or may not be aligned into common command or task groups may affiliate to attain a specific objective with which each is concerned. This is an *interest group.* Employees who band together to have their vacation schedule altered, to support a peer who has been fired, or to seek increased fringe benefits represent the formation of a united body to further their common interest.

Groups often develop because the individual members have one or more common characteristics. We call these formations *friendship groups.* Social allegiances, which frequently extend outside the work situation, can be based on, for example, similar age, support for "Big Red" Nebraska football, having attended the same college, or holding similar political views.

Informal groups provide a very important function by satisfying their members' social needs. Because of interactions that result from the close proximity of work stations or tasks, we find workers playing golf together, riding to and from work together, lunching together, and spending their breaks around the water cooler together. We must recognize that these types of interactions among individuals, even though informal, deeply affect their behavior and performance.

◼ WHY DO PEOPLE JOIN GROUPS?

There is no single reason why individuals join groups. Because most people belong to a number of groups, it's obvious that different groups provide different benefits to their members. The most popular reasons for joining a group are related to our needs for security, status, self-esteem, affiliation, power, and goal achievement.

Security

"There's strength in numbers." By joining a group, we can reduce the insecurity of standing alone—we feel stronger, have fewer self-doubts, and are more resistant to threats. New employees are particularly vulnerable to a sense of isolation and turn to the group for guidance and support. However, whether we are talking about new employees or those with years on the job, we can state that few individuals like to stand alone. We get reassurances from interacting with others and being part of a group. This often explains the appeal of unions—if management creates an environment in which employees feel insecure, they are likely to turn to unionization to reduce their feelings of insecurity.

Status

"I'm a member of our company's running team. Last month, at the National Corporate Relays, we won the national championship. Didn't you see our picture in the company newsletter?" These comments demonstrate the role that a group can play in giving prestige. Inclusion in a group viewed as important by others provides recognition and status for its members.

Self-Esteem

"Before I was asked to pledge Phi Omega Chi, I felt like a nobody. Being in a fraternity makes me feel much more important." This quote demonstrates that groups can provide people with feelings of self-worth. That is, in addition to conveying status to those outside the group, membership can also give increased feelings of worth to the group members themselves. Our self-esteem is bolstered, for example, when we are accepted by a highly valued group. Being assigned to a task force whose purpose is to review and make recommendations for the location of the company's new corporate headquarters can fulfill one's needs for competence and growth, as well as for status.

Affiliation

"I'm independently wealthy, but I wouldn't give up my job. Why? Because I really like the people I work with!" This quote, from a $45,000-a-year purchasing agent who inherited several million dollars' worth of real estate, verifies that groups can fulfill our social needs. People enjoy the regular interaction that comes with group membership. For many people, these on-the-job interactions are their primary source for fulfilling their needs for affiliation. For almost all people, work groups significantly contribute to fulfilling their needs for friendship and social relations.

Power

"I tried for two years to get the plant management to increase the number of female rest rooms on the production floor to the same number as the men have. It was like talking to a wall. But I got about fifteen other women who were production employees together and we jointly presented our demands to management. The construction crews were in here adding female rest rooms within ten days!"

This episode demonstrates that one of the appealing aspects of groups is that they represent power. What often cannot be achieved individually becomes possible through group action. Of course, this power may not be sought only to make demands on others. It may be desired merely as a countermeasure. In order to protect themselves from unreasonable demands by management, individuals may align with a group.

Informal groups additionally provide opportunities for individuals to exercise power over others. For individuals who desire to influence others, groups can offer power without a formal position of authority in the organization. As a group leader, you may be able to make requests of group members and obtain compliance without any of the responsibilities that traditionally go with formal managerial positions. So, for people with a high power need, groups can be a vehicle for fulfillment.

Goal Achievement

"I'm part of a three-person team studying how we can cut our company's transportation costs. They've been going up at over 30 percent a year for several years now so the corporate controller assigned representatives from cost accounting, shipping, and marketing to study the problem and make recommendations."

This task group was created to achieve a goal that would be considerably more difficult if pursued by a single person. There are times when it takes more than one person to accomplish a particular task—there is a need to pool talents, knowledge, or power in order to get a job completed. In such instances, management will rely on the use of a formal group.

■ GROUP STRUCTURE

Three concepts underlie a basic understanding of group structure—roles, norms, and status. These seem, on the surface, everyday terms. But in order to understand and analyze group behavior, a thorough understanding of the theory on which these concepts are built is fundamental. This section provides a clear explanation and definition of each concept.

Roles

Shakespeare said, "All the world's a stage, and all the men and women merely players." Using the same metaphor, all group members are actors, each playing a *role*. A role is a set of expected behavior patterns attributed to someone occupying a given position in a social unit. The understanding of role behavior would be dramatically simplified if each of us chose one role and played it regularly and consistently. Unfortunately, we are required to play a number of diverse roles, both on and off our jobs. As we shall see, one of the tasks in understanding behavior is grasping the role that a person is currently playing.

For example, on his job, Bill Patterson is a plant manager with Electrical Industries, a large electrical equipment manufacturer in Phoenix. He has a number of roles that he fulfills on that job: Electrical Industries employee, member of middle management, electrical engineer, and the primary company spokesman in the community. Off the job, Bill Patterson finds himself in still more roles: husband, father, Catholic, Rotarian, tennis player, member of the Thunderbird Country Club, and president of his homeowner's association. Many of these roles are compatible; some create conflicts. For instance, how does his religious involvement influence his managerial decisions regarding layoffs, expense account padding, or providing accurate information to government agencies? A recent offer of promotion requires Bill to relocate, yet his family very much wants to stay in Phoenix. Can the role demands of his job be reconciled with the demands of husband and father roles?

The issue should be clear: Like Bill Patterson, we all are required to play a number of roles, and our behavior varies with the role we are playing. Bill's behavior when he attends church on Sunday morning is different from his behavior on the golf course later that same day. We act differently in the role of student from when we play husband or wife, or boyfriend or girl-friend.

Role Identity. Certain attitudes and actual behaviors are consistent with a role, and they create the *role identity*. People have the ability to shift roles rapidly when they recognize the situation and its demands clearly require major changes. For instance, when union stewards were promoted to foreman positions, it was found their attitudes changed from pro-union to pro-management within a few months of their promotion. When these promotions had to be rescinded later because of economic difficulties in the firm, it was found the demoted foremen had once again adopted their pro-union attitudes.

Role Perception. One's view of how one is supposed to act in a given situation is a *role perception*. Based on an interpretation of how we believe we are supposed to behave, we engage in certain types of behavior.

Where do we get these perceptions? From stimuli all around us—friends, books, movies, television. Undoubtedly many of today's young surgeons formed their role identities from their perception of Hawkeye on "M.A.S.H." It also seems reasonable that many current law enforcement officers learned their roles from reading Joseph Wambaugh novels or watching "Dirty Harry" movies. Tomorrow's lawyers will certainly be influenced by characters on "L.A. Law." Of course, the primary reason that apprenticeship programs exist in many trades and professions is to allow individuals to watch an expert so they can learn to act as they are supposed to.

Role Expectations. *Role expectations* are defined as how others believe you should act in a given situation. How you behave is determined, to a large part, by the role defined in the context in which you are acting. The role of a Supreme Court justice is viewed as having propriety and dignity, whereas a football coach is seen as aggressive, dynamic, and inspirational to his players. In the same context, we might be surprised to learn the neighborhood priest moonlights during the week as a bartender. Why? Because our role expectations of priests and bartenders tend to be considerably different. Role stereotypes are role expectations concentrated into generalized categories.

During the last four decades we have seen a major change in the general population's role stereotypes of females. In the 1950s, a woman's role was to stay home, take care of the house, raise children, and generally care for her husband. Today, most of us no longer hold this stereotype. Young girls can aspire to be doctors, lawyers, and astronauts as well as the more traditional positions of nurse, schoolteacher, secretary, or homemaker. In other words, many of us have changed role expectations of women and, similarly, many women carry new role perceptions.

In the workplace, it can be helpful to look at the topic of role expectations through the perspective of the *psychological contract.* An unwritten agreement exists between employees and their employer. This psychological contract sets out mutual expectations—what management expects from workers and vice versa. In effect, this contract defines the behavioral expectations that accompany every role. Management is expected to treat employees justly, provide acceptable working conditions, clearly communicate what is a fair day's work and give feedback on how well the employee is doing. Employees are expected to respond by demonstrating a good attitude, following directions, and showing loyalty to the organization.

What happens when role expectations as implied in the psychological contract are not met? If management is derelict in keeping up its part of the bargain, we can expect negative repercussions on employee performance and satisfaction. When employees fail to live up to expectations, the result is usually some form of disciplinary action up to and including firing.

The psychological contract should be recognized as a powerful determinant of behavior in organizations. It points out the importance of communicating accurately role expectations.

Role Conflict. When an individual is confronted by divergent role expectations, the result is *role conflict.* It exists when an individual finds that compliance with one role requirement may make more difficult the compliance with another. At the extreme it would include situations where two or more role expectations are mutually contradictory.

Many believe the topic of role conflict is the most critical role concept in attempting to explain behavior. This, for example, is one of the classic problems of college presidents, a fact that became highly evident in the late 1960s. The college president is forced to reconcile diverse role expectations by faculty, students, board members, alumni, and other administrators. The behavior expectations that are perceived as acceptable by one group are often totally in disagreement with the expectations of other groups.

Our previous discussion of the many roles Bill Patterson had to deal with included several role conflicts—for instance, Bill's attempt to reconcile the expectations placed on him as head of his family and as an executive with Electrical Industries. The former emphasizes stability and concern for the desire of his wife and children to remain in Phoenix. Electrical Industries, on the other hand, expects its employees to be responsive to the needs and requirements of the company. Although it might be in Bill's financial and career interests to accept a relocation, the conflict is the choice between family and career role expectations.

All of us have faced and will continue to face role conflicts. The critical issue, from our standpoint, is how conflicts, imposed by divergent expectations within the organization, have an impact on behavior. Certainly they increase internal tension and frustration. There are a number of behavioral responses one may engage in. For example, one can give a formalized bureaucratic response. The conflict is then resolved by relying on the rules, regulations, and procedures that govern organizational activities. For example, a plant controller, faced with the conflicting requirements imposed by the corporate controller's office and his own plant manager, decides in favor of his immediate boss, the plant manager. Similarly, many college professors create a formal environment in class by calling their students Mr. and Ms., and expecting to be called Professor in order to avoid allowing friendships to interfere with the objective requirements of the professorial role. Other behavioral responses may include withdrawal, stalling, negotiation, or, as we found in our discussion of dissonance in Chapter 3, redefining the facts or the situation to make them appear congruent.

Norms

On the first Friday of every month, the six men and two women who make up the executive board of Consolidated Foods meet to review the company's prior month's performance. Upon arriving at the meeting, the executives exchange handshakes. At the meeting's conclusion, and again before departing, they shake hands. But at a recent dinner party given by one of the executives and at which the other seven were in attendance, the male and female executives greeted each other with kisses. Similarly, upon saying goodnight at the end of the evening, they again exchanged kisses. Why handshakes on one occasion and kisses on another? Norms!

All groups have established *norms,* that is, acceptable standards of behavior shared by the group's members. Norms tell members what they ought or ought not to do under certain circumstances. From an individual's standpoint, they tell what is expected in certain situations. When agreed to and accepted by the group, norms act as a means of influencing the behavior of group members with a minimum of external controls. Norms may differ among groups, communities, and societies, but each has its own set of them.

Formalized norms are written up in organizational manuals, which set out rules and procedures for employees to follow. However, the majority of norms are informal. We do not need someone to tell us that throwing paper airplanes or engaging in prolonged bull sessions at the water cooler is unacceptable behavior when the "big boss from New York" is touring the office. Similarly, we all know that when we are in an employment interview discussing what we did not like about our previous job, there are certain things we should not talk about (difficulty in getting along with co-workers or our supervisor), while it is very appropriate to talk about other things (inadequate opportunities for advancement, or unimportant and meaningless work). Evidence indicates that even high school students recognize that in such interviews certain answers are more socially desirable than others.

Students are very good at quickly assimilating classroom norms. Depending on the environment created by the instructor, the norms may support unequivocal acceptance of the material suggested by the instructor, or, at the other extreme, students may be expected to question and challenge the instructor on any point that is unclear. For example, in most classroom situations, the norms dictate that one not engage in loud, boisterous discussion that makes it impossible to hear the lecturer, nor humiliate the instructor by pushing him or her too far, even if one has obviously located a weakness in something the instructor has said. Should some individuals in the classroom group behave in such a way as to violate these norms, we can expect pressure to be applied against the deviant members to bring their behavior into conformity with group standards.

The Hawthorne Studies.   It is generally agreed among behavioral scientists that full-scale appreciation of the importance norms play in influencing worker behavior did not occur until the early 1930s. This enlightenment grew out of a series of studies undertaken at Western Electric Company's Hawthorne Works in Chicago between 1924 and 1932.[1] Originally initiated by Western Electric officials and later overseen by Harvard professor Elton Mayo, the Hawthorne studies concluded that a worker's behavior and sentiments were closely related, that group influences were significant in affecting individual behavior, that group standards were highly effective in establishing individual worker output, and that money was less a factor in determining worker output than group standards, sentiments, and security. Let us briefly review the Hawthorne investigations and demonstrate the importance of these findings in explaining group behavior.

The Hawthorne researchers began by examining the relation between the physical environment and productivity. Illumination and other working conditions were selected to represent this physical environment. The researchers' initial findings contradicted their anticipated results.

---

[1] Elton Mayo, *The Human Problems of an Industrial Civilization* (New York: Macmillan, 1933); and Fritz J. Roethlisberger and William J. Dickson, *Management and the Worker* (Cambridge, MA: Harvard University Press, 1939).

They began with illumination experiments with various groups of workers. The researchers manipulated the intensity of illumination upward and downward, while at the same time noting changes in group output. Results varied, but one thing was clear: In no case was the increase or decrease in output in proportion to the increase or decrease in illumination. So the researchers introduced a control group: An experimental group was presented with varying intensity of illumination, while the controlled unit worked under a constant illumination intensity. Again, the results were bewildering to the Hawthorne researchers. As the light level was increased in the experimental unit, output rose for each group. But to the surprise of the researchers, as the light level was dropped in the experimental group, productivity continued to increase in both. In fact, a productivity decrease was observed in the experimental group only when the light intensity had been reduced to that of moonlight. The Hawthorne researchers concluded that illumination intensity was only a minor influence among the many influences that affected an employee's productivity, but they could not explain the behavior they had witnessed.

As a follow-up to the illumination experiments, the researchers began a second set of experiments in the relay assembly test room at Western Electric. A small group of women was isolated from the main work group so their behavior could be more carefully observed. They went about their job of assembling small telephone relays in a room laid out similar to their normal department. The only significant difference was the placement in the room of a research assistant who acted as an observer—keeping records of output, rejects, working conditions, and a daily log sheet describing everything that happened. Observations covering a multiyear period found that this small group's output increased steadily. The number of personal absences and those due to sickness were approximately one-third of those recorded by women in the regular production department. What became evident was that this group's performance was significantly influenced by its status of being a "special" group. The women in the test room thought that being in the experimental group was fun, that they were in sort of an elite group, and that management was concerned with their interest by engaging in such experimentation.

A third study in the bank wiring observation room was introduced to ascertain the effect of a sophisticated wage incentive plan. The assumption was that individual workers would maximize their productivity when they saw it was directly related to economic rewards. The most important finding coming out of this study was that employees did not individually maximize their outputs. Rather, their output became controlled by a group norm that determined what was a proper day's work. Output was not only being restricted, but individual workers were giving erroneous reports. The total for a week would check with the total week's output, but the daily reports showed a steady level output regardless of actual daily production. What was going on?

Interviews determined that the group was operating well below its capability and was leveling output in order to protect itself. Members were afraid that if they significantly increased their output, the unit incentive rate would be cut, the expected daily output would be increased, layoffs might occur, or slower workers would be reprimanded. So the group established its idea of a fair output—neither too much nor too little. They helped each other out to ensure their reports were nearly level.

The norms the group established included a number of "don'ts." *Don't* be a rate-buster, turning out too much work. *Don't* be a chiseler, turning out too little work. *Don't* be a squealer on any of your peers.

How did the group enforce these norms? Their methods were neither gentle nor subtle. They included sarcasm, name calling, ridicule, and even physical punches to the upper arm of members who violated the group's norms. Members would also ostracize individuals whose behavior was against the group's interest.

The Hawthorne studies made an important contribution to our understanding of group behavior—particularly the significant place that norms have in determining individual work behavior.

Common Norms in Organizations. An organization's norms are like an individual's fingerprints—each is unique. Yet there are still common classes of norms that appear in most organizations.

Probably the most widespread norms, as demonstrated in the Hawthorne studies, relate to levels of *effort* and *performance*. Work groups typically provide their members with very explicit cues on how hard they should work, their level of output, when to look busy, when it's acceptable to goof off, and the like. These norms are extremely powerful in affecting an individual employee's performance—capable of modifying significantly a performance prediction based solely on the employee's ability and level of personal motivation.

Some organizations have formal *dress* codes. However, even in their absence, norms frequently develop to dictate the kind of clothing that should be worn to work. College seniors, interviewing for their first postgraduate job, pick up this norm quickly. Every spring on college campuses throughout the country, those interviewing for jobs can usually be spotted—they're the ones walking around in the dark gray or blue pinstriped suits. They are enacting the dress norms they have learned are expected in professional positions. Of course, what connotes acceptable dress in one organization may be very different from another. Faculty members in the Graduate Schools of Business at Harvard and UCLA may teach the same subject matter, but the social norms at Harvard dictate a much more formal dress attire than exists at the West Coast school.

Few managers appreciate employees who disparage the organization. Similarly, professional employees and those in the executive ranks recognize that most employers view with a great deal of disfavor those who actively look for another job. If such people are unhappy, they know to keep their job search secret. These examples demonstrate that *loyalty* norms are widespread in organizations. This concern for demonstrating loyalty, by the way, often explains why ambitious aspirants to top management positions in an organization willingly take work home at night, come in on weekends, and accept transfers to cities where they would otherwise not prefer to live.

The "How" and "Why" of Norms. *How* do norms develop? *Why* are they enforced? The following offers answers to these two questions.

Norms typically develop gradually as group members learn what behaviors are necessary for the group to function effectively. Of course, critical events in the group might short-circuit the process and act quickly to solidify new norms. Most norms develop in one or more of the following four ways: (1) *Explicit statements made by a group member*—often the group's supervisor or a powerful member. The group leader might, for instance, specifically say that no personal phone calls are allowed during working hours or that coffee breaks are to be kept to ten minutes. (2) *Critical events in the group's history.* These set important precedents. A bystander is injured while standing too close to a machine, and, from that point on, members of the work group regularly monitor each other to ensure that no one other than the operator gets within 5 feet of any machine. (3) *Primacy.* The first behavior pattern that emerges in a group frequently sets group expectations. Friendship groups of students often stake out seats near each other on the first day of class and become perturbed if an outsider takes the seats they consider theirs in a later class. (4) *Carry-over behaviors from past situations.* Group members bring expectations with them from other groups of which they have been members. This can explain why work groups typically prefer to add new members who are similar to current ones in background and experience. This is likely to increase the probability that the expectations they bring are consistent with those already held by the group.

But groups do not establish or enforce norms for every conceivable situation. The norms the group will enforce tend to be those that are important to it. A norm is important: (1) *If it facilitates the group's survival.* Groups don't like to fail, so they look to enforce those norms that increase their chances for success. This means they will try to protect themselves from interference from other groups or individuals. (2) *If it increases the predictability of group members' behaviors.* Norms that increase predictability enable group members to anticipate each other's actions and to prepare appropriate responses. (3) *If it reduces embarrassing interpersonal problems for group members.* Norms are important that ensure the satisfaction of their members and prevent as much interpersonal discomfort as possible. (4) *If it allows members to express the central values of the group and clarify what is distinctive about the group's identity.* Norms that encourage expression of the group's values and distinctive identity help to solidify and maintain the group.

Conformity. As a member of a group, you desire continued acceptance by the group. Because of this you are susceptible to conforming to the group's norms. There is considerable evidence that groups can place strong pressures on individual members to change their attitudes and behaviors to conform to the group's standard.

Do individuals conform to the pressures of all the groups they belong to? Obviously not, because people belong to many groups and their norms vary. In some cases, they may even have contradictory norms. So what do people

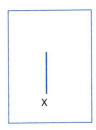
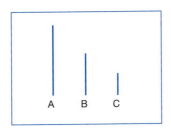

do? They conform to the important groups to which they belong or hope to belong. The important groups have been referred to as *reference* groups and are characterized as ones in which the person is aware of the other members, defines himself or herself as a member (or would like to be a member), and feels the group members are significant to him or her. The implication, then, is that *all* groups do not impose equal conformity pressures on their members.

The impact that group pressures for conformity can have on an individual member's judgment and attitudes was demonstrated in the now classic studies by Solomon Asch.[2] Asch made up groups of seven or eight people, who sat in a classroom and were asked to compare two cards held by the experimenter. One card had one line, the other had three lines of varying length. As shown in Exhibit 7–1, one of the lines on the three-line card was identical to the line on the one-line card. Also, as shown in Exhibit 7–1, the difference in line length was quite obvious; under ordinary conditions, subjects made less than 1 percent errors. The object was to announce aloud which of the three lines matched the single line. But what happens if all the members in the group begin to give incorrect answers? Will the pressures to conform result in the unsuspecting subject (USS) altering his or her answer to align with the others? That was what Asch wanted to know. So he arranged the group so only the USS was unaware that the experiment was "fixed." The seating was prearranged so the USS was the last to announce his or her decision.

The experiment began with several sets of matching exercises. All the subjects gave the right answers. On the third set, however, the first subject gave an obviously wrong answer—for example, saying "C" in Exhibit 7–1. The next subject gave the same wrong answer, and so did the others until it got to the unsuspecting subject. He knew "B" was the same as "X," yet everyone had said "C." The decision confronting the USS was this: Do you state a perception publicly that differs from the preannounced position of the others? Or do you give an answer that you strongly believe is incorrect in order to have your response agree with the other group members?

The results obtained by Asch demonstrated that over many experiments and many trials, subjects conformed in about 35 percent of the trials; that is,

2 Solomon E. Asch, "Effects of Group Pressure upon the Modification and Distortion of Judgments," in *Groups, Leadership and Men,* ed. Harold Guetzkow (Pittsburgh: Carnegie Press, 1951), pp. 177–90.

the subjects gave answers they knew were wrong but that were consistent with the replies of other group members.

What can we conclude from this study? The results suggest there are group norms that press us toward conformity. We desire to be one of the group and avoid being visibly different. We can generalize further to say that when an individual's opinion of objective data differs significantly from that of others in the group, he or she feels extensive pressure to align his or her opinion to conform with those of the others.

Status

While teaching a college course on adolescence a few years ago, the instructor asked the class to list things that contributed to status when they were in high school. The list was long, including such activities as being on a varsity athletic team, being able to cut class without getting caught, and having your own car. Then the instructor asked the students to list things that didn't contribute to status. Again, it was easy for the students to create a long list—getting straight A's, having your mother drive you to school, and so forth. Finally, the students were asked to develop a third list—those things that didn't matter one way or the other. There was a long silence. Finally, a young woman in the back row volunteered, "In high school, nothing didn't matter."

Status permeates far beyond the walls of high school. It would not be incorrect to rephrase the preceding quotation to read, "In the status hierarchy of life, nothing doesn't matter." In spite of the fact that most of us are quick to declare how unimportant status is, most of us are greatly concerned with acquiring status symbols. We live in a class-structured society. In spite of attempts to make our world more egalitarian, we have made little movement toward a classless society. As far back as scientists have been able to trace human groupings, we have had chiefs and Indians, noblemen and peasants, the haves and the have-nots. This continues to be the case today. Even the smallest group will develop roles, rites, and rituals to differentiate its members. Status is an important factor in understanding behavior because it is a significant motivator and has major behavioral consequences when individuals see a disparity between what they perceive their status to be and what others perceive it to be.

Status is a prestige grading, position, or rank within a group. It may be formally imposed by a group; that is, organizationally imposed, through titles or amenities like "the heavyweight champion of the world" or "most congenial." We are all familiar with the trappings associated with high organizational status—large offices with thick carpeting, impressive titles, high pay and fringe benefits, preferred work schedules, and so on. Whether management acknowledges the existence of a status hierarchy, organizations are filled with amenities that are not uniformly available to everyone and, hence, carry status value.

More often, we deal with status in an informal sense. Status may be informally acquired by such characteristics as education, age, gender, skill, or experience. Anything can have status value if others in the group evaluate it as such. But just because status is informal does not mean it is less important or there is less agreement on who has it or who does not. This was supported when individuals were asked to rank the status of their high school class-mates a number of years following graduation. The respondents were able to place former classmates into a status hierarchy and the rankings were almost identical. We can and do place people into status categories, and there appears to be high agreement among members as to who is high, low, and in the middle.

In his classic restaurant study, William F. Whyte demonstrated the importance of status.[3] Whyte proposed that people work more smoothly if high-status personnel customarily originate action for lower-status person-nel. He found a number of instances where, when those of lower status were initiating action, this created a conflict between formal and informal status systems. For example, he cited one instance in which waitresses passed their customers' orders directly on to countermen—and thus low-status servers were initiating action for high-status cooks. By the simple addition of an aluminum spindle to which the order could be hooked, a buffer was created, thus allowing the countermen to initiate action on orders when they felt ready.

Whyte also noted that in the kitchen, supply men secured food supplies from the chefs. This was, in effect, a case of low-skilled employees initiating action upon the high skilled. Conflict was stimulated when several supply men explicitly and implicitly urged the chefs to "get a move on." However, Whyte observed that one supply man had little trouble. He gave the chef the order and asked the chef to call him when it was ready, thus reversing the ini-tiating process. In Whyte's analysis, he suggested several changes in proce-dures, which aligned interactions more closely with the accepted status hier-archy and resulted in substantial improvements in worker relations and effec-tiveness.

It is important for group members to believe the status hierarchy is equi-table. When inequity is perceived, it creates disequilibrium resulting in vari-ous types of corrective behavior.

The concept of equity, presented in Chapter 4, applies to status. Individuals expect rewards to be proportionate to costs incurred in obtaining those rewards. If Sally and Betty are the two finalists for the position of head nurse in a hospital, and it is clear Sally has more seniority and better prepara-tion for assuming the promotion, Betty will view the selection of Sally as equitable. However, if Betty is chosen because she is the daughter-in-law of the hospital director, Sally will see there is an injustice.

The trappings that go with formal positions are also important elements in maintaining equity. If we believe there is an inequity between the per-ceived ranking of an individual and the status accoutrements he or she is given by the organization, we are experiencing status incongruence. Some

---

3 William F. Whyte, "The Social Structure of the Restaurant," *American Journal of Sociology* (January 1954), pp. 302–8.

examples of incongruence are the supervisor earning less than her subordinates, the more desirable office location being held by a lower-ranking individual, or paid country club membership being provided by the company for division managers but not for vice presidents. Employees expect the things an individual has and receives to be congruent with his or her status.

In spite of our acknowledgement that groups generally agree within themselves on status criteria and hence tend to rank individuals fairly closely, individuals can find themselves in conflict when they move between groups whose status criteria are different or where groups are formed of individuals with heterogeneous backgrounds. Businesspeople may use income, total wealth, or size of the companies they run as determinants. Government bureaucrats might use the size of their agencies. Academics may use the number of grants received or articles published. Blue-collar workers may use years of seniority, job assignments, or bowling scores. Where groups are made up of heterogeneous individuals or where heterogeneous groups are forced to be interdependent, there is a potential for status differences to initiate conflict as the group attempts to reconcile and align the differing hierarchies.

■ CONTINGENCY VARIABLES

Several contingency variables have been identified that improve our ability to explain and predict group behavior. Among these variables are individual personality characteristics, group size, and the degree of heterogeneity among members.

Personality Characteristics

There has been a great deal of research on the relationship between personality traits and group attitudes and behavior. The general conclusion is that attributes that tend to have a positive connotation in our culture tend to be positively related to group productivity, morale, and cohesiveness. These include traits such as sociability, self-reliance, and independence. In contrast, negatively evaluated characteristics such as authoritarianism, dominance, and unconventionality tend to be negatively related to the dependent variables.

Is any one personality characteristic a good predictor of group behavior? The answer is "No." The magnitude of the effect of any *single* characteristic is small, but taken *together,* the consequences for group behavior are of major significance. We can conclude, therefore, that personality characteristics of group members play an important part in determining behavior in groups.

Group Size

Does the size of a group affect the group's overall behavior? The answer to this question is a definite "Yes," but the effect depends on the group's goal.

The evidence indicates, for instance, that smaller groups are faster at completing tasks than are larger ones. However, if the group is engaged in problem solving, large groups consistently get better marks than their smaller counterparts. Translating these results into specific numbers is a bit more hazardous, but we can offer some parameters. Large groups (those with a dozen or more members) are good for gaining diverse input. So if the goal of the group is fact finding, larger groups should be more effective. On the other hand, smaller groups are better at doing something productive with that input. Groups of approximately seven members, therefore, tend to be more effective for action taking.

One of the most important findings related to the size of a group has been labeled "social loafing." It directly challenges the logic that the productivity of the group as a whole should at least equal the sum of the productivity of each individual in that group.

A common stereotype about groups is that the sense of team spirit spurs individual effort and enhances the group's overall productivity. In the late 1920s, a German psychologist named Ringelmann compared the results of individual and group performance on a rope-pulling task. He expected the group's effort would be equal to the sum of the efforts of individuals within the group. That is, three people pulling together should exert three times as much pull on the rope as one person, and eight people should exert eight times as much pull. Ringelmann's results, however, did not confirm his expectations. Groups of three people exerted a force only two-and-a-half times the average individual performance. Groups of eight collectively achieved less than four times the solo rate.

Replications of Ringelmann's research with similar tasks have generally supported his findings. Increases in group size are inversely related to individual performance. More may be better in the sense that the total productivity of a group of four is greater than one or two, but the individual productivity of each group member declines.

What causes this social loafing effect? It may be due to a belief that others in the group are not pulling their own weight. If you see others as lazy or inept, you can reestablish equity by reducing your effort. Another explanation is the dispersion of responsibility. Because the results of the group cannot be attributed to any single person, the relationship between an individual's input and the group's output is clouded. In such situations, individuals may be tempted to take a free ride and coast on the group's efforts. In other words, there will be a reduction in efficiency where individuals think their contribution cannot be measured.

For OB, the implications of this effect on work groups are significant. Where managers utilize collective work situations to enhance morale and teamwork, they must also provide means by which individual efforts can be identified. If this is not done, management must weigh the potential losses in productivity against any possible gains in worker satisfaction.

The research on group size also leads us to two additional conclusions: (1) Groups with an odd number of members tend to be preferred over those with an even number, and (2) groups composed of five or seven members do a pretty good job of extracting the best elements of both small and large groups. The preference for an odd number of members eliminates the possibility of ties. Groups made up of five or seven members are large enough to form a majority and allow for diverse input yet avoid the negative outcomes often associated with large groups such as domination by a few members, development of subgroups, inhibited participation by some members, and excessive time taken to reach a decision.

Member Diversity

Most group activities require a variety of skills and knowledge. Given this requirement, it would be reasonable to conclude that heterogeneous groups— those made up of dissimilar individuals—would be more likely to have diverse abilities and information and should be more effective than homogeneous groups. Research studies substantiate this conclusion.

When a group is heterogeneous in terms of personalities, opinions, abilities, skills, and perspectives, there is an increased probability that the group will possess the needed characteristics to complete its tasks effectively. The group may be more imbued with conflict and less expedient as diverse positions are introduced and assimilated, but the evidence generally supports the conclusion that heterogeneous groups perform more effectively than those that are homogeneous.

Incidentally, this research argues well for the value of gender, racial, ethnic, and age diversity in work groups and teams. People of diversity bring experiences and ways of seeing the world that can result in a wider range of perspectives, more creativity, and other positive group outcomes.

■ GROUP COHESIVENESS

This section determines whether cohesiveness, as a group characteristic, is desirable. And, if it is, should management actively seek to create work groups that are highly cohesive?

Intuitively, it would appear that groups with a lot of internal disagreement and a lack of cooperative spirit would complete their tasks less effectively than would groups in which individuals generally agree, cooperate, and like each other. Research to test this intuition has focused on the concept of *group cohesiveness,* defined as the degree to which members are attracted to one another and share the group's goals. That is, the more members are attracted to each other and the more the group's goals align with their individual goals, the greater the group's cohesiveness. In the following pages, we review the factors that have been found to influence group cohesiveness and then look at the effect of cohesiveness on group productivity.

Determinants of Cohesiveness

What factors determine whether group members will be attracted to one another? Cohesiveness can be affected by such factors as time spent together, the severity of initiation, group size, external threats, and previous successes.

Time Spent Together. If you rarely get an opportunity to see or interact with other people, you're unlikely to be attracted to them. The amount of time people spend together, therefore, influences cohesiveness. As people spend more time together, they become more friendly. They naturally begin to talk, respond, gesture, and engage in other interactions. These interactions typically lead to discovery of common interests and increased attraction.

The opportunity for group members to spend time together is dependent on their physical proximity. We would expect more close relationships among members who are located close to one another rather than far apart. People who live on the same block, ride in the same car pool, or share a common office are more likely to become a cohesive group because the physical distance between them is minimal. For instance, among clerical workers in one organization, it was found that the distance between their desks was the single most important determinant of the rate of interaction between any two of the clerks.

Severity of Initiation. The more difficult it is to get into a group, the more cohesive that group becomes. The hazing through which fraternities typically put their pledges is meant to screen out those who don't want to "pay the price" and to intensify the desire of those who do to become fraternity actives. But group initiation needn't be as blatant as hazing. The competition to be accepted to a good medical school results in first-year medical school classes that are highly cohesive. The common initiation rites—applications, test taking, interviews, and the long wait for a final decision—all contribute to creating this cohesiveness. Similarly, the months or often years that an apprentice trade worker must put in to develop his or her skills before being advanced to journeyman status results in union journeymen generally being a cohesive group.

Group Size. If group cohesiveness tends to increase with the time members are able to spend together, it seems logical that cohesiveness should decrease as group size increases, since it becomes more difficult for a member to interact with all the members. This is generally what the research indicates. As group size expands, interaction with all members becomes more difficult, as does the ability to maintain a common goal. Not surprisingly, too, as a single group's size increases, the likelihood of cliques forming also increases. The creation of groups within groups tends to decrease overall cohesiveness.

External Threats. Most of the research supports the proposition that a group's cohesiveness will increase if the group comes under attack from external sources. Management threats frequently bring together an otherwise disar-rayed union. Efforts by management unilaterally to redesign even one or two jobs or to discipline one or two employees occasionally grab local headlines when the entire work force walks out in support of the "abused" few. These examples illustrate a cooperative phenomenon that can develop within a group when it is attacked from outside.

While a group generally moves toward greater cohesiveness when threat-ened by external agents, this does not occur under all conditions. If group members perceive their group may not meet an attack well, then the group becomes less important as a source of security, and cohesiveness will not nec-essarily increase. Additionally, if members believe the attack is directed at the group merely because of its existence and that it will cease if the group is abandoned or broken up, there is likely to be a decrease in cohesiveness.

Previous Successes. Everyone loves a winner! If a group has a history of pre-vious successes, it builds an esprit de corps that attracts and unites members. Successful firms find it easier to attract and hire new employees. The same holds true for successful research groups, well-known and prestigious univer-sities, and winning athletic teams. When Bill Bowerman was head track coach at the University of Oregon during the 1960s, he never had trouble attracting the country's top track and field athletes to his campus. The best athletes wanted to come to Oregon because of Bowerman's highly successful program. In fact, Bowerman claims never to have initiated contact with an athlete. In contrast to track coaches at other major universities, if an athlete wanted to compete at Oregon, he had to prove his interest by taking the first step. By the same token, for those readers who harbor ambitions to attend a top-quality graduate school of business, you should recognize that the success of these schools attracts large numbers of aspiring candidates—many have 10 or more applicants for every vacancy. Again, everyone loves a winner!

Effects of Cohesiveness on Group Productivity

The previous section indicates that, generally speaking, group cohesiveness is increased when members spend time together and undergo a severe initia-tion, when the group size is small, when external threats exist, and when the group has a history of previous successes. But is increased cohesiveness always desirable from the point of view of management? Is it related to increased productivity?

Research has generally shown that highly cohesive groups are more effec-tive than those with less cohesiveness, but the relationship is more complex than merely allowing us to say high cohesiveness is good. First, high cohesive-ness is both a cause and an outcome of high productivity. Second, the relation-ship is moderated by the degree to which the group's attitude aligns with its formal goals or those of the larger organization of which it is a part.

Cohesiveness influences productivity and productivity influences cohe-siveness. Camaraderie reduces tension and provides a supportive environ-

Cohesiveness

	High	Low
High	Strong increase in productivity	Moderate increase in productivity
Low	Decrease in productivity	No significant effect on productivity

Alignment of group and organizational goals

EXHIBIT 7-2   *RELATIONSHIP OF COHESIVENESS TO PRODUCTIVITY*

ment for the successful attainment of group goals. But as already noted, the successful attainment of group goals and the members' feelings of having been a part of a successful unit can serve to enhance the commitment of members. Basketball coaches, for example, are famous for their endearment of teamwork. They believe that if the team is going to win games, members have to learn to play together. Popular coaching phrases include, "There are no individuals on this team" and "We win together, or we lose together." The other side of this view, however, is that winning reinforces camaraderie and leads to increased cohesiveness; that is, successful performance leads to increased intermember attractiveness and sharing.

More important has been the recognition that the relationship of cohesiveness and productivity depends on the alignment of the group's attitude with its formal goals, or for work groups, those of the larger organization of which it is a part. The more cohesive a group, the more its members will follow its goals. If these attitudes are favorable (i.e., high output, quality work, cooperation with individuals outside the group), a cohesive group will be more productive than a less cohesive group. But if cohesiveness is high and attitudes unfavorable, there will be decreases in productivity. If cohesiveness is low and there is support of goals, productivity increases but less than in the high cohesiveness–high support situation. Where cohesiveness is low and attitudes are not in support of the organization's goal, there seems to be no significant effect of cohesiveness on productivity. These conclusions are summarized in Exhibit 7–2.

■ GROUP BEHAVIOR MODEL

Now we want to synthesize the factors that influence group performance, member satisfaction, and group cohesiveness into a group behavior model

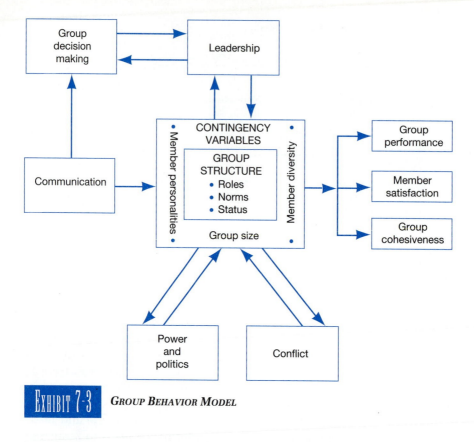

EXHIBIT 7-3   *GROUP BEHAVIOR MODEL*

(see Exhibit 7–3). This model not only summarizes the key concepts introduced in this chapter but also demonstrates how the topics we discuss in the
next four chapters—communication, group decision making, leadership,
power, politics, and conflict—interrelate.

The core of our group behavior model is the group's structure. Every
group has roles, norms, and a status hierarchy that define its structure.
However, the effect of group structure on the outcome variables is moderated
by the personality characteristics of the group's members, as well as the size
and composition of the group.

While leadership provides direction to a group, it is through collective communication and decision making that leaders and group members
interact. That is, communication and decision making provide the "grease"
that facilitates the potential synergistic gains from group interaction. Of
course, that interaction also creates power differences and the potential for
political maneuvers and conflicts. As we show in Chapters 10 and 11, politics and conflict are not necessarily bad. Sometimes they improve a
group's performance. But they can be dysfunctional by reducing, or even
completely offsetting, any of the synergistic benefits created through group
interaction.

■ BUILDING EFFECTIVE TEAMS

Are work teams and groups the same thing? Not necessarily. *Work teams* are formal groups, made up of interdependent individuals, responsible for the attainment of a goal. So all work teams are groups, but only formal groups can be work teams.

Teams are increasingly becoming a major device around which work is being organized. In the United States alone, 10 million or more people are doing their jobs as part of a team. And that number is sure to grow over the next several years.

Why the popularity of teams? They build esprit de corps, they allow for faster operating decisions, they stimulate ideas for improving work processes, and they often lead to higher performance than can be achieved by the same individuals working alone. But teams are by no means automatic productivity enhancers. High-performance teams have certain characteristics. The following should guide you if you decide to use teams as a central building block for work activities.

Clear Goals. High-performance teams have both a clear understanding of the goal to be achieved and a belief that the goal embodies a worthwhile or important result. Moreover, the importance of these goals encourages individuals to sublimate personal concerns to these team goals. In effective teams, members are committed to the team's goals, know what they are expected to accomplish, and understand how they will work together to achieve these goals.

Relevant Skills. Effective teams are composed of competent individuals. They have the necessary technical skills and abilities to achieve the desired goals and the personal characteristics required to achieve excellence while working well with others. This second point is important and often overlooked. Not everyone who is technically competent has the skills to work well as a team member. High-performing teams have members who possess both technical and interpersonal skills.

Mutual Trust. Effective teams are characterized by high mutual trust among members. That is, members believe in the integrity, character, and ability of each other. But as you know from personal relationships, trust is fragile. It takes a long time to build and can be easily destroyed. Also, since trust begets trust and distrust begets distrust, maintaining trust requires careful attention by management.

The climate of trust within a group tends to be strongly influenced by the organization's culture and the actions of management. Organizations that value openness, honesty, and collaborative processes, and which additionally encourage employee involvement and autonomy are likely to create trusting cultures. Exhibit 7–4 lists six recommended actions that can help managers build and maintain trust.

EXHIBIT 7-4   SIX SUGGESTIONS TO HELP MANAGERS BUILD TRUST

1. *Communicate.* Keep team members and subordinates informed by explaining decisions and policies, and providing accurate feedback. Be candid about your own problems and limitations.

2. *Be supportive.* Be available and approachable. Encourage and support team members' ideas.

3. *Be respectful.* Delegate real authority to team members and listen to their ideas.

4. *Be fair.* Give credit where it's due, be objective and impartial in performance evaluations, and be generous with your praise.

5. *Be predictable.* Be consistent in your daily affairs. Make good on your explicit and implied promises.

6. *Demonstrate competence.* Develop the admiration and respect of team members by demonstrating technical and professional ability and good business sense.

Source: Adapted from Fernando Bartolomé, "Nobody Trusts the Boss Completely—Now What?" *Harvard Business Review* (March–April 1989), pp. 135–42.

Unified Commitment. Members of an effective team exhibit intense loyalty and dedication to the team. They're willing to do anything that has to be done to help their team succeed. We call this loyalty and dedication *unified commitment.*

Studies of successful teams have found that members identify with their team. Members redefine themselves to include membership in the team as an important aspect of the self. Unified commitment, then, is characterized by dedication to the team's goals and a willingness to expend extraordinary amounts of energy to achieve it.

Good Communication. Not surprisingly, effective teams are characterized by good communication. Members are able to convey messages between each other in a form that is readily and clearly understood. This includes nonverbal as well as spoken messages. Good communication is also characterized by a healthy dose of feedback from team members and management. This helps guide team members and correct misunderstandings. Like a couple who have been together for many years, members on high-performing teams are able to share ideas and feelings quickly and efficiently.

Negotiating Skills. When jobs are designed around individuals, job descriptions, rules and procedures, and other forms of formalized documentation clarify employee roles. Effective teams, on the other hand, tend to be flexible and continually making adjustments. This requires team members to possess adequate negotiating skills. Problems and relationships are regularly changing in teams, requiring members to confront and reconcile differences.

The Right Kind of Leadership. Effective leaders can motivate a team to follow them through the most difficult situations. How? They help clarify goals. By overcoming inertia, they demonstrate that change is possible. And they increase the self-confidence of team members, helping them to more fully realize their potential.

Importantly, the best leaders are not necessarily directive or controlling. Increasingly, effective team leaders take the role of coach and facilitator. They help guide and support the team, but they don't control it. For some traditional managers, changing their role from boss to facilitator—from giving orders to working *for* the team—is a difficult transition. While most managers relish the newfound shared authority or come to understand its advantages through leadership training, some hard-nosed dictatorial managers are just ill-suited to the team concept and must be transferred or replaced.

Internal and External Support. The final ingredient to make an effective team is a supportive climate. Internally, the team should be provided with a sound infrastructure. This includes proper training, an understandable measurement system so team members can evaluate their overall performance, an incentive program that recognizes and rewards team activities, and a supportive human resource system. The right infrastructure should support members and reinforce behaviors that lead to high levels of performance. External support requires that management provide the team with the resources it needs to get the job done.

■ IMPLICATIONS FOR MANAGERS

In order to accomplish work tasks, the individuals who make up an organization are typically united into departments, committees, or other forms of work groups. In addition to these formal groups, individuals also create informal groups based on common interests or friendships. It is important for managers to look at employees as members of a group because, in reality, group behavior is not merely the summation of the individual behavior of its members. The group itself adds an additional dimension to its members' behavior.

How is it relevant to understanding group behavior to know that a Maryland woman, for example, has to reconcile her roles of mother, Methodist, Democrat, councilwoman, and police officer with the City of Baltimore? Knowledge of the role that a person is attempting to enact can make it easier for us to deal with the person, for we have insight into her expected behavior patterns. Also, knowledge of a job incumbent's role makes it easier for others to work with her, for she should behave in ways consistent with others' expectations. In other words, when a person plays out her role as it is supposed to be played, it improves the ability of others to predict the behavior of the role incumbent. We can predict an individual's behavior in new encounters by superimposing the role requirements of the situation on her.

Knowledge of an incumbent's role perception and others expectations can also be beneficial in predicting role conflict and possibly explaining the behavior of the individual experiencing the conflict.

Norms control group member behavior by establishing standards of right or wrong. If we know the norms of a given group, it can help us to explain the attitudes and behaviors of its members. Where norms support high output, we can expect individual performance to be markedly higher than where group norms aim to restrict output. Similarly, acceptable standards of absence will be dictated by the group norms. Given the inverse correlation between satisfaction and turnover, it would also be reasonable to assume that if the group's norms reinforce complaining and consistent outward demonstration of job dissatisfaction, the propensity for members to terminate employment may be greater. On the other hand, members may enjoy this complaining and it may not affect turnover rates. To illustrate, it is not unusual for union members to play the role of a so-called abused and exploited worker. The group may establish such a role stereotype as part of the norm. In such cases, it may have no real influence on satisfaction or quit rates.

Can managers control group norms? Not completely, but they can influence them. By making explicit statements about desirable behaviors, by regularly reinforcing these preferred behaviors, and by linking rewards to the acceptance of preferred norms, managers can exert some degree of influence over group norms.

Status inequities within a group divert activity away from goal accomplishment and direct it toward resolving the inequities. When inequities exist, managers may find that group members reduce their work effort, attempt to undermine the activities of those members with higher status, or pursue similar dysfunctional behaviors. To the degree that a manager controls status accoutrements, he or she should ensure that they are distributed carefully and consistently with status equity. Inequities are likely to have a negative motivational impact on the group.

Should managers seek cohesive groups? Our answer is a qualified "Yes." The qualification lies in the degree of alignment between the group and the organization's goals. Managers should attempt to create work groups whose goals are consistent with those of the organization. If this is achieved, then high group cohesiveness will make a positive contribution to the group's performance.

Finally, an increasing number of managers are using work teams as a basic organizing mechanism. If you use work teams, you should ensure they have clear goals and appropriate support; members have competent technical, interpersonal, and negotiating skills; you act to build and maintain trust and unified commitment; you and the team members work to facilitate good communication; and you provide leadership by being a coach and facilitator.

SUGGESTIONS FOR FURTHER READING

GEORGE, JENNIFER M., "Extrinsic and Intrinsic Origins of Perceived Social Loafing in Organizations," *Academy of Management Journal,* March 1992, pp. 191–202.

GUZZO, RICHARD A., AND GREGORY P. SHEA, "Group Performance and Intergroup Relations in Organizations," in M.D. Dunnette and L.M. Hough, eds., *Handbook of Industrial & Organizational Psychology,* Vol. 3 (Palo Alto, CA: Consulting Psychologists Press, 1992), pp. 269–313.

HACKMAN, J. RICHARD, "Group Influences on Individuals in Organizations," in M.D. Dunnette and L.M. Hough, eds., *Handbook of Industrial & Organizational Psychology,* Vol. 3 (Palo Alto, CA: Consulting Psychologists Press, 1992), pp. 199–267.

JONES, STEPHEN R.G., "Was There a Hawthorne Effect?" *American Journal of Sociology,* November 1992, pp. 451–68.

KATZENBACH, JON R., AND DOUGLAS K. SMITH, *The Wisdom of Teams: Creating the High-Performance Organization* (Boston: Harvard Business School Press, 1993).

KEYTON, JOANN, AND JEFF SPRINGSTON, "Redefining Cohesiveness in Groups," *Small Group Research,* May 1990, pp. 234–54.

SUNDSTROM, ERIC, KENNETH P. DE MEUSE, AND DAVID FUTRELL, "Work Teams: Applications and Effectiveness," *American Psychologist,* February 1990, pp. 120–33.

WORCHEL, S., W. WOOD, AND J.A. SIMPSON (eds.), *Group Process and Productivity* (Newbury Park, CA: Sage, 1991).

CHAPTER 8

COMMUNICATION AND GROUP DECISION MAKING

After reading this chapter, you should be able to:

1. Describe the communication process
2. Contrast the three common small-group networks
3. Identify factors affecting the use of the grapevine
4. Describe common barriers to effective communication
5. List four rules for improving cross-cultural communication
6. Outline behaviors associated with providing effective feedback
7. Identify the behaviors related to effective active listening
8. List the advantages and disadvantages of group decision making
9. Describe the symptoms of groupthink

Probably the most frequently cited source of interpersonal conflict is poor communication. Because we spend nearly 70 percent of our waking hours communicating—writing, reading, speaking, listening—it seems reasonable to conclude that one of the most inhibiting forces to successful group performance is a lack of effective communication.

No group can exist without communication: the transference of meaning among its members. It is only through transmitting meaning from one person to another that information and ideas can be conveyed. Communication, however, is more than merely imparting meaning. It must also be understood. In a group where one member speaks only German and the others do not know German, the individual speaking German will not be fully understood. Therefore, communication must include both the *transference* and *understanding* of meaning.

An idea, no matter how great, is useless until it is transmitted and understood by others. Perfect communication, if there were such a thing, would exist when a thought or idea was transmitted so the mental picture perceived by the receiver was exactly the same as that envisioned by the sender. Although elementary in theory, perfect communication is never achieved in practice, for reasons we expand on later.

Before making too many generalizations concerning communication and problems in communicating effectively, we should construct a model to depict and explain the components in the communication process.

■ THE COMMUNICATION PROCESS

Before communication can take place, a purpose, expressed as a message to be conveyed, is needed. It passes between a source (the sender) and a receiver. The message is encoded (converted to a symbolic form) and passed by way of some medium (channel) to the receiver, who retranslates (decodes) the message initiated by the sender. The result is a transference of meaning from one person to another.

Exhibit 8–1 depicts this communication process. This model is made up of seven parts: (1) the communication source, (2) encoding, (3) the message, (4) the channel, (5) decoding, (6) the receiver, and (7) feedback.

The *source* initiates a message by encoding a thought. The *message* is the actual physical product from the source *encoding*. When we speak, the speech is the message. When we write, the writing is the message. When we gesture, the movements of our arms and the expressions on our faces are the message. The *channel* is the medium through which the message travels. It is selected by the source, who must determine whether to use a formal or informal channel. Formal channels are established by the organization and transmit messages that relate to the professional activities of members. They traditionally follow the authority chain within the organization. Other forms of messages, such as personal or social, follow the informal channels in the organization.

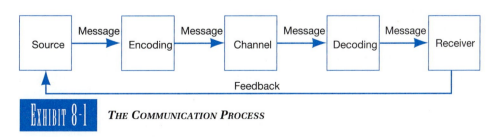

EXHIBIT 8-1   *THE COMMUNICATION PROCESS*

The *receiver* is the object to whom the message is directed. But before the message can be received, the symbols in it must be translated into a form that can be understood by the receiver. This is the *decoding* of the message. The final link in the communication process is a feedback loop. *Feedback* is the check on how successful we have been in transferring our messages as originally intended. It determines whether understanding has been achieved.

■ POPULAR WAYS TO COMMUNICATE

How do group members transfer meaning between and among each other? There are three basic methods. People essentially rely on oral, written, and nonverbal communication.

The Obvious: Oral and Written Communication

The chief means of conveying messages is oral communication. Speeches, formal one-on-one and group discussions, and the informal rumor mill or grapevine are popular forms of oral communication.

The advantages of oral communication are speed and feedback. A verbal message can be conveyed and a response received in a minimal amount of time. If the receiver is unsure of the message, rapid feedback provides for early detection by the sender and, hence, allows for early correction.

The major disadvantage of oral communication surfaces in organizations, or whenever the message has to be passed through a number of people. The more people a message must pass through, the greater the potential distortion. If you ever played the game "telephone" at a party, you know the problem. Each person interprets the message in his or her own way. The message's content, when it reaches its destination, is often very different from the original. In an organization, where decisions and other communiqués are verbally passed up and down the authority hierarchy, there exists considerable opportunity for messages to become distorted.

Written communications include memos, letters, electronic mail, fax transmissions, organizational periodicals, notices placed on bulletin boards, or any other device that is transmitted via written words or symbols.

Why would a sender choose to use written communications? They're tangible and verifiable. Typically, both the sender and receiver have a record of the communication. The message can be stored for an indefinite period of time. If there are questions concerning the content of the message, it is physically available for later reference. This is particularly important for complex and lengthy communications. The marketing plan for a new product is likely to contain a number of tasks spread out over several months. By putting it in writing, those who have to initiate the plan can readily refer to it over the life of the plan. A final benefit of written communication comes from the process itself. Except in rare instances, such as when you're presenting a formal speech, you're more careful with the written word than the oral word. You're forced to think more thoroughly about what you want to convey in a written message. Thus written communications are more likely to be well thought out, logical, and clear.

Of course, written messages have their drawbacks. They're time consuming. You could convey far more information to a college instructor in a one-hour oral exam than in a one-hour written exam. In fact, you could probably say the same thing in ten to fifteen minutes that it would take you an hour to write. So while writing may be more precise, it also consumes a great deal of time. The other major disadvantage is feedback, or lack of it. Oral communication allows the receiver to respond rapidly to what he thinks he hears. However, written communication does not have a built-in feedback mechanism. The result is that the mailing of a memo is no assurance it has been received and, if received, there is no guarantee the recipient will interpret it as the sender intended. The latter point is also relevant in oral communiqués, except it's easy in such cases merely to ask the receiver to summarize what you've said. An accurate summary presents feedback evidence that the message has been received and understood.

The Not-So-Obvious: Nonverbal Communication

Some of the most meaningful communications are not conveyed verbally or in writing. These are the "not-so-obvious" nonverbal communications.

Every time we verbally give a message to someone, we also impart a nonverbal message. In some instances, the nonverbal component may stand alone. For example, in a singles bar, a glance, a stare, a smile, a frown, and a provocative body movement all convey meaning. Obviously, no discussion of communication would be complete without consideration of this not-so-obvious dimension of communication. For our purposes, we define nonverbal communication to include body movements, the intonations or emphasis we give to words, facial expressions, and the physical distance between the sender and receiver.

The academic study of body motions has been labeled *kinesics.* It refers to gestures, facial configurations, and other movements of the body. But it is a relatively new field, and it has been subject to far more conjecture and popularizing than the research findings support. Hence, while we acknowledge the fact that body movement is an important segment of the study of communication and behavior, conclusions must, of necessity, be guarded. Recognizing this qualification, let us briefly consider the ways body motions convey meaning.

It can be argued that every *body movement* has a meaning and no movement is accidental. For example, through body language we say "Help me, I'm lonely"; "Take me, I'm available"; "Leave me alone, I'm depressed." And rarely do we send our messages consciously. We act out our state of being with nonverbal body language. We lift one eyebrow for disbelief. We rub our noses for puzzlement. We clasp our arms to isolate ourselves or to protect ourselves. We shrug our shoulders for indifference, wink one eye for intimacy, tap our fingers for impatience, slap our forehead for forgetfulness.

While we may disagree with the specific meanings of the movements just described, body language adds to, and often complicates, verbal communication. A body position or movement does not by itself have a precise or universal meaning, but when it is linked with spoken language, it gives fuller meaning to a sender's message.

If you read the verbatim minutes of a meeting, you could not grasp the impact of what was said in the same way you could if you had been there or saw the meeting on video. Why? There is no record of nonverbal communication. The emphasis given to words or phrases is missing. To illustrate how *intonations* can change the meaning of a message, consider the student in class who asks the instructor a question. The instructor replies, "What do you mean by that?" The student's reaction will be different depending on the tone of the instructor's response. A soft, smooth tone creates a different meaning from an intonation that is abrasive with strong emphasis placed on the last word.

The *facial expression* of the instructor in the previous illustration also conveys meaning. A snarling face says something different from a smile. Facial expressions, along with intonations, can show arrogance, aggressiveness, fear, shyness, and other characteristics that would never be communicated if you read a transcript of what had been said.

The way individuals space themselves in terms of *physical distance* also has meaning. What is considered proper spacing is largely dependent on cultural norms. For example, what is considered a businesslike distance in some European countries would be viewed as intimate in many parts of North America. If someone stands closer to you than is considered appropriate, it may indicate aggressiveness or sexual interest; if farther away than usual, it may mean disinterest or displeasure with what is being said.

It is important for the receiver to be alert to these nonverbal aspects of communication. You should look for nonverbal cues as well as listen to the literal meaning of a sender's words. You should particularly be aware of contradictions between the messages. Your boss may say she is free to talk to you about a pressing budget problem, but you may see nonverbal signals suggesting this is *not* the time to discuss the subject. Regardless of what is being said, an individual who frequently glances at her wristwatch is giving the message that she would prefer to terminate the conversation. We misinform others when we express one emotion verbally, such as trust, but nonverbally communicate a contradictory message that reads, "I don't have confidence in you." These contradictions often suggest that "actions speak louder (and more accurately) than words."

■ COMMUNICATION NETWORKS

The channels by which information flows are critical once we move beyond groups of two or three individuals. The way a group structures itself will determine the ease and availability with which members can transmit information.

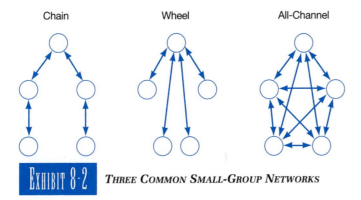

Chain   Wheel   All-Channel

EXHIBIT 8-2   *THREE COMMON SMALL-GROUP NETWORKS*

Formal Small-Group Networks

Most studies of communication networks have taken place in groups created in a laboratory setting. As a result, the research conclusions tend to be constrained by the artificial setting and limited to small groups. Three common small-group networks are shown in Exhibit 8–2; these are the chain, wheel, and all-channel. The chain rigidly follows the formal chain of command. The wheel relies on the leader to act as the central conduit for all the group's communication. The all-channel permits all group members to actively communicate with each other. The all-channel network is most often characterized in practice by the problem-solving task force, where all group members are free to contribute.

The effectiveness of each network depends on the goals of the group. For instance, if speed is important, the wheel and all-channel networks are most effective. For accuracy, choose the chain or wheel. The wheel is best for allowing leaders to emerge. And if member satisfaction is important, the all-channel network is best and the wheel worst. The point is that no single network will be best for all occasions.

The Informal Group Communication Network

The previous discussion of networks emphasized formal communication patterns, but the formal system is not the only communication system in a group or organization. Let us, therefore, now turn our attention to the informal system—where information flows along the well-known *grapevine,* and rumors can flourish.

A classic study of the grapevine was reported 40 years ago.[1] The researcher investigated the communication pattern among 67 managerial personnel in a small manufacturing firm. The basic approach used was to learn

---

[1] Keith Davis, "Management Communication and the Grapevine," *Harvard Business Review* (September-October 1953), pp. 43–49.

from each communication recipient how he first received a given piece of information and then trace it back to its source. It was found that, while the grapevine was an important source of information, only 10 percent of the executives acted as liaison individuals, that is, passed the information on to more than one other person. For example, when one executive decided to resign to enter the insurance business, 81 percent of the executives knew about it, but only 11 percent transmitted this information on to others.

Two other conclusions from this study are also worth noting. Information on events of general interest tended to flow between the major functional groups (production, sales) rather than within them. Also, no evidence surfaced to suggest that any one group consistently acted as liaisons; rather, different types of information passed through different liaison persons.

An attempt to replicate this study among employees in a small state government office also found that only 10 percent act as liaison individuals.[2] This is interesting, since the replication contained a wider spectrum of employees, including rank-and-file as well as managerial personnel. However, the flow of information in the government office took place within, rather than between, functional groups. It was proposed that this discrepancy might be due to comparing an executive-only sample against one which also included rank-and-file workers. Managers, for example, might feel greater pressure to stay informed and thus cultivate others outside their immediate functional group. Also, in contrast to the findings of the original study, the replication found that a consistent group of individuals acted as liaisons by transmitting information in the government office.

Is the information that flows along the grapevine accurate? The evidence indicates that about 75 percent of what is carried is accurate. But what conditions foster an active grapevine? What gets the rumor mill rolling?

It is frequently assumed that rumors start because they make titillating gossip. This is rarely the case. Rumors emerge as a response to situations that are *important* to us, where there is *ambiguity,* and under conditions that arouse *anxiety.* Work situations frequently contain these three elements, which explains why rumors flourish in organizations. The secrecy and competition that typically prevail in large organizations—around such issues as the appointment of new bosses, the relocation of offices, and the realignment of work assignments—create conditions that encourage and sustain rumors on the grapevine. A rumor will persist either until the wants and expectations creating the uncertainty underlying the rumor are fulfilled, or until the anxiety is reduced.

What can we conclude from the preceding discussion? Certainly the grapevine is an important part of any group or organization's communication network and is well worth understanding. It identifies for managers those confusing issues that employees consider important and that create anxiety. It acts, therefore, as both a filter and a feedback mechanism, picking up the

---

    [2] Harold Sutton and Lyman W. Porter, "A Study of the Grapevine in a Governmental Organization," *Personnel Psychology* (Summer 1968), pp. 223–30.

issues that employees consider relevant. For employees, the grapevine is particularly valuable for translating formal communications into their group's own jargon. Maybe more importantly, again from a managerial perspective, it seems possible to analyze grapevine information and to predict its flow, given that only a small set of individuals (around 10 percent) actively pass on information to more than one other person. By assessing which liaison individuals will consider a given piece of information to be relevant, we can improve our ability to explain and predict the pattern of the grapevine.

■ BARRIERS TO EFFECTIVE COMMUNICATION

A number of barriers can retard or distort effective communication. In this section, we highlight a half-dozen of these barriers.

Filtering

Filtering refers to a sender's purposely manipulating information so it will be seen more favorably by the receiver. For example, when a manager tells his boss what he feels his boss wants to hear, he is filtering information.

   The major determinant of filtering is the number of levels in an organization's structure. The more vertical levels in the organization's hierarchy, the more opportunities there are for filtering.

Selective Perception

We have mentioned selective perception before in this book. It appears again because the receiver, in the communication process, sees and hears things in a selective way, based on his needs, motivations, experience, background, and other personal characteristics. The receiver also projects his interests and expectations into communications as he decodes them. The employment interviewer who expects a female job candidate to put family before career is likely to *see* that in female candidates, regardless of whether the candidates feel that way or not. As we said in Chapter 3, we don't see reality but rather we interpret what we see and call it reality.

Gender Styles

Men and women use oral communication for different reasons. In so doing, gender becomes a barrier to effective communication between the sexes.

   Research evidence indicates that men use talk to emphasize status, while women use it to create connection. That is, women speak and hear a language of connection and intimacy; and men speak and hear a language of status and independence. So, for many men, conversations are primarily a means to preserve independence and maintain status in a hierarchical social order. For many women, conversations are negotiations for closeness in which people try to seek and give confirmation and support. For example, men frequently complain that women talk on and on about their problems. Women criticize men for not listening. What's happening is that when men hear a problem, they want to assert their desire for independence and control by providing solutions. Women, on the other hand, view relating a problem as a way to promote closeness. The women present the problem to gain support and connection, not to get the male's advice.

Emotions

How the receiver feels at the time of receipt of a communication message will influence how he or she interprets it. The same message received when you're angry or distraught is often interpreted differently from when you're happy. Extreme emotions such as jubilation or depression are most likely to hinder effective communication. In such instances, we are most prone to disregard our rational and objective thinking processes, and substitute emotional judgments.

Language

Words mean different things to different people. Age, education, and cultural background are three of the more obvious variables that influence the language a person uses and the definitions he gives to words. The language of William F. Buckley, Jr., is clearly different from that of a factory worker who has earned only a high school diploma. The latter, in fact, would undoubtedly have trouble understanding much of Buckley's vocabulary. In an organization, employees usually come from diverse backgrounds. Further, the grouping of employees into departments creates specialists who develop their own jargon or technical language. In large organizations, members are also frequently widely dispersed geographically—even operating in different countries—and individuals in each locale will use terms and phrases that are unique to their area. The existence of vertical levels can also cause language problems. For instance, differences in meaning with regard to words such as *incentives* and *quotas* have been found at different levels in management. Top managers often speak about the need for incentives and quotas, yet these terms imply manipulation and create resentment among many lower managers.

The point is that while you and I both speak a common language— English—our usage of that language is far from uniform. If we knew how each of us modified the language, communication difficulties would be minimized. The problem is that members in an organization usually don't know how those with whom they interact have modified the language. Senders tend to assume that the words and terms they use mean the same to the receiver as they do to them. This is often incorrect, thus creating communication difficulties.

Nonverbal Cues

Earlier we noted that nonverbal communication is an important way in which people convey messages to others. But nonverbal communication is almost always accompanied by oral communication. As long as the two are in agreement, they act to reinforce each other. My boss's words tell me he is angry, his tone and body movements indicate anger; so I can conclude, probably correctly, that he is angry. When nonverbal cues are inconsistent with the oral message, however, the receiver becomes confused and the clarity of the message suffers.

■ CROSS-CULTURAL COMMUNICATION

Effective communication is difficult under the best of conditions. Cross-cultural factors clearly create the potential for increased communication problems.[3]

The encoding and decoding of messages into symbols is based on an individual's cultural background and, as a result, is not the same for each person. The greater the differences in backgrounds between sender and receiver, the greater the differences in meanings attached to particular words or behaviors. People from different cultures see, interpret, and evaluate things differently, and consequently act on them differently.

When communicating with people from a different culture, what can you do to reduce misperceptions, misinterpretations, and misevaluations? Following these four rules can be helpful:

1. *Assume differences until similarity is proven.* Most of us assume that others are more similar to us than they actually are. But people from different countries often are very different from us. So you are far less likely to err if you assume others are different from you rather than assuming similarity until difference is proven.

2. *Emphasize description rather than interpretation or evaluation.* Interpreting or evaluating what someone has said or done, in contrast to description, is based more on the observer's culture and background than on the observed situation. As a result, delay judgment until you've had sufficient time to observe and interpret the situation from the perspectives of all cultures involved.

3. *Practice empathy.* Before sending a message, put yourself in the receiver's shoes. What are his or her values, experiences, and frames of reference? What do you know about his or her education, upbringing, and background that can give you added insight? Try to see the other person as he or she really is.

4. *Treat your interpretations as a working hypothesis.* Once you've developed an explanation for a new situation or think you empathize with someone from a foreign culture, treat your interpretation as a hypothesis that needs further testing rather than as a certainty. Carefully assess the feedback provided by receivers to see if it confirms your hypothesis. For important decisions or communiqués, you can also check with other foreign and home-country colleagues to make sure your interpretations are on target.

---

[3] This section is based on Nancy J. Adler, *International Dimensions of Organizational Behavior,* 2nd ed. (Boston: PWS-Kent, 1991), pp. 83–84.

■ IMPLICATIONS FOR MANAGERS

Given the barriers to communication, what can managers do to minimize problems and attempt to overcome these barriers? The following suggestions should be helpful in making communication more effective.

Use Feedback

Many communication problems can be attributed directly to misunderstandings and inaccuracies. These are less likely to occur if the manager ensures that the feedback loop is utilized in the communication process (see Exhibit 8–3). This feedback can be verbal, written, or nonverbal.

If a manager asks a receiver, "Did you understand what I said?", the response to this question represents feedback. But the "yes" or "no" type of feedback can definitely be improved upon. The manager can ask a set of questions relating to a message in order to determine whether or not the message was

---

 IMPROVING FEEDBACK SKILLS

The following specific suggestions can help managers to be more effective in providing feedback to others.

1. *Focus on specific behaviors.* Feedback should be specific rather than general. For example, in place of saying, "You have a bad attitude," a manager might say, "Bob, I'm concerned with your attitude toward your work. You were a half hour late to yesterday's staff meeting, and then you told me you hadn't read the preliminary report we were discussing. Today you tell me you're taking off three hours early for a dental appointment." This tells Bob why he is being criticized.

2. *Keep feedback impersonal.* Feedback should be job related. Never criticize someone personally because of an inappropriate action. Telling people they're "stupid," "incompetent," or the like is almost always counterproductive.

3. *Keep feedback goal oriented.* If a manager has to say something negative, he or she should make sure it's directed toward the *recipient's* goals. A manager should ask whom the feedback is supposed to help. If the answer is essentially that "I've got something I just want to get off my chest," then he or she should not speak.

4. *Make feedback well timed.* Feedback is most meaningful to a recipient when there is a very short interval between his or her behavior and the receipt of feedback about that behavior.

5. *Ensure understanding.* Is the feedback concise and complete enough so the recipient clearly and fully understands the communication? Managers should consider having the recipient rephrase the content of the feedback to see whether it fully captures the intended meaning.

6. *Direct negative feedback toward behavior that is controllable by the recipient.* There's little value in reminding a person of a shortcoming over which he or she has no control. Negative feedback, therefore, should be directed toward behavior the recipient can do something about.

---

received as intended. Better yet, the manager can ask the receiver to restate the message, in his or her own words. If the manager then hears what was intended, understanding and accuracy should be enhanced. Feedback can also be more subtle than the direct asking of questions or the summarizing of the message by the receiver. General comments can give the manager a sense of a receiver's reaction to a message. Additionally, performance appraisals, salary reviews, and promotion decisions represent important, but more subtle, forms of feedback.

Feedback, of course, does not have to be conveyed in words. Actions *can* speak louder than words. For instance, a sales manager sends out a directive to her staff describing a new monthly sales report that all sales personnel will need to complete. If some of the salespeople fail to turn in the new report, this is a type of feedback. It should suggest to her that she needs to clarify further her initial directive. Similarly, when you give a speech to a group of people, you watch their eyes and look for other nonverbal clues to tell you whether group members are getting your message or not. This may explain why television performers on situation comedy shows prefer to tape their programs in front of a live audience. Immediate laughter and applause, or their absence, convey to the performers whether they are getting their message across.

Simplify Language

Since language can be a barrier, a manager should seek to structure messages in ways that will make them clear and understandable. Words should be chosen carefully. The manager needs to simplify his or her language and consider the audience to whom a message is directed, so the language will be compatible with the receiver. Remember, effective communication is achieved when a message is both received and *understood.* Understanding is improved by simplifying the language used in relation to the audience intended. This means, for example, that a hospital administrator should always try to communicate in clear and easily understood terms and that the language used for conveying messages to the surgical staff should be purposely different from that used with employees in the admissions office. Jargon can facilitate understanding when it is used with other group members who speak that language, but it can cause innumerable problems when used outside that group.

Listen Actively

When someone talks, we hear. But, too often, we don't listen. Listening is an active search for meaning, while hearing is passive (see Exhibit 8–4). When you listen, two people, the receiver and the sender, are thinking.

Many of us are poor listeners. Why? Because it's difficult and because it's usually more satisfying to be on the offensive. Listening, in fact, is often more tiring than talking. It demands intellectual effort. Unlike hearing, active listening demands total concentration. The average person speaks at a rate of about 150 words per minute, whereas we have the capacity to listen at the rate of over 1,000 words per minute. The difference obviously leaves idle brain time and opportunities for mind wandering.

EXHIBIT 8-4 *IMPROVING ACTIVE LISTENING SKILLS*

The following specific suggestions can help managers to be more effective active listeners.

1. *Make eye contact.* While we listen with our ears, people judge whether we're listening by looking at our eyes. Making eye contact with the speaker focuses one's attention, reduces the potential for distractions, and encourages the speaker.

2. *Exhibit affirmative head nods and appropriate facial expressions.* The effective listener shows interest in what is being said through nonverbal signals. Affirmative head nods and appropriate facial expressions, when added to good eye contact, convey to the speaker that one is listening.

3. *Avoid distracting actions or gestures.* The other side of showing interest is avoiding actions that suggest the manager's mind is somewhere else. Actions like looking at one's watch, shuffling papers, or playing with a pencil make the speaker feel one is bored or uninterested.

4. *Ask questions.* The critical listener analyzes what he or she hears and asks questions. This provides clarification, ensures understanding, and assures the speaker one is listening.

5. *Paraphrase.* The effective listener uses phrases like, "What I hear you saying is..." or "Do you mean...?" This acts as an excellent control device to check on whether one is listening carefully. It is also a control for accuracy.

6. *Avoid interrupting the speaker.* Let the speaker complete his or her thought before responding. Don't try to guess where the speaker's thoughts are going.

7. *Don't overtalk.* Most of us would rather speak our own ideas than listen to what someone else says. Too many of us listen only because it's the price we have to pay to get people to let us talk. While talking may be more fun and silence may be uncomfortable, it's impossible to talk and listen at the same time. The good listener recognizes this fact and doesn't overtalk.

Active listening is enhanced when the receiver develops empathy with the sender, that is, when the receiver tries to place himself in the sender's position. Since senders differ in attitudes, interests, needs, and expectations, empathy makes it easier to understand the actual content of a message. An empathetic listener reserves judgment on the message's content and carefully listens to what is being said. The goal is to improve one's ability to receive the full meaning of a communication, without having it distorted by premature judgments or interpretations.

Constrain Emotions

It would be naive to assume that a manager always communicates in a fully rational manner. Yet we know emotions can severely cloud and distort the transference of meaning. If we're emotionally upset over an issue, we're more likely to misconstrue incoming messages, and we may fail to express clearly and accurately our outgoing messages. What can the manager do? The best approach is to defer further communication until composure is regained.

Watch Your Nonverbal Cues

Assuming that actions speak louder than words, it's important to watch your actions to make sure they align with, and reinforce, the words that go along with them. We noted that nonverbal messages carry a great deal of weight. Given this fact, the effective communicator watches his or her nonverbal cues to ensure that they, too, convey the message desired.

Use the Grapevine

You can't eliminate the grapevine. What managers should do, therefore, is use it and make it work for them.

Managers can use the grapevine to transmit information rapidly, to test the reaction to various decisions prior to their final consummation, and as a valuable source of feedback when the managers themselves are grapevine members. Of course, the grapevine can carry damaging rumors that reduce the effectiveness of formal communication. To lessen this potentially destructive force, managers should make good use of formal channels by ensuring that they regularly carry the relevant and accurate information that employees seek.

■ GROUP DECISION MAKING

One of the more obvious applications of communication concepts is in the area of group decision making. We know that, today, many decisions in organizations are made by groups or committees. The communicative interaction in a group decision can either increase or decrease the quality of the decision over that made by an individual alone. In the following pages, we review both the advantages and disadvantages of group decisions in contrast to individual decisions. In addition, we compare their effectiveness and efficiency and offer four techniques for improving group decision making.

Advantages

Individual and group decisions each have their own set of strengths. Neither is ideal for all situations. The following list identifies the major advantages that groups offer over individuals in the making of decisions:

1. **More complete information and knowledge.** Two heads can be better than one. There is more information in a group than typically resides with one individual. So groups can provide more diverse input into the decision.
2. **Increases acceptance of a solution.** Many decisions fail after the final choice has been made because people do not accept the solution. However, if people who will be affected by a decision and who will be instrumental in implementing it are able to participate in the decision itself, they will be more likely to accept it and encourage others to accept it. Participation in the process increases the

commitment and motivation of those who will carry out the decision. Since members are reluctant to fight or undermine a decision they helped to develop, group decisions increase acceptance of the final solution and facilitate its implementation.

3. **Increases legitimacy.** North American society fosters democratic methods. The group decision-making process is consistent with democratic ideals and, therefore, may be perceived as more legitimate in North America and other democratic societies than decisions made by a single person. When an individual decision maker fails to consult with others before making a decision, the fact that the decision maker has complete power can create the perception that the decision was made autocratically and arbitrarily.

Disadvantages

Of course, group decisions are not without drawbacks. The following lists the major *disadvantages* to group decision making:

1. **Time consuming.** It takes time to assemble a group. The interaction that takes place once the group is in place is frequently inefficient. The result is that groups take more time to reach a solution than would be the case if an individual were making the decision.

2. **Pressures to conform.** There are social pressures in groups. The desire by group members to be accepted and considered as an asset to the group can result in squashing any overt disagreement, thus encouraging conformity among viewpoints.

3. **Ambiguous responsibility.** Group members share responsibility, but who is actually responsible for the final outcome? In an individual decision, it is clear who is responsible. In a group decision, the responsibility of any single member is watered down and less clearly defined.

Effectiveness and Efficiency

Whether groups are more effective than individuals depends on the criteria you use for defining effectiveness. In terms of *accuracy,* group decisions will tend to be correct more often. The evidence indicates that, on the average, groups make better decisions than individuals. This doesn't mean, of course, that *all* groups will outperform *every* individual. Rather, group decisions have been found to be better than those that would be reached by the average individual in the group. However, they are seldom better than the performance of the best individual.

If decision effectiveness is defined in terms of *speed,* individuals are superior. Group decision processes are characterized by give and take, which consumes time.

Effectiveness may mean the degree to which a solution demonstrates *creativity.* If creativity is important, groups tend to be more effective than individuals. However, this assumes the group leader successfully limits conformity pressures.

A final criterion for effectiveness is the degree of *acceptance* the final solution achieves. As noted previously, group decisions, because they have input from more people, are likely to develop solutions that will be more widely accepted.

The effectiveness of group decision making has also been shown to be influenced by the size of the group. The larger the group, the greater the opportunity for heterogeneous representation. On the other hand, increased size requires more coordination and increased time to allow all members to contribute. What this means is that groups probably should not be too large—a minimum of five, a maximum of about fifteen. In fact, as noted in the previous chapter, groups of five and, to a lesser extent, seven appear to be the most effective. Because they are odd numbers, strict deadlocks are avoided. Such groups are large enough for members to shift roles and withdraw from embarrassing positions, but still small enough for quieter members to participate actively in discussions.

Effectiveness should not be considered without also assessing efficiency. In terms of efficiency, groups almost always stack up a poor second to the individual decision maker. With few exceptions, group decision making consumes more work hours than if an individual were to tackle the same problem alone. The exception tends to be those instances where, to achieve comparable quantities of diverse input, the single decision maker must spend a great deal of time reviewing files and talking to people. Because groups can include members from diverse areas, the time spent searching for information can be reduced. However, as we noted, these advantages in efficiency tend to be the exception. Groups are generally less efficient than individuals. In deciding whether to use groups, then, primary consideration must be given to assessing whether increases in effectiveness are more than enough to offset the losses in efficiency.

Groupthink and Groupshift

Two by-products of group decision making have received a considerable amount of attention by researchers in OB. As we show here, these two phenomena have the potential to affect the group's ability to appraise alternatives objectively and arrive at quality decision solutions.

The first phenomenon, called *groupthink,* is related to norms. It describes situations in which group pressures for conformity deter the group from critically appraising unusual, minority, or unpopular views. The second phenomenon is called *groupshift.* It indicates that in discussing a given set of alternatives and arriving at a solution, group members tend to exaggerate the initial positions they hold. In some situations, caution dominates, and there is a conservative shift. More often, however, the evidence indicates that groups tend toward a risky shift.

Groupthink. Have you ever felt like speaking up in a meeting, classroom, or informal group, but decided against it? One reason may have been shyness. On the other hand, you may have been a victim of groupthink, the phenomenon that occurs when group members become so enamored of seeking concurrence, the norm for consensus overrides the realistic appraisal of alternative courses of action and the full expression of deviant, minority, or unpopular views. It describes a deterioration in an individual's mental efficiency, reality testing, and moral judgment as a result of group pressures.[4]

We've all seen the symptoms of the groupthink phenomenon:

1. Group members rationalize any resistance to the assumptions they have made. No matter how strongly the evidence may contradict their basic assumptions, members behave so as to reinforce those assumptions continually.

2. Members apply direct pressures on those who momentarily express doubts about any of the group's shared views or who question the validity of arguments supporting the alternative favored by the majority.

3. Those members who have doubts or hold differing points of view seek to avoid deviating from what appears to be group consensus by keeping silent about misgivings and even minimizing to themselves the importance of their doubts.

4. There appears to be an illusion of unanimity. If someone does not speak, it is assumed he or she is in full accord. In other words, abstention becomes viewed as a "Yes" vote.

Groupthink appears to be closely aligned with the conclusions Asch drew in his experiments with a lone dissenter. Individuals who hold a position different from that of the dominant majority are under pressure to suppress, withhold, or modify their true feelings and beliefs. As members of a group, we find it more pleasant to be in agreement—to be a positive part of the group—than to be a disruptive force, even if disruption is necessary to improve the effectiveness of the group's decisions.

Groupshift. In comparing group decisions with the individual decisions of members within the group, evidence indicates there are differences. In some cases, the group decisions are more conservative than the individual decisions. More often, the shift is toward greater risk.[5]

What appears to happen in groups is that the discussion leads to a significant shift in the positions of members toward a more extreme position in the direction they were already leaning before the discussion. So conservative types become more cautious and the more aggressive types take on more risk. The group discussion tends to *exaggerate* the initial position of the group.

The groupshift can be viewed as actually a special case of groupthink. The decision of the group reflects the dominant decision-making norm that develops during the group's discussion. Whether the shift in the group's decision is toward greater caution or more risk depends on the dominant prediscussion norm.

---

[4] Irving L. Janis, *Groupthink* (Boston: Houghton Mifflin, 1982).

[5] M.A. Wallach, N. Kogan, and D.J. Bem, "Group Influence on Individual Risk Taking," *Journal of Abnormal and Social Psychology*, Vol. 65 (1962), pp. 75-86.

The greater occurrence of the shift toward risk has generated several explanations for the phenomenon. It's been argued, for instance, that the discussion creates familiarization among the members. As they become more comfortable with each other, they also become more bold and daring. But probably the most plausible explanation of the shift toward risk is that the group diffuses responsibility. Group decisions free any single member from accountability for the group's final choice. Greater risk can be taken because even if the decision fails, no one member can be held wholly responsible.

Improving Group Decision Making

The most common form of group decision making takes place in face-to-face interacting groups. But as our discussion of groupthink demonstrated, interacting groups often censor themselves and pressure individual members toward conformity of opinion. Brainstorming, nominal group and Delphi techniques, and electronic meetings have been proposed as ways to reduce many of the problems inherent in the traditional interacting group.

Brainstorming. *Brainstorming* is meant to overcome pressures for conformity in the interacting group that retard the development of creative alternatives. It does this by utilizing an idea-generation process that specifically encourages any and all alternatives, while withholding any criticism of those alternatives.

In a typical brainstorming session, a half-dozen to a dozen people sit around a table. The group leader states the problem in a clear manner so it is understood by all participants. Members then "free-wheel" as many alternatives as they can in a given length of time. No criticism is allowed, and all the alternatives are recorded for later discussion and analysis. That one idea stimulates others and that judgments of even the most bizarre suggestions are withheld until later encourages group members to "think the unusual."

Brainstorming, however, is merely a process for generating ideas. The next three techniques go further by offering methods of actually arriving at a preferred solution.

Nominal Group Technique. The nominal group restricts discussion or interpersonal communication during the decision-making process, hence the term *nominal group technique.* Group members are all physically present, as in a traditional committee meeting, but the members are required to operate independently. Specifically, the following steps take place:

1. Members meet as a group but, before any discussion takes place, each member independently writes down his or her ideas on the problem.
2. This silent period is followed by each member presenting one idea to the group. Each member takes his or her turn, going around the table, presenting a single idea until all ideas have been presented and recorded (typically on a flip chart or chalkboard). No discussion takes place until all ideas have been recorded.
3. The group then discusses the ideas for clarity and evaluates them.

4. Each group member silently and independently ranks the ideas. The final decision is determined by the idea with the highest aggregate ranking.

The chief advantage of this technique is that it permits the group to meet formally but does not restrict independent thinking, as so often happens in the traditional interacting group.

Delphi Technique. A more complex and time-consuming alternative is the Delphi technique. It is similar to the nominal group except it does not require the physical presence of the group members. This is because the Delphi technique never allows the group members to meet face to face. The following steps characterize the Delphi technique:

1. The problem is identified and members are asked to provide potential solutions through a series of carefully designed questionnaires.
2. Each member anonymously and independently completes the first questionnaire.
3. Results of the first questionnaire are compiled at a central location, transcribed, and reproduced.
4. Each member receives a copy of the results.
5. After viewing the results, members are again asked for their solutions. The results typically trigger new solutions or cause changes in the original position.
6. Steps 4 and 5 are repeated as often as necessary until consensus is reached.

Like the nominal group technique, the Delphi technique insulates group members from the undue influence of others. Because it does not require the physical presence of the participants it has some interesting applications. For instance, Boeing can use the technique to query its sales managers in Tokyo, Paris, London, New York, Toronto, Mexico City, and Melbourne about what equipment should be offered as standard on the new 787. The cost of bringing the executives together at a central location is avoided, yet input is obtained from Boeing's major markets. Of course, the Delphi technique has its drawbacks. The method is extremely time consuming. It is frequently inapplicable where a speedy decision is necessary. Additionally, the method may not develop the rich array of alternatives that the interacting or nominal groups do. The ideas that can surface from the heat of face-to-face interaction may never arise.

Electronic Meetings. The most recent approach to group decision making blends the nominal group technique with sophisticated computer technology. It's called the *electronic meeting*.

Once the technology is in place, the concept is simple. Up to 50 people sit around a horseshoe-shaped table, empty except for a series of computer terminals. Issues are presented to participants and they type their responses onto their computer screen. Individual comments, as well as aggregate votes, are displayed on a projection screen in the room.

The major advantages of electronic meetings are anonymity, honesty, and speed. Participants can anonymously type any message they want and it flashes on the screen for all to see at the push of a participant's board key. It also allows people to be brutally honest without penalty. And it's fast because chitchat is eliminated, discussions don't digress, and many participants can "talk" at once without stepping on one another's toes.

Experts claim that electronic meetings are as much as 55 percent faster than traditional face-to-face meetings. Phelps Dodge Mining, for instance, used the approach to cut its annual planning meeting from several days down to 12 hours. Yet there are drawbacks to this technique. Those who can type fast can outshine those who are verbally eloquent but lousy typists; those with the best ideas don't get credit for them; and the process lacks the information richness of face-to-face oral communication. But although this technology is currently in its infancy, the future of group decision making is very likely to include extensive use of electronic meetings.

■ IMPLICATIONS FOR MANAGERS

In contrast to decisions made by individuals alone, group decisions are more time consuming, more prone to conformity pressures, and more likely to cloud responsibility. However, group solutions are often more accurate, creative, and acceptable than those reached by a single individual. So whether managers choose to make a decision themselves or use a group depends on factors such as accountability, the importance of the decision, and how quickly it needs to be made.

If you use group decision making, you'll particularly want to try to manage groupthink. To lessen the likelihood of groupthink, you should encourage member input, especially from those who are less active in the discussion; and avoid expressing your preferred solution early in the group's discussion because this tends to limit critical analysis and significantly increases the likelihood that the group will adopt this solution as the final choice. You might also want to consider one or more of the techniques presented, such as brainstorming or electronic meetings, as a means to lessen conformity pressures.

ℐUGGESTIONS FOR FURTHER READING

CLAMPITT, P.G., *Communicating for Managerial Effectiveness* (Newbury Park, CA: Sage, 1991).

GALLUPE, R. BRENT, A.R. DENNIS, W.H. COOPER, J.S. VALACICH, L.M. BASTIANUTTI, AND J.F. NUNAMAKER, JR., "Electronic Brainstorming and Group Size," *Academy of Management Journal,* June 1992, pp. 350–69.

GOLEN, S., "A Factor Analysis of Barriers to Effective Listening," *Journal of Business Communication,* Winter 1990, pp. 25–36.

HANEY, WILLIAM V., *Communication and Interpersonal Relations,* 6th ed. (Homewood, IL: Richard D. Irwin, 1992).

LENGEL, ROBERT H., AND RICHARD L. DAFT, "The Selection of Communication Media as an Executive Skill," *Academy of Management Executive,* August 1988, pp. 225–32.

NOON, MIKE, AND RICK DELBRIDGE, "News from Behind My Hand: Gossip in Organizations," *Organization Studies,* Vol. 14, No. 1, 1993, pp. 23–36.

REILLY, BERNARD J., AND JOSEPH A. DIANGELO, JR., "Communication: A Cultural System of Meaning and Value," *Human Relations,* February 1990, pp. 129–40.

TANNEN, DEBORAH, *You Just Don't Understand: Women and Men in Conversation* (New York: Ballantine, 1990).

CHAPTER 9

LEADERSHIP

After reading this chapter, you should be able to:

1. Summarize the conclusions of trait theories

2. Identify the limitations of behavioral theories

3. Describe Fiedler's contingency model

4. Summarize the path-goal theory

5. List the contingency variables in the leader-participation model

6. Explain gender differences in leadership styles

7. Identify the characteristics associated with charismatic leadership

It has been accepted as a truism that good leadership is essential to business, to government, and to the countless groups and organizations that shape the way we live, work, and play. If leadership is such an important factor, the critical issue is: What makes a great leader? The tempting answer to give is: Great followers! While there is some truth to this response, the issue is far more complex.

■ WHAT IS LEADERSHIP?

Leadership is the ability to influence a group toward the achievement of goals. The source of this influence may be formal, such as that provided by the possession of managerial rank in an organization. Since management positions come with some degree of formally designated authority, an individual may assume a leadership role as a result of the position he or she holds in the organization. But not all leaders are managers nor, for that matter, are all managers leaders. Just because an organization provides its managers with certain rights is no assurance they will be able to lead effectively. We find nonsanctioned leadership, that is, the ability to influence that arises outside of the formal structure of the organization, is as important or more important than formal influence. In other words, leaders can emerge from within a group as well as being formally appointed.

■ TRANSITIONS IN LEADERSHIP THEORIES

The leadership literature is voluminous, and much of it is confusing and contradictory. In order to make our way through this "forest," we consider four approaches to explaining what makes an effective leader. The first sought to find universal personality traits that leaders had to some greater degree than nonleaders. The second approach tried to explain leadership in terms of the behavior that a person engaged in. Both of these approaches proved to be false starts, based on their erroneous and oversimplified conception of leadership. The third looked to contingency models to explain the inadequacies of previous leadership theories in reconciling and bringing together the diversity of research findings. Most recently, we have returned to traits but with a different twist. Now the search is on to find the qualities or traits that are held by charismatic leaders. In this chapter, we present the contributions and limitations of each of the four approaches and conclude by attempting to ascertain the value of the leadership literature in explaining and predicting behavior.

■ TRAIT THEORIES

If one were to describe a leader based on the general connotations presented in today's media, one might list qualities such as intelligence, charisma, decisiveness, enthusiasm, strength, bravery, integrity, self-confidence, and so on—possibly eliciting the conclusion that effective leaders must be one part Boy Scout and two parts Jesus Christ. The search for characteristics such as those listed that would differentiate leaders from nonleaders occupied the early psychologists who studied leadership.

Is it possible to isolate one or more personality traits in individuals we generally acknowledge as leaders—Winston Churchill, Susan B. Anthony, Martin Luther King, Jr., John F. Kennedy, Nelson Mandela, Ted Turner—that nonleaders do not possess? We may agree that these individuals meet our definition of a leader, but they represent individuals with utterly different characteristics. If the concept of traits were to be proved valid, specific characteristics had to be found that all leaders possess.

Research efforts at isolating these traits resulted in a number of dead ends. If the search was to identify a set of traits that would always differentiate leaders from followers and effective from ineffective leaders, the search failed. Perhaps it was a bit optimistic to believe a set of consistent and unique traits could apply across the board to all effective leaders, whether they were in charge of the Hell's Angels, the Church of Jesus Christ of Latter-Day Saints, Playboy Enterprises, the Shell Oil Company, or the Walt Disney Company.

However, attempts to identify traits consistently associated with leadership have been more successful. Six traits on which leaders differ from nonleaders include (1) drive and ambition, (2) the desire to lead and influence others, (3) honesty and integrity, (4) self-confidence, (5) intelligence, and (6) in-depth technical knowledge related to their area of responsibility.

Yet traits alone are not sufficient for explaining leadership. Their primary failing is that they ignore situational factors. Possessing the appropriate traits only makes it more likely that an individual will be an effective leader. He or she still has to take the right actions. And what "the right actions" are in one situation is not necessarily right for a different situation. So while there has been some resurgent interest in traits during the past decade, a major movement away from trait theorists began as early as the 1940s. Leadership research from the late 1940s through the mid-1960s emphasized the preferred behavioral styles that leaders demonstrated.

■ BEHAVIORAL THEORIES

The inability to strike gold in the trait mines led researchers to look at the behaviors that specific leaders exhibited. They wondered if there was something unique in the way effective leaders behave. For example, do they tend to be more democratic than autocratic?

Not only, it was hoped, would the behavioral approach provide more definitive answers about the nature of leadership but, if successful, it would have practical implications quite different from those of the trait approach. If trait research had been successful, it would have provided a basis for selecting the right person to assume formal positions in groups and organizations requiring leadership. In contrast, if behavioral studies were to turn up critical behavioral determinants of leadership, we could *train* people to be leaders. The difference between trait and behavioral theories, in terms of application, lies in their underlying assumptions. If trait theories were valid, then leaders are basically born: You either have it or you don't. On the other hand, if there were specific behaviors that identified leaders, then we could teach leadership—we could design programs that implanted these behavioral patterns in individuals who desired to be effective leaders. This was surely a more exciting avenue, for it would mean the supply of leaders could be expanded. If training worked, we could have an infinite supply of effective leaders.

A number of studies looked at behavioral styles. We briefly review the two most popular studies: the Ohio State group and the University of Michigan group. Then we see how the concepts these studies developed could be used to create a grid for looking at and appraising leadership styles.

Ohio State Studies

The most comprehensive and replicated of the behavioral theories resulted from research that began at Ohio State University in the late 1940s. These studies sought to identify independent dimensions of leader behavior. Beginning with over a thousand dimensions, they eventually narrowed the list into two categories that substantially accounted for most of the leadership behavior described by subordinates. They called these two dimensions initiating structure and consideration.

Initiating structure refers to the extent to which a leader is likely to define and structure his or her role and those of subordinates in the search for goal attainment. It includes behavior that attempts to organize work, work relationships, and goals. The leader characterized as high in initiating structure could be described in terms such as assigns group members to particular tasks, expects workers to maintain definite standards of performance, and emphasizes the meeting of deadlines.

Consideration is described as the extent to which a person is likely to have job relationships characterized by mutual trust, respect for subordinates' ideas, and regard for their feelings. This type of leader shows concern for his followers' comfort, well-being, status, and satisfaction. A leader high in consideration could be described as one who helps subordinates with personal problems, is friendly and approachable, and treats all subordinates as equals.

Extensive research, based on these definitions, found that leaders high in initiating structure *and* consideration (a "high-high" leader) tended to achieve high subordinate performance and satisfaction more frequently than those who rated low on either initiating structure, consideration, or on both. However, the "high-high" style did not *always* result in positive consequences. For example, leader behavior characterized as high on initiating structure led to greater rates of grievances, absenteeism and turnover, and lower levels of job satisfaction for workers performing routine tasks. Other studies found that high consideration was negatively related to performance ratings of the leader by his superior. In conclusion, the Ohio State studies suggested the "high-high" style generally resulted in positive outcomes, but enough exceptions were found to indicate that situational factors needed to be integrated into the theory.

University of Michigan Studies

Leadership studies undertaken at the University of Michigan's Survey Research Center, at about the same time as those being done at Ohio State, had similar research objectives: to locate behavioral characteristics of leaders that appeared to be related to measures of performance effectiveness.

The Michigan group also came up with two dimensions of leadership behavior, which they labeled *employee oriented* and *production oriented*. Leaders who were employee oriented were described as emphasizing interpersonal relations; they took a personal interest in the needs of their subordinates and accepted individual differences among members. The production-oriented leaders, in contrast, tended to emphasize the technical or task aspects of the job—their main concern was in accomplishing their group's tasks, and the group members were a means to that end.

The conclusions arrived at by the Michigan researchers strongly favored the leaders who were employee oriented in their behavior. Employee-oriented leaders were associated with higher group productivity and higher job satis-

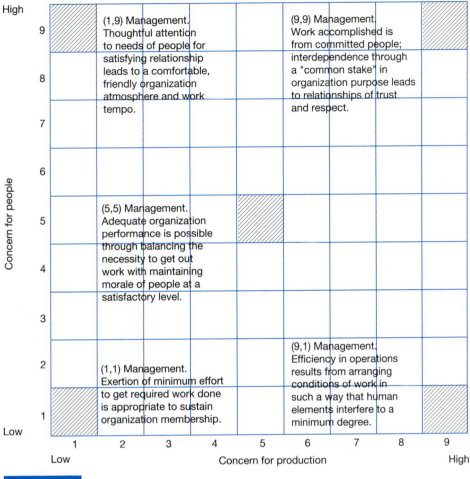

High

9   (1,9) Management. Thoughtful attention to needs of people for satisfying relationship leads to a comfortable, friendly organization atmosphere and work tempo.

(9,9) Management. Work accomplished is from committed people; interdependence through a "common stake" in organization purpose leads to relationships of trust and respect.

5   (5,5) Management. Adequate organization performance is possible through balancing the necessity to get out work with maintaining morale of people at a satisfactory level.

(9,1) Management. Efficiency in operations results from arranging conditions of work in such a way that human elements interfere to a minimum degree.

(1,1) Management. Exertion of minimum effort to get required work done is appropriate to sustain organization membership.

Concern for people

Low

1   2   3   4   5   6   7   8   9

Low   Concern for production   High

EXHIBIT 9-1   *THE MANAGERIAL GRID*

Source: Robert R. Blake, Jane S. Mouton, Louis B. Barnes, and Larry E. Greiner, "Breakthrough in Organization Development," *Harvard Business Review*, November-December 1964, p. 136. Copyright © 1964 by the President and Fellows of Harvard College; all rights reserved.

faction. Production-oriented leaders tended to be associated with lower group productivity and lower job satisfaction.

The Managerial Grid

A graphic portrayal of a two-dimensional view of leadership style has been developed by Blake and Mouton.[1] They propose a *managerial grid* based on the

---

[1] Robert R. Blake and Jane S. Mouton, *The Managerial Grid* (Houston: Gulf, 1964).

styles of "concern for people" and "concern for production," which essentially represent the Ohio State dimensions of consideration and initiating structure or the Michigan dimensions of employee oriented and production oriented.

The grid, depicted in Exhibit 9–1, has 9 possible positions along each axis, creating 81 different positions in which the leader's style may fall. The grid does not show results produced, but rather the dominating factors in a leader's thinking in regard to getting results.

Based on the findings from the research Blake and Mouton conducted, they concluded that managers perform best under a 9,9 style, as contrasted, for example, with a 9,1 or the 1,9 leader. Unfortunately, the grid offers a better framework for conceptualizing leadership style than for presenting any tangible new information in clarifying the leadership quandary, since there is little substantive evidence to support the conclusion that a 9,9 style is most effective in all situations.

Summary of Behavioral Theories

We have described the most popular and important of the attempts to explain leadership in terms of the behavior exhibited by the leader. Unfortunately, there was very little success in identifying consistent relationships between patterns of leadership behavior and group performance. General statements could not be made because results would vary over different ranges of circumstances. What was missing was consideration of the situational factors that influence success or failure. For example, it seems unlikely that Martin Luther King, Jr., would have been a great leader of his people at the turn of the century, yet he was in the 1950s and 1960s. Would Ralph Nader have risen to lead a consumer activist group had he been born in 1834 rather than 1934, or in Costa Rica rather than Connecticut? It seems quite unlikely, yet the behavioral approaches we have described could not clarify these situational factors.

■ CONTINGENCY THEORIES

It became increasingly clear to those who were studying the leadership phenomenon that predicting leadership success was more complex than isolating a few traits or preferable behaviors. The failure to obtain consistent results led to a new focus on situational influences. The relationship between leadership style and effectiveness suggested that under condition a, style x would be appropriate, while style y would be more suitable for condition b, and style z for condition c. But what were the conditions a, b, c, and so forth? It was one thing to say that leadership effectiveness was dependent on the situation, and another to be able to isolate those situational conditions.

Many studies have attempted to isolate the critical situational factors that affect leadership effectiveness. To illustrate, some of the more popular variables have included the type of task being performed, the style of the leader's immediate supervisor, group norms, time demands, and the organization's culture.

Three contingency theories have received the bulk of attention: Fiedler, path-goal, and leader-participation. We review each in this section. We also take a look at gender as a contingency variable. Although there is no specific contingency theory that directly addresses gender, an expanding body of research compares male and female leadership styles. Given that women have been moving rapidly into organizational leadership positions in recent years, it is important to give some attention to this issue.

Fiedler Model

The first comprehensive contingency model for leadership was developed by Fred Fiedler.[2] His model proposes that effective group performance depends on the proper match between the leader's style of interacting with his or her subordinates and the degree to which the situation gives control and influence to the leader. Fiedler developed an instrument, which he called the least-preferred co-worker (LPC) questionnaire, that purports to measure whether a person is task oriented or relationship oriented. Further, he isolated three situational criteria—leader-member relations, task structure, and position power—that he believes can be manipulated so as to create the proper match with the behavioral orientation of the leader. In a sense, the Fiedler model is an outgrowth of trait theory, since the LPC questionnaire is a simple psychological test. However, Fiedler goes significantly beyond trait and behavioral approaches by attempting to isolate situations, relating his personality measure to his situational classification, and then predicting leadership effectiveness as a function of the two.

The preceding description of the Fiedler model is somewhat abstract. Let us now look at the model more closely.

Fiedler believes an individual's basic leadership style is a key factor in leadership success. So he began by trying to find out what that basic style is. Fiedler created the LPC questionnaire for this purpose. It contains 16 contrasting adjectives (such as pleasant-unpleasant, efficient-inefficient, open-guarded, supportive-hostile). The questionnaire then asks the respondent to think of all the co-workers he or she has ever had and to describe the one person he or she *least enjoyed* working with by rating that person on a scale of 1 to 8 for each of the 16 sets of contrasting adjectives. Fiedler believes that based on the respondents' answers to this LPC questionnaire, he can determine their basic leadership style. If the least-preferred co-worker is described in relatively positive terms (a high LPC score), then the respondent is primarily interested in good personal relations with this co-worker. That is, if you essentially describe the person you are least able to work with in favorable terms, Fiedler would label you relationship oriented. In contrast, if the least-preferred co-worker is seen in relatively unfavorable terms (a low LPC score), the respon-

---

2 Fred E. Fiedler, *A Theory of Leadership Effectiveness* (New York: McGraw-Hill, 1967).

dent is primarily interested in productivity and thus would be labeled task oriented. Notice that Fiedler assumes an individual's leadership style is fixed, that is, either relationship oriented or task oriented. As we show in a moment, this is important because it means that if a situation requires a task-oriented leader and the person in that leadership position is relationship oriented, either the situation has to be modified or the leader removed and replaced if optimum effectiveness is to be achieved. Fiedler argues that leadership style is innate to a person—you *can't* change your style to fit changing situations!

After an individual's basic leadership style has been assessed through the LPC, it is necessary to match the leader with the situation. The three situational factors or contingency dimensions identified by Fiedler are defined as follows:

1. **Leader-member relations**—the degree of confidence, trust, and respect subordinates have in their leader
2. **Task structure**—the degree to which the job assignments are structured or unstructured
3. **Position power**—the degree of influence a leader has over power variables such as hiring, firing, discipline, promotions, and salary increases

So the next step in the Fiedler model is to evaluate the situation in terms of these three contingency variables. Leader-member relations are either good or poor, task structure either high or low, and position power either strong or weak.

Fiedler states the better the leader-member relations, the more highly structured the job, and the stronger the position power, the more control or influence the leader has. For example, a very favorable situation (where the leader would have a great deal of control) might involve a payroll manager who is well respected and whose subordinates have confidence in him or her (good leader-member relations), where the activities to be done—such as wage computation, check writing, report filing—are specific and clear (high task structure), and the job provides considerable freedom to reward and punish subordinates (strong position power). On the other hand, an unfavorable situation might be the disliked chairman of a voluntary United Way fund-raising team. In this job, the leader has very little control. Altogether, by mixing the three contingency variables, there are potentially eight different situations or categories in which a leader could find himself or herself.

With knowledge of an individual's LPC and an assessment of the three contingency variables, the Fiedler model proposes matching them up to achieve maximum leadership effectiveness. Based on Fiedler's study of over 1,200 groups, where he compared relationship versus task-oriented leadership styles in each of the eight situational categories, he concluded that task-oriented leaders tend to perform better in situations that are *very favorable* to them and in situations that are *very unfavorable* (see Exhibit 9–2). So Fiedler would predict that when faced with a category I, II, III, VII, or VIII situation, task-oriented leaders perform better. Relationship-oriented leaders, however, perform better in moderately favorable situations—categories IV through VI.

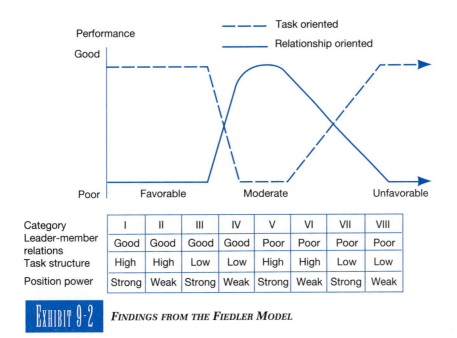

Performance

- - - - Task oriented
——— Relationship oriented

Category	I	II	III	IV	V	VI	VII	VIII
Leader-member relations	Good	Good	Good	Good	Poor	Poor	Poor	Poor
Task structure	High	High	Low	Low	High	High	Low	Low
Position power	Strong	Weak	Strong	Weak	Strong	Weak	Strong	Weak

EXHIBIT 9-2 *FINDINGS FROM THE FIEDLER MODEL*

Given Fiedler's findings, how would you apply them? You would seek to match leaders and situations. Individuals' LPC scores would determine the type of situation for which they were best suited. That situation would be defined by evaluating the three contingency factors of leader-member relations, task structure, and position power. But remember that Fiedler views an individual's leadership style as being fixed. Therefore, there are really only two ways in which to improve leader effectiveness. First, you can change the leader to fit the situation. Analogous to a baseball game, management can reach into its bullpen and put in a right-handed pitcher or a left-handed pitcher, depending on the situational characteristics of the hitter. So, for example, if a group situation rates as highly unfavorable but is currently led by a relationship-oriented manager, the group's performance could be improved by replacing that manager with one who is task oriented. The second alternative would be to change the situation to fit the leader. That could be done by restructuring tasks or increasing or decreasing the power that the leader has to control factors such as salary increases, promotions, and disciplinary actions. To illustrate, assume a task-oriented leader were in a category IV situation. If this leader could increase his or her position power, then the leader would be operating in category III and the leader-situation match would be compatible for high group performance.

One should not surmise that Fiedler has closed all the gaps and put to rest all the questions underlying leadership effectiveness. Research finds that the Fiedler model predicts all except category II when laboratory studies are reviewed; however, when field studies are analyzed, the model produces supportive evidence for only categories II, V, VII, and VIII. So we have conflicting results depending on the type of studies used.

As a whole, reviews of the major studies undertaken to test the overall validity of the Fiedler model lead to a generally positive conclusion. That is, there is considerable evidence to support the model. But additional variables are probably needed if an improved model is to fill in some of the remaining gaps. Moreover, there are problems with the LPC and the practical use of the model that need to be addressed. For instance, the logic underlying the LPC is not well understood and studies have shown that respondents' LPC scores are not stable. Also, the contingency variables are complex and difficult for practitioners to assess. It's often difficult in practice to determine how good the leader-member relations are, how structured the task is, and how much position power the leader has.

Our conclusion is that Fiedler has clearly made an important contribution toward understanding leadership effectiveness. His model has been the object of much controversy and probably will continue to be. Field studies fall short of providing full support and the model could benefit by including additional contingency variables. But Fiedler's work continues to be a dominant input in the development of a contingency explanation of leadership effectiveness.

Path-Goal Theory

Currently, one of the most respected approaches to leadership is the path-goal theory. Developed by Robert House, *path-goal theory* is a contingency model of leadership that extracts key elements from the Ohio State leadership research on initiating structure and consideration and the expectancy theory of motivation.[3]

The essence of the theory is that it's the leader's job to assist his or her followers in attaining their goals and to provide the necessary direction and/or support to ensure their goals are compatible with the overall objectives of the group or organization. The term *path-goal* is derived from the belief that effective leaders clarify the path to help their followers get from where they are to the achievement of their work goals and make the journey along the path easier by reducing roadblocks and pitfalls.

According to path-goal theory, a leader's behavior is *acceptable* to subordinates to the degree that it is viewed by them as an immediate source of satisfaction or as a means of future satisfaction. A leader's behavior is *motivational* to the degree that it (1) makes subordinate need satisfaction contingent on effective performance and (2) provides the coaching, guidance, support, and rewards that are necessary for effective performance. To test these statements, House identified four leadership behaviors. The *directive leader* lets subordinates know what is expected of them, schedules work to be done, and

---

[3] Robert J. House, "A Path-Goal Theory of Leader Effectiveness," *Administrative Science Quarterly* (September 1971), pp. 321–38.

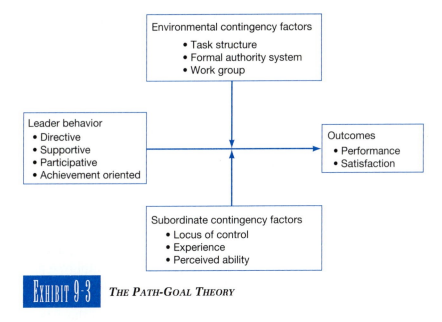

EXHIBIT 9-3 *THE PATH-GOAL THEORY*

gives specific guidance on how to accomplish tasks. This closely parallels the Ohio State dimension of initiating structure. The *supportive leader* is friendly and shows concern for the needs of subordinates. This is essentially synonymous with the Ohio State dimension of consideration. The *participative leader* consults with subordinates and uses their suggestions before making a decision. The *achievement-oriented leader* sets challenging goals and expects subordinates to perform at their highest level. In contrast to Fiedler's view of a leader's behavior, House assumes leaders are flexible. Path-goal theory implies the same leader can display any or all of these behaviors depending on the situation.

As Exhibit 9–3 illustrates, path-goal theory proposes two classes of situational or contingency variables that moderate the leadership behavior-outcome relationship—those in the *environment* that are outside the control of the subordinate (task structure, the formal authority system, and the work group) and those that are part of the personal characteristics of the *subordinate* (locus of control, experience, and perceived ability). Essentially the theory proposes that leader behaviors should complement these contingency variables. So the leader will be ineffective when his or her behavior is redundant with sources of environmental structure or incongruent with subordinate characteristics.

Following are examples of hypotheses that have evolved out of path-goal theory:

- Directive leadership leads to greater satisfaction when tasks are ambiguous or stressful than when they are highly structured and well laid out.

- Supportive leadership results in high employee performance and satisfaction when subordinates are performing structured tasks.
- Directive leadership is likely to be perceived as redundant among subordinates with high perceived ability or with considerable experience.
- The more clear and bureaucratic the formal authority relationships, the more leaders should exhibit supportive behavior and deemphasize directive behavior.
- Directive leadership will lead to higher employee satisfaction when there is substantive conflict within a work group.
- Subordinates with an internal locus of control (those who believe they control their own destiny) will be more satisfied with a participative style.
- Subordinates with an external locus of control will be more satisfied with a directive style.
- Achievement-oriented leadership will increase subordinates' expectancies that effort will lead to high performance when tasks are ambiguously structured.

Research to validate hypotheses such as these are generally encouraging. The evidence supports the logic underlying the theory. That is, employee performance and satisfaction are likely to be positively influenced when the leader compensates for things lacking in either the employee or the work setting. However, the leader who spends time explaining tasks when those tasks are already clear or the employee has the ability and experience to handle them without interference is likely to see such directive behavior as redundant or even insulting.

What does the future hold for path-goal theory? Its framework has been tested and appears to have moderate to high empirical support. We can, however, expect to see more research focused on refining and extending the theory by incorporating additional contingency variables.

Leader-Participation Model

Back in 1973, Victor Vroom and Phillip Yetton developed a leader-participation model that related leadership behavior and participation in decision making.[4] Recognizing that task structures have varying demands for routine and nonroutine activities, these researchers argued that leader behavior must adjust to reflect the task structure. Vroom and Yetton's model was normative—it provided a sequential set of rules that should be followed in determining the form and amount of participation in decision making, as determined by different types of situations. The model was a decision tree incorporating seven contingencies (whose relevance could be identified by making "yes" or "no" choices) and five alternative leadership styles.

More recent work by Vroom and Arthur Jago has resulted in a revision of this model.[5] The new model retains the same five alternative leadership

---

[4] Victor H. Vroom and Phillip W. Yetton, *Leadership and Decision Making* (Pittsburgh: University of Pittsburgh Press, 1973).

[5] Victor H. Vroom and Arthur G. Jago, *The New Leadership: Managing Participation in Organizations* (Englewood Cliffs, NJ: Prentice Hall, 1988).

EXHIBIT 9-4 **CONTINGENCY VARIABLES IN THE REVISED LEADER-PARTICIPATION MODEL**

1. Importance of the decision
2. Importance of obtaining subordinate commitment to the decision
3. Whether the leader has sufficient information to make a good decision
4. How well structured the problem is
5. Whether an autocratic decision would receive subordinate commitment
6. Whether subordinates buy into the organization's goals
7. Whether there is likely to be conflict among subordinates over solution alternatives
8. Whether subordinates have the necessary information to make a good decision
9. Time constraints on the leader that may limit subordinate involvement
10. Whether costs to bring geographically dispersed subordinates together is justified
11. Importance to the leader of minimizing the time it takes to make the decision
12. Importance of using participation as a tool for developing subordinate decision skills

Source: Based on Victor H. Vroom and Arthur G. Jago, *The New Leadership: Managing Participation in Organizations* (Englewood Cliffs, NJ: Prentice Hall, 1988), pp. 111–12.

styles—from the leader making the decision completely by him or herself to sharing the problem with the group and developing a consensus decision—but expands the contingency variables to 12. These are listed in Exhibit 9–4.

Research testing both the original and revised leader-participation model has been encouraging. But unfortunately, the model is far too complex for the typical manager to use on a regular basis. In fact, Vroom and Jago have developed a computer program to guide managers through all the decision branches in the revised model.

We obviously can't do justice to the model's sophistication in this discussion. What's important, however, is that Vroom and his associates have provided us with some solid, empirically supported insights into contingency variables that you should consider when choosing your leadership style.

Gender as a Contingency Variable: Do Males and Females Lead Differently?

Women often use a different leadership style than men and that different style can be a plus in the dynamic organizational world of the 1990s. Those are the most important conclusions we can make based on studies linking gender and leadership style.[6]

Women tend to adopt a more democratic leadership style. They encourage participation, share power and information, and attempt to enhance followers' self-worth. They lead through inclusion and rely on their charisma,

---

[6] See, for instance, Alice H. Eagly, Mona G. Makhijani, and Bruce G. Klonsky, "Gender and the Evaluation of Leaders: A Meta-Analysis," *Psychological Bulletin* (January 1992), pp. 3–22.

expertise, contacts, and interpersonal skills to influence others. Men, on the other hand, are more likely to use a directive command-and-control style. They rely on the formal authority of their position for their influence base.

Given that men have historically held the great majority of leadership positions in organizations, it is tempting to assume that the existence of differences between men and women would automatically work to favor men. It doesn't. In today's organizations, flexibility, teamwork, trust, and information sharing are replacing rigid structures, competitive individualism, control, and secrecy. The best managers listen, motivate, and provide support to their people. And many women seem to do those things better than men. As a specific example, the expanded use of cross-functional teams in organizations means that effective managers must become skillful negotiators. The leadership styles women typically use can make them better at negotiating, as they are less likely than men to focus on wins, losses, and competition. They tend to treat negotiations in the context of a continuing relationship—trying hard to make the other party a winner in his or her own and others' eyes.

■ TRAIT THEORIES UPDATED: CHARISMATIC LEADERSHIP

Most of the leadership theories discussed in this chapter have involved transactional leaders. These people guide or motivate their followers in the direction of established goals by clarifying role and task requirements. There is another type of leader who inspires followers to transcend their own self-interests for the good of the organization and who is capable of having a profound and extraordinary effect on his or her followers. These are transformational or charismatic leaders. Ted Turner, Jesse Jackson, Mother Teresa, General Douglas MacArthur, and Franklin D. Roosevelt are of this latter type. By the force of their personal abilities they transform their followers by raising their sense of the importance and value of their tasks. "I'd walk through fire if my boss asked me" is the kind of support that charismatic leaders inspire.

What characteristics differentiate charismatic leaders from noncharismatic ones? Five attributes seem most important:

Self-confidence. They have complete confidence in their judgment and ability.

A vision. This is an idealized goal that proposes a future better than the status quo. The greater the disparity between this idealized goal and the status quo, the more likely that followers will attribute extraordinary vision to the leader.

Strong convictions in that vision. Charismatic leaders are perceived as being strongly committed. They are perceived as willing to take on high personal risk, incur high costs, and engage in self-sacrifice to achieve their vision.

Behave out of the ordinary. Leaders with charisma engage in behavior that is perceived as novel, unconventional, and counter to norms. When successful, these behaviors evoke surprise and admiration in followers.

Perceived as a change agent. Charismatic leaders are perceived as agents of radical change rather than as caretakers of the status quo.

What can we say about the charismatic leader's impact on his or her followers' attitudes and behavior? One study found that followers of charismatic leaders were more self-assured, experienced more meaningfulness in their work, reported more support from their leaders, worked longer hours, saw their leaders as more dynamic, and had higher performance ratings than the followers of the noncharismatic but effective leaders. Another study found that people working under charismatic leaders were more productive and satisfied than those working under leaders who relied on the more traditional transactional behaviors of initiating structure and consideration. Two studies, of course, provide only a limited set of information from which to generalize. We need more research on this subject. However, the early evidence is encouraging.

■ A FINAL THOUGHT: SOMETIMES LEADERSHIP IS IRRELEVANT!

We conclude this chapter by challenging the notion that some leadership style *will always* be effective *regardless* of the situation. Leadership may not always be important. Data from numerous studies collectively demonstrate that, in many situations, whatever behaviors leaders exhibit are irrelevant. Certain individual, job, and organizational variables can act as substitutes for leadership, negating the formal leader's ability to exert either positive or negative influence over subordinate attitudes and effectiveness.

For instance, characteristics of subordinates such as their experience, training, professional orientation, or need for independence can neutralize the effect of leadership. These characteristics can replace the need for a leader's support or ability to create structure and reduce task ambiguity. Similarly, jobs that are inherently unambiguous and routine or that are intrinsically satisfying may place fewer demands on the leadership variable. Finally, organizational characteristics like explicit formalized goals, rigid rules and procedures, or cohesive work groups can act in the place of formal leadership.

The preceding comments should not be surprising. After all, in Chapter 3 and subsequent chapters, we introduced independent variables that have been documented to impact on employee performance and satisfaction. Yet supporters of the leadership concept have tended to place an undue burden on this variable for explaining and predicting behavior. It is too simplistic to consider subordinates as guided to goal accomplishments based solely on the behavior of their leader. It is important, therefore, to recognize explicitly that leadership is merely another independent variable in explaining organizational behavior. In some situations it may contribute a lot toward explaining employee productivity, absence, turnover, and satisfaction; but in other situations, it may contribute little toward that end.

Even charismatic leadership may not be the panacea that many in the public and media think it is. While charismatic leaders may be ideal for pulling a group or organization through a crisis, they often perform poorly after the crisis subsides and ordinary conditions return. The forceful, confident behavior that was needed during the crisis now becomes a liability. Charismatic managers are often self-possessed, autocratic, and given to thinking that their opinions have a greater degree of certainty than they merit. These behaviors then tend to drive good people away and can lead their organizations down dangerous paths.

■ IMPLICATIONS FOR MANAGERS

The topic of leadership certainly doesn't lack for theories. But from an overview perspective, what does it all mean? Let's try to identify commonalities among the leadership theories and attempt to determine what, if any, practical value the theories hold for managers.

Careful examination discloses that the concepts of "task" and "people"— often expressed in more elaborate terms that hold substantially the same meaning—permeate most of the theories. The task dimension is called just that by Fiedler, but it goes by the name of "initiating structure" for the Ohio State group, "directive" by path-goal supporters, "production orientation" by the Michigan researchers, and "concern for production" by Blake and Mouton. The people dimension gets similar treatment, going under such aliases as "consideration," "supportive," and "employee-oriented" or "relationship-oriented" leadership. It seems clear that leadership behavior can be shrunk down to two dimensions—task and people—but researchers continue to differ as to whether the orientations are two ends of a single continuum (you could be high on one or the other but not both) or two independent dimensions (you could be high or low on both).

How should we interpret the findings presented in this chapter? Some traits have shown, over time, to be modest predictors of leadership effectiveness. But the fact that a manager possessed intelligence, drive, self-confidence, or the like would by no means assure us that his or her subordinates would be productive and satisfied employees. The ability of these traits to predict leadership success is just not that strong.

The early task-people approaches (the Ohio State, Michigan, and managerial grid theories) also offer us little substance. The strongest statement one can make based on these theories is that leaders who rate high in people orientation should end up with satisfied employees. The research is too mixed to make predictions regarding employee productivity or the effect of a task orientation on productivity and satisfaction.

Controlled laboratory studies designed to test the Fiedler model, in aggregate, have generally supported the theory. But field studies provide more limited support. We suggest that when category II, V, VII, and VIII situations exist, the utilization of the LPC instrument to assess whether this is a leader-situation match and the use of that information to predict employee productivity and satisfaction are warranted.

The path-goal model provides a framework for explaining and predicting leadership effectiveness that has developed a solid, empirical foundation. It recognizes that a leader's success depends on adjusting his or her style to the environment that the leader is placed in and the individual characteristics of followers.

In spite of the leader-participation model's complexity, efforts to validate it have been encouraging. One investigation, for example, found that leaders who were high in agreement with the model had subordinates with higher productivity and higher satisfaction than those leaders who were low in agreement with the model. For our purposes, its greatest contribution is in identifying a set of contingency variables that you should consider before choosing a leadership style.

SUGGESTIONS FOR FURTHER READING

BASS, BERNARD M., *Bass and Stogdill's Handbook of Leadership*, 3rd ed. (New York: Free Press, 1990).

CONGER, JAY A., AND R.N. KANUNGO, eds., *Charismatic Leadership* (San Francisco: Jossey-Bass, 1988).

GEMMILL, GARY, AND JUDITH OAKLEY, "Leadership: An Alienating Social Myth?" *Human Relations*, February 1992, pp. 113–29.

HOUSE, ROBERT J., AND JANE M. HOWELL, "Personality and Charismatic Leadership," *Leadership Quarterly*, Summer 1992, pp. 81–108.

PODSAKOFF, PHILIP M., BRIAN P. NIEHOFF, SCOTT B. MACKENZIE, AND MARGARET L. WILLIAMS, "Do Substitutes for Leadership Really Substitute for Leadership? An Empirical Examination of Kerr and Jermier's Situational Leadership Model," *Organizational Behavior and Human Decision Processes*, February 1993, pp. 1–44.

WHEATLEY, MARGARET J., *Leadership and the New Science* (San Francisco: Berrett-Koehler, 1992).

YUKL, GARY, *Leadership in Organizations*, 3rd ed. (Englewood Cliffs, NJ: Prentice Hall, 1994).

YUKL, GARY, AND DAVID D. VAN FLEET, "Theory and Research on Leadership in Organizations," in M.D. Dunnette and L.M. Hough, eds., *Handbook of Industrial & Organizational Psychology*, 2nd ed., Vol. 3 (Palo Alto, CA: Consulting Psychologists Press. 1992), pp. 148–97.

CHAPTER 10

POWER
AND POLITICS

After reading this chapter, you should be able to:

1. Define *power*
2. Contrast *bases* and *sources* of power
3. Explain what creates dependency in power relationships
4. Describe how power is central to understanding sexual harassment
5. Define *political behavior*

6. Describe the importance of a political perspective
7. Explain the factors contributing to political behavior in organizations
8. Identify seven techniques for managing the impression you make on others

Power may be the last dirty word. It is easier for most of us to talk about money or even sex than it is to talk about power. People who have it, deny it; people who want it, try not to appear to be seeking it; and those who are good at getting it, are secretive about how they got it.

In this chapter, we show that power determines what goals a group will pursue and how the group's resources will be distributed among its members. Further, we show how group members with good political skills use their power to influence the distribution of resources in their favor.

■ A DEFINITION OF POWER

Power refers to a capacity that A has to influence the behavior of B, so that B does something he or she would not otherwise do. This definition implies (1) a *potential* that need not be actualized to be effective, (2) a *dependence* relationship, and (3) that B has some *discretion* over his or her own behavior. Let's look at each of these points more closely.

Power may exist but not be used. It is, therefore, a capacity or potential. Arthur Fonzarelli, appearing nightly in reruns of "Happy Days," has power. Everyone is afraid of "The Fonz," yet he has never actually had to use his power to get others to comply with his wishes. They respond in fear that he *might* use his physical force but, as long as no one calls his bluff, his capacity to influence others is as effective as if he actually used physical force. Our point again is that one can have power but not impose it.

Probably the most important aspect of power is that it is a function of dependence. The greater B's dependence on A, the greater is A's power in the relationship. Dependence, in turn, is based on alternatives that B perceives and the importance that B places on the alternative(s) that A controls. A person can have power over you only if he or she controls something you desire. If you want a college degree, have to pass a certain course to get that degree, and your current instructor is the only faculty member in the college who teaches that course, he or she has power over you. Your alternatives are definitely limited and you place a high degree of importance on obtaining a passing grade. Similarly, if you're attending college on funds provided entirely by your parents, you probably recognize the power they hold over you. You are dependent on them for financial support. But once you're out of school, have a job, and are making a solid income, your parents' power is reduced significantly. Who among us, though, has not known or heard of the rich relative who is able to control a large number of family members merely through the implicit or explicit threat of writing them out of the will?

For A to get B to do something he or she otherwise would not do means B must have the discretion to make choices. At the extreme, if B's job behavior is so programmed that he is allowed no room to make choices, he obviously is constrained in his ability to do something other than what he is doing. For instance, job descriptions, group norms, organizational rules and regulations, as well as community laws and standards constrain people's choices. As a nurse, you may be dependent on your supervisor for continued employment. But in spite of this dependence, you're unlikely to comply with her request to perform heart surgery on a patient or steal several thousand dollars from petty cash. Your job description and laws against stealing constrain your ability to make these choices.

■ CONTRASTING LEADERSHIP AND POWER

A careful comparison of our description of power with our description of leadership in the previous chapter should bring the recognition that the two concepts are closely intertwined. Leaders use power as a way to attain group goals. Leaders achieve goals, and power is a means for facilitating their achievement.

What differences are there between the two terms? One difference relates to goal compatibility. Power does not require goal compatibility, merely dependence. Leadership, on the other hand, requires some congruence between the goals of the leader and the led. The other difference deals with the direction that research on the two concepts has taken. Leadership research, for the most part, emphasizes style. It seeks answers to questions like these: How supportive should a leader be? How much decision making should be shared with subordinates? In contrast, the research on power has tended to encompass a broader area and focus on tactics for gaining compliance. It has gone beyond the individual as exerciser because power can be used by groups as well as individuals to control other individuals or groups.

■ BASES AND SOURCES OF POWER

Where does power come from? What is it that gives an individual or group influence over others? The early answer to these questions was a five-category classification scheme identified by French and Raven.[1] They proposed five bases or sources of power that they termed coercive, reward, expert, legitimate, and referent power. Coercive power depends on fear; reward power is derived from the ability to distribute anything of value (typically money, favorable performance appraisals, interesting work assignments, friendly colleagues, and preferred work shifts or sales territories); expert power refers to influence that is derived from special skills or knowledge; legitimate power is based on the formal rights one receives as a result of holding an authoritative position or role in an organization; and referent power develops out of others' admiration for an individual and their desire to model their behavior and attitudes after that person. While French and Raven's classification scheme provided an extensive repertoire of possible bases of power, their categories created ambiguity because they confused bases of power with sources of power. The result was much overlapping. We can improve our understanding of the power concept by separating bases and sources to develop clearer and more independent categories.

The term *bases* of power refers to what the powerholder has that gives him or her power. Assuming you're the powerholder, your bases are what you control that enables you to manipulate the behavior of others. There are four power bases—coercive power, reward power, persuasive power, and knowledge power. We describe each in detail in a moment.

How are *sources* of power different from bases of power? The answer is that sources tell us where the powerholder gets his or her power bases. That is, sources refer to how you come to control the bases of power. There are four sources—the position you hold, your personal characteristics, your expertise, and the opportunity you have to receive and obstruct information. Each of these are also discussed in a moment.

Let us now turn back to the four bases of power and define them.

---

[1] J.R.P. French, Jr. and Bertram Raven, "The Bases of Social Power," in *Studies in Social Power*, ed. D. Cartwright (Ann Arbor: University of Michigan, Institute for Social Research, 1959), pp. 150–67.

Bases of Power

Coercive Power. The coercive base depends on fear. One reacts to this power out of fear of the negative ramifications that might result if one fails to comply. It rests on the application, or the threat of application, of physical sanctions such as infliction of pain, deformity, or death; the generation of frustration through restriction of movement; or the controlling through force of basic physiological or safety needs.

In the 1930s, when John Dillinger went into a bank, held a gun to the teller's head, and asked for the money, he was incredibly successful at getting compliance to his request. His power base? Coercive. A loaded gun gives its holder power because others are fearful they will lose something they hold dear—their lives.

At the organizational level, A has coercive power over B if A can dismiss, suspend, or demote B, assuming B values his or her job. Similarly, if A can assign B work activities that B finds unpleasant or can treat B in a manner B finds embarrassing, A possesses coercive power over B.

Reward Power. The opposite of coercive power is the power to reward. People comply with the wishes of another because it will result in positive benefits; therefore, one who can distribute rewards that others view as valuable will have power over them. Our definition of rewards is here limited only to material rewards. These would include salaries and wages, commissions, fringe benefits, and the like.

Persuasive Power. Persuasive power rests on the allocation and manipulation of symbolic rewards. If you can decide who is hired, manipulate the mass media, control the allocation of status symbols, or influence a group's norms, you have persuasive power. For instance, when a teacher uses the class climate to control a deviant student, or when a union steward arouses the members to use their informal power to bring a deviant member into line, you are observing examples of persuasive power.

Knowledge Power. Knowledge, or access to information, is the final base of power. We can say that when an individual in a group or organization controls unique information, and when that information is needed to make a decision, that individual has knowledge-based power.

To summarize, the bases of power refer to what the powerholder controls that enables him or her to manipulate the behavior of others. The coercive base of power is the control of punishment; the reward base is the control of material rewards; the persuasive base is the control of symbolic rewards; and the knowledge base is the control of information.

Sources of Power

Position Power. In formal groups and organizations, probably the most frequent access to one or more of the power bases is one's structural position. A teacher's position includes significant control over symbols, a secretary frequently is privy to important information, and the head coach of an NFL team has substantial coercive resources at his disposal. All of these bases of power are achieved as a result of the formal position each holds within a structural hierarchy.

Personal Power. Personality traits were discussed in Chapter 3 and again in the previous chapter on leadership. They reappear within the topic of power when we acknowledge the fact that one's personal characteristics can be a source of power. If you are articulate, domineering, physically imposing, or possessed of that mystical quality called charisma, you hold personal characteristics that may be used to get others to do what you want.

Expert Power. Expertise is a means by which the powerholder comes to control specialized information (rather than the control itself, which we have discussed as the knowledge base of power). Those who have expertise in terms of specialized information can use it to manipulate others. Expertise is one of the most powerful sources of influence, especially in a technologically oriented society. As jobs become more specialized, we become increasingly dependent on experts to achieve goals. So, while it is generally acknowledged that physicians have expertise and hence expert power—when your doctor talks, you listen—you should also recognize that computer specialists, tax accountants, solar engineers, industrial psychologists, and other specialists are able to wield power as a result of their expertise.

Opportunity Power. Finally, being in the right place at the right time can give a person the opportunity to exert power. One need not hold a formal position in a group or organization to have access to information that is important to others or be able to exert coercive influence. An example of how one can use an opportunity to create a power base is the story of Lyndon Johnson, when he was a student at Southwestern Texas State Teachers College. He had a job as special assistant to the college president's personal secretary.

> As special assistant, Johnson's assigned job was simply to carry messages from the president to the department heads and occasionally to other faculty members. Johnson saw that the rather limited function of messenger had possibilities for expansion, for example, encouraging recipients of the messages to transmit their own communications through him. He occupied a desk in the president's outer office, where he took it upon himself to announce the arrival of visitors. These added services evolved from a helpful convenience into an aspect of the normal process of presidential business. The messenger had become an appointments secretary, and, in time, faculty members came to think of Johnson as a funnel to the president. Using a technique which was later to serve him in achieving mastery over the Congress, Johnson turned a rather insubstantial service into a process through which power was exercised.[2]

---

[2] Doris Kearns, "Lyndon Johnson and the American Dream," *The Atlantic Monthly* (May 1976), p. 41.

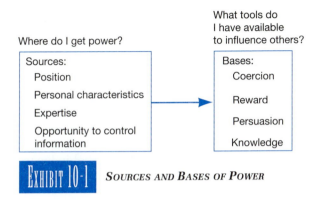

Where do I get power?

Sources:
  Position
  Personal characteristics
  Expertise
  Opportunity to control
  information

What tools do
I have available
to influence others?

Bases:
  Coercion
  Reward
  Persuasion
  Knowledge

EXHIBIT 10-1   *SOURCES AND BASES OF POWER*

Johnson eventually broadened his informal duties to include handling the president's political correspondence and preparing his reports for state agencies. Regularly, he accompanied the college president on his trips to the state capital with the president eventually relying on his young apprentice for political counsel. Certainly this represents an example of someone using an opportunity to redefine his job and to give himself power.

Summary

The foundation for understanding power begins by identifying where power comes from (sources) and, given that one has the means to exert influence, what it is that one manipulates (bases). Exhibit 10–1 depicts the relationship between sources and bases. Sources are the means. Individuals can use their position in the structure, rely on personal characteristics, develop expertise, or take advantage of opportunities to control information. Control of one or more of these sources allows the powerholder to manipulate the behavior of others via coercion, reward, persuasion, or knowledge bases. To reiterate, sources are *where* you get power. Bases are *what* you manipulate. Those who seek power must develop a source of power. Then, and only then, can they acquire a power base.

■ DEPENDENCY: THE KEY TO POWER

Earlier in this chapter we noted the important relationship between power and dependence. In this section, we show how an understanding of dependency is central to furthering our understanding of power itself.

The General Dependency Postulate

Let's begin with a general postulate: *The greater B's dependency on A, the greater power A has over B*. When you possess anything that others require but that you alone control, you make them dependent on you and, therefore, you gain power over them. Dependency, then, is inversely proportional to the alternative sources of supply. If something is plentiful, possession of it will not increase your power. If everyone is intelligent, intelligence gives no special advantage. Similarly, among the superrich, money is no longer power. But as the old saying goes, "In the land of the blind, the one-eyed man is king!" If you can create a monopoly by controlling information, prestige, or anything that others crave, they become dependent on you. Conversely, the more you can expand your options, the less power you place in the hands of others. This explains, for example, why most organizations use many suppliers rather than give their business to only one. It also explains why so many of us aspire to financial independence. Financial independence reduces the power others can have over us.

What Creates Dependency?

Dependency is increased when the resource you control is *important* and *scarce*.

Importance. If nobody wants what you've got, it's not going to create dependency. To create dependency, therefore, the thing(s) you control must be perceived as important. It's been found, for instance, that organizations seek to avoid uncertainty. We should, therefore, expect that those individuals or groups who can absorb an organization's uncertainty will be understood to control an important resource. For instance, a study of industrial organizations found that the marketing departments in these firms were consistently rated as the most powerful. It was concluded by the researcher that the most critical uncertainty facing these firms was selling their products. This might suggest that during a labor strike, the organization's negotiating representatives have increased power or that engineers, as a group, would be more powerful at Intel than at Procter & Gamble. These inferences appear to be generally valid. Labor negotiators do become more powerful within the personnel area and the organization as a whole during periods of labor strife. An organization such as Intel, which is a technological company, is dependent on its engineers to maintain its product quality. And, at Intel, engineers are clearly the most powerful group. At Procter & Gamble, marketing is the name of the game, and marketers are the most powerful group. These examples support not only the view that the ability to reduce uncertainty increases a group's importance and, hence, its power but also that what's important is situational. It varies among organizations and undoubtedly also varies over time within any given organization.

Scarcity. As noted previously, if something is plentiful, possession of it will not increase your power. A resource needs to be perceived as scarce to create dependency.

This can help to explain how low-ranking members in an organization, who have important knowledge not available to high-ranking members, gain power over the high-ranking members. Possession of a scarce resource—in this case, important knowledge—makes the high-ranking member dependent on the low-ranking member. This also helps to make sense out of behaviors of low-ranking members that, otherwise, might seem illogical, such as destroying the procedure manuals that describe how a job is done, refusing to train people in their job or even to show others exactly what they do, creating specialized language and terminology that inhibit others from understanding their jobs, or operating in secrecy so the activity will appear more complex and difficult than it really is.

The scarcity-dependency relationship can further be seen in the power of occupational categories. Individuals in occupations in which the supply of personnel is low relative to demand can negotiate compensation and benefit packages far more attractive than can those in occupations where there is an abundance of candidates. College administrators have no problem today finding English instructors. The market for accounting teachers, in contrast, is extremely tight, with the demand high and the supply limited. The result is that the bargaining power of accounting faculty allows them to negotiate higher salaries, lighter teaching loads, and other benefits.

■ POWER IN GROUPS: COALITIONS

Those "out of power" and seeking to be "in" will first try to increase their power individually. Why spread the spoils if one doesn't have to? But if this proves ineffective, the alternative is to form a coalition. There *is* strength in numbers.

The natural way to gain influence is to become a powerholder. Therefore, those who want power will attempt to build a personal power base. But in many instances, this may be difficult, risky, costly, or impossible. In such cases, efforts will be made to form a coalition of two or more "outs" who, by joining together, can each better themselves at the expense of those outside the coalition.

In the late 1960s, college students found by joining together to form a student power group they could achieve ends that had been impossible individually. Historically, employees in organizations who were unsuccessful in bargaining on their own behalf with management resorted to labor unions to bargain for them. In recent years, even some managers have joined unions after finding it difficult individually to exert power to attain higher wages and greater job security.

What predictions can we make about coalition formation? First, coalitions in organizations often seek to maximize their size. In political science theory, coalitions move the other way—they try to minimize their size. They tend to be just large enough to exert the power necessary to achieve their objectives. But legislatures are different from organizations in that legislators make the policy decisions that are then carried out by separate administrators or managers. Decision making in organizations does not end with merely selecting from among a set of alternatives. The decision must also be implemented. In organizations, the implementation of and commitment to the decision is at least as important as the decision itself. It's necessary, therefore, for coalitions in organizations to seek a broad constituency to support the coalition's objectives. This means expanding the coalition to encompass as many interests as possible. This coalition expansion to facilitate consensus building, of course, is more likely to occur in organizational cultures where cooperation, commitment, and shared decision making are highly valued. In autocratic and hierarchically controlled organizations, the maximization of the coalition's size is less likely to be sought.

Another prediction about coalitions relates to the degree of interdependence within the organization. More coalitions will likely be created where there is a great deal of task and resource interdependence. In contrast, there will be less interdependence among subunits and less coalition formation activity where subunits are largely self-contained or resources are abundant.

Finally, coalition formation will be influenced by the actual tasks that workers perform. The more routine the task of a group, the greater the likelihood coalitions will form. The more the work that people do is routine, the greater their substitutability for each other and, thus, the greater their dependence. To offset this dependence, they can be expected to resort to a coalition. We see, therefore, that unions appeal more to low-skill and nonprofessional workers than to skilled and professional types. Of course, where the supply of skilled and professional employees is high relative to their demand or where organizations have standardized traditionally unique jobs, we would expect even these incumbents to find unionization attractive.

■ POWER AND SEXUAL HARASSMENT

The issue of sexual harassment received increasing attention by corporations and the media in the 1980s because of the growing ranks of female employees, especially in nontraditional work environments. But it was the congressional hearings in the fall of 1991 in which law professor Anita Hill graphically accused Supreme Court nominee Clarence Thomas of sexual harassment that challenged organizations to reassess their harassment policies and practices.

Legally, sexual harassment is defined as unwelcome advances, requests for sexual favors, and other verbal or physical conduct of a sexual nature. But there is a great deal of disagreement about what *specifically* constitutes sexual harassment. Organizations have made considerable progress in the last few years toward limiting overt forms of sexual harassment of female employees. This includes unwanted physical touching, recurring requests for dates when it is made clear the woman is not interested, and coercive threats that a woman will lose her job if she refuses a sexual proposition. The problems today are likely to surface around more subtle forms of sexual harassment— unwanted looks or comments; sexual artifacts, like nude calendars, in the workplace; or misinterpretation of where the line between "being friendly" ends and "harassment" begins.

Most studies confirm that the concept of power is central to understanding sexual harassment.[3] This seems to be true whether the harassment comes from a supervisor, a co-worker, or even a subordinate.

The supervisor-employee dyad best characterizes an unequal power relationship, where position power gives the supervisor the capacity to reward and coerce. Supervisors give subordinates their assignments, evaluate their performance, make recommendations for salary adjustments and promotions, and even decide whether an employee retains his or her job. These decisions give a supervisor power. Since subordinates want favorable performance reviews, salary increases, and the like, it's clear supervisors control resources that most subordinates consider important and scarce. It's also worth noting that individuals who occupy high-status roles (like management positions) sometimes believe that sexually harassing female subordinates is merely an extension of their right to make demands on lower status individuals. Because of power inequities, sexual harassment by one's boss typically creates the greatest difficulty for those who are being harassed. If there are no witnesses, it is her word against his. Are there others this boss has harassed and, if so, will they come forward? Because of the supervisor's control over resources, many of those who are harassed are afraid of speaking out for fear of retaliation by the supervisor.

While co-workers don't have position power, they can have influence and use it to sexually harass peers. In fact, although co-workers appear to engage in somewhat less severe forms of harassment than do supervisors, co-workers are the most frequent perpetrators of sexual harassment in organizations. How do co-workers exercise power? Most often it's by providing or withholding information, cooperation, and support. For example, the effective performance of most jobs requires interaction and support from co-workers. This is especially true nowadays as work is assigned to teams. By threatening to withhold or delay providing information that's necessary for the successful achievement of your work goals, co-workers can exert power over you.

Although it doesn't get nearly the attention that harassment by a supervisor does, women in positions of power can be subjected to sexual harassment from males who occupy less powerful positions within the organization. This is usually achieved by the subordinate devaluing the woman through highlighting traditional gender stereotypes (such as helplessness, passivity, lack of career commitment) that reflect negatively on the woman in power. Why would a subordinate engage in such practices? To attempt to gain some power over the higher ranking female or to minimize power differentials.

The topic of sexual harassment is about power. It's about an individual controlling or threatening another individual. It's wrong. Moreover, it's illegal. But you can understand how sexual harassment surfaces in organizations if you analyze it in power terms.

---

[3] The following is based on Jeanette N. Cleveland and Melinda E. Kerst, "Sexual Harassment and Perceptions of Power: An Under-Articulated Relationship," *Journal of Vocational Behavior* (February 1993), pp. 49–67.

■ POLITICS: POWER IN ACTION

When people get together, power will be exerted. People want to carve out a niche from which to exert influence, to earn rewards, and to advance their careers. When employees in organizations convert their power into action, they are engaged in politics. Those with good political skills have the ability to use their bases of power effectively.

A Definition of Political Behavior

There have been no shortages of definitions for organizational politics. Essentially, however, they have focused on the use of power to affect decision making in the organization or on behaviors by members that are self-serving and organizationally nonsanctioned. For our purposes, we define *political behavior* in organizations as *those activities that are not required as part of one's formal role in the organization, but that influence, or attempt to influence, the distribution of advantages and disadvantages within the organization.*

This definition encompasses key elements from what most people mean when they talk about organizational politics. Political behavior is *outside* one's specified job requirements. The behavior requires some attempt to use one's *power* bases. Our definition encompasses efforts to influence the goals, criteria, or processes used for *decision making* when we state that politics is concerned with the distribution of advantages and disadvantages within the organization. Our definition is broad enough to include such varied political behaviors as withholding key information from decision makers, whistle-blowing, spreading rumors, leaking confidential information about organizational activities to the media, exchanging favors with others in the organization for mutual benefit, or lobbying on behalf of or against a particular individual or decision.

The Importance of a Political Perspective

Those who fail to acknowledge political behavior ignore the reality that organizations are political systems. It would be nice if all organizations or formal groups within organizations could be described as supportive, harmonious, trusting, collaborative, or cooperative. A nonpolitical perspective can lead one to believe that employees will always behave in ways consistent with the interests of the organization. In contrast, a political view can explain much of what may seem to be irrational behavior in organizations. It can help to explain, for instance, why employees withhold information, restrict output, attempt to "build empires," publicize their successes, hide their failures, distort performance figures to make themselves look better, and engage in similar activities that appear to be at odds with the organization's desire for effectiveness and efficiency.

Factors Contributing to Political Behavior

Recent research and observation have identified a number of factors that appear to be associated with political behavior. Some are individual characteristics, derived from the unique qualities of the people whom the organization employs; others are a result of the organization's culture or internal environment.

Individual Factors. At the individual level, researchers have identified certain personality characteristics, needs, and other individual factors that are likely to be related to political behavior. Employees who are authoritarian, have a high-risk propensity, or possess an external locus of control act politically with less regard for the consequences to the organization. A high need for power, autonomy, security, or status is also a major contributor to an employee's tendency to engage in political behavior.

Organizational Factors. Political activity is probably more a function of the organization's culture than of individual differences. Why? Because most organizations have a large number of employees with the characteristics we listed, yet the presence of political behavior varies widely.

While we acknowledge the role that individual differences can play in fostering politicking, the evidence more strongly supports that certain cultures promote politics. Cultures characterized by low trust, role ambiguity, unclear performance evaluation systems, zero-sum reward allocation practices, and democratic decision making will create opportunities for political activities to be nurtured.

The less trust there is within the organization, the higher the level of political behavior. So high trust should suppress the level of political behavior.

Role ambiguity means the prescribed behaviors of the employee are not clear. There are fewer limits, therefore, to the scope and functions of the employee's political actions. Since political activities are defined as those not required as part of one's formal role, the greater the role ambiguity, the more one can engage in political activity with little chance of its being visible.

The practice of performance evaluation is far from a perfected science. The more that organizations use subjective criteria in the appraisal, emphasize a single outcome measure, or allow significant time to pass between an action and its appraisal, the greater the likelihood an employee can get away with politicking. Subjective performance criteria create ambiguity. The use of a single outcome measure encourages individuals to do whatever is necessary to look good on that measure, but often at the expense of performing well on other important parts of the job that are not being appraised. The amount of time that elapses between an action and its appraisal is also a relevant factor. The longer the time period, the more unlikely the employee will be held accountable for his or her political behaviors.

The more an organization's culture emphasizes the zero-sum or win-lose approach to reward allocations, the more employees will be motivated to engage in politicking. The zero-sum approach treats the reward "pie" as fixed so that any gain one person or group achieves has to come at the expense of another person or group. If I win, you must lose! If $10,000 in annual raises is to be distributed among five employees, then any employee who gets more than

$2,000 takes money away from one or more of the others. Such a practice encourages making others look bad and increasing the visibility of what you do.

In the last 25 years there has been a general move in North America toward making organizations less autocratic. While much of this trend has been more in theory than in practice, it is undoubtedly true that in many organizations, managers are being asked to behave more democratically. Managers are told they should allow subordinates to advise them on decisions and they should rely to a greater extent on group input into the decision process. Such moves toward democracy, however, are not necessarily desired by individual managers. Many managers sought their positions in order to have legitimate power to make unilateral decisions. They fought hard and often paid high personal costs to achieve their influential positions. Sharing their power with others rubs directly against their desires. The result is that managers may use the required teams, committees, conferences, and group meetings in a superficial way—as arenas for maneuvering and manipulating.

Impression Management

We know people have an ongoing interest in how others perceive and evaluate them. For example, North Americans spend billions of dollars on diets, health club memberships, cosmetics, and plastic surgery—all intended to make them more attractive to others. Being perceived positively by others should have benefits for people in organizations. It might, for instance, help them initially to get the jobs they want in an organization and, once hired, to get favorable evaluations, superior salary increases, and more rapid promotions. In a political context, it might help sway the distribution of advantages in their favor.

The process by which individuals attempt to control the impression others form of them is called *impression management*. It's a subject that only quite recently has gained the attention of OB researchers. In this section we review impression management (IM) techniques and ascertain whether they actually work in organizations.

Techniques. Most of the attention given to IM techniques has centered on seven verbal self-presentation behaviors that individuals use to manipulate information about themselves. Let's briefly define them and give an example of each.

> **Self-descriptions**. These are statements made by a person that describe such personal characteristics as traits, abilities, feelings, opinions, and personal lives. An example: A job applicant tells an interviewer, "I got my Harvard M.B.A. even though I suffer from dyslexia."
>
> **Conformity**. Agreeing with someone else's opinion in order to gain his or her approval. An example: A manager tells his boss, "You're absolutely right on your reorganization plan for the western regional office. I couldn't agree with you more."
>
> **Accounts**. Excuses, justifications, or other explanations of a predicament-creating event aimed at minimizing the apparent severity of the predicament. An

example: Sales manager to boss, "We failed to get the ad in the paper on time but no one responds to those ads anyway."

Apologies. Admitting responsibility for an undesirable event and simultaneously seeking to get a pardon for the action. An example: Employee to boss, "I'm sorry I made a mistake on the report. Please forgive me."

Acclaiming. Explanation of favorable events by someone in order to maximize the desirable implications for that person. An example: A salesperson informs a peer, "The sales in our division have nearly tripled since I was hired."

Flattery. Complimenting others about their virtues in an effort to make oneself appear perceptive and likeable. An example: New sales trainee to peer, "You handled that client's complaint *so* tactfully! I could never have handled that as well as you did."

Favors. Doing something nice for someone to gain that person's approval. An example: Salesperson to prospective client, "I've got two tickets to the theatre for tonight that I can't use. Take them. Consider it a thank you for taking the time to talk with me."

Keep in mind that nothing in IM implies the impressions people convey are necessarily false (although, of course, they sometimes are). You can, for instance, *actually* believe that ads contribute little to sales in your region or that you *are* the key ingredient in the tripling of your division's sales. But misrepresentation can have a high cost. If the image claimed is false, you may be discredited. If you "cry wolf" once too often, no one is likely to believe you when the wolf really comes. So one must be cautious not to be perceived as insincere or manipulative.

Are there situations where individuals are more likely to misrepresent themselves or more likely to get away with it? Yes—when the situation is characterized by high uncertainty or ambiguity. These situations provide relatively little information for challenging a fraudulent claim and reduce the risks associated with misrepresentation.

Effectiveness. Only a few studies have been undertaken to test the effectiveness of IM techniques and these have been essentially limited to determining whether IM behavior is related to job interview success. This makes a particularly relevant area of study since applicants are clearly attempting to present positive images of themselves and there are relatively objective outcome measures (written assessments and typically a hire-don't hire recommendation).

The evidence demonstrates that using IM behaviors seems to work. In one study, for instance, interviewers felt that those applicants for a position as a customer-service representative who used IM techniques performed better in the interview, and they seemed somewhat more inclined to hire these people. Moreover, the researchers considered applicants' credentials and concluded it was the IM techniques alone that influenced the interviewers. That is, it didn't seem to matter if applicants were well or poorly qualified. If they used IM techniques, they did better in the interview. Of course, it could be argued that since the job for which applicants were being considered—customer-service representative—was a public contact position, self-presentation may be a job-relevant skill and more important than such qualifications as college major, grades, or prior work experience. Nevertheless, IM techniques seem to work in interviews.

The Ethics of Behaving Politically

We conclude our discussion of politics by providing some ethical guidelines for political behavior. While there are no clear-cut ways to differentiate ethical from unethical politicking, there are some questions you should consider.

Exhibit 10–2 illustrates a decision tree to guide ethical actions. The first question you need to answer addresses self-interest versus organizational goals. Ethical actions are consistent with the organization's goals. Spreading untrue rumors about the safety of a new product introduced by your company, in order to make that product's design group look bad, is unethical. However, there may be nothing unethical if a department head exchanges favors with her division's purchasing manager in order to get a critical contract processed quickly.

The second question concerns the rights of other parties. If the department head described in the previous paragraph went down to the mail room during her lunch hour and read through the mail directed to the purchasing manager—with the intent of "getting something on him" so he'll expedite your contract—she would be acting unethically. She would have violated the purchasing manager's right to privacy.

The final question that needs to be addressed relates to whether the political activity conforms to standards of equity and justice. The department head that inflates the performance evaluation of a favored employee and deflates the evaluation of a disfavored employee—then uses these evaluations to justify giving the former a big raise and nothing to the latter—has treated the disfavored employee unfairly.

Unfortunately, the answers to the questions in Exhibit 10–2 are often argued in ways to make unethical practices seem ethical. Powerful people, for example, can become very good at explaining self-serving behaviors in terms of the organization's best interests. Similarly, they can persuasively argue that unfair actions are really fair and just. Our point is that immoral people can

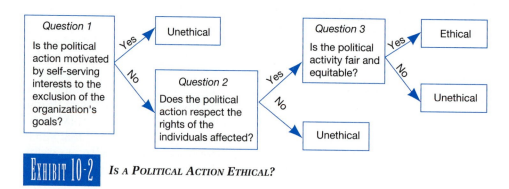

EXHIBIT 10-2 *IS A POLITICAL ACTION ETHICAL?*

justify almost any behavior. Those who are powerful, articulate, and persuasive are most vulnerable because they are likely to be able to get away with unethical practices successfully. When faced with an ethical dilemma regarding organizational politics, try to answer the questions in Exhibit 10–2 truthfully. And if you have a strong power base, recognize the ability of power to corrupt. Remember, it's a lot easier for the powerless to act ethically, for no other reason than they typically have very little political discretion to exploit.

■ IMPLICATIONS FOR MANAGERS

If you want to get things done in a group or organization, it helps to have power. As a manager who wants to maximize your power, you will want to increase others' dependence on you. You can, for instance, increase your power in relation to your boss by developing knowledge or a skill that he needs and for which he perceives no ready substitute. But power is a two-way street. You will not be alone in attempting to build your power sources. Others, particularly subordinates, will be seeking to make you dependent on them. The result is a continual battle. While you seek to maximize others' dependence on you, you will be seeking to minimize your dependence on others. And, of course, others you work with will be trying to do the same.

The effective manager accepts the political nature of organizations. By assessing behavior in a political framework, you can better predict the actions of others and use this information to formulate political strategies that will gain advantages for you and your work unit.

$\mathcal{S}$UGGESTIONS FOR FURTHER READING

DRORY, AMOS, "Perceived Political Climate and Job Attitudes," *Organization Studies*, Vol. 14, No. 1, 1993, pp. 59–71.

FERRIS, GERALD R., AND K. MICHELE KACMAR, "Perceptions of Organizational Politics," *Journal of Management*, March 1992, pp. 93–116.

GIACALONE, ROBERT A., AND PAUL ROSENFELD, *Applied Impression Management: How Image-Making Affects Managerial Decisions* (Newbury Park, CA: Sage, 1991).

HINKIN, TIMOTHY R., AND CHESTER R. SCHRIESHEIM, "Relationships between Subordinate Perceptions and Supervisor Influence Tactics and Attributed Bases of Supervisory Power," *Human Relations*, March 1990, pp. 221–37.

KEYS, BERNARD, AND THOMAS CASE, "How to Become an Influential Manager," *Academy of Management Executive*, November 1990, pp. 38–51.

KRACHKHARDT, DAVID, "Assessing the Political Landscape: Structure, Cognition, and Power in Organizations, " *Administrative Science Quarterly*, June 1990, pp. 342–69.

PFEFFER, JEFFREY, *Managing with Power* (Boston: Harvard Business School Press, 1992).

YUKL, GARY, AND CECILIA M. FALBE, "Importance of Different Power Sources in Downward and Lateral Relations," *Journal of Applied Psychology*, June 1991, pp. 416–23.

CONFLICT AND NEGOTIATION

After reading this chapter, you should be able to:

1. Define *conflict*
2. Differentiate between the traditional, human relations, and interactionist views of conflict
3. Contrast functional from dysfunctional conflict
4. Describe the five conflict-handling orientations

5. Outline the conflict process
6. Contrast distributive and integrative bargaining
7. Identify decision biases that hinder effective negotiation
8. Explain ways for individuals to improve their negotiating skills

It has been said conflict is a theme that has occupied the thinking of man more than any other—with the exception of God and love. It has been only recently, though, that conflict has become a major area of interest and research for students of organizational behavior. The evidence suggests that this interest has been well placed: The type and intensity of conflict *does* affect group behavior.

■ A DEFINITION OF CONFLICT

There has been no shortage of definitions for conflict. In spite of the divergent meanings the term has acquired, several common themes underlie most definitions. Conflict must be *perceived* by the parties to it. Whether conflict exists or not is a perception issue. If no one is aware of a conflict, it is generally agreed no conflict exists. Of course, conflicts perceived may not be real while many situations that otherwise could be described as conflictive are not because the group members involved do not perceive the conflict. For a conflict to exist, therefore, it must be perceived. Additional commonalities among most conflict definitions are the concepts of *opposition*, *scarcity*, and *blockage*, and the assumption there are two or more parties whose interests or goals appear to be incompatible. Resources—money, jobs, prestige, power, for example—are not unlimited, and their scarcity encourages blocking behavior. The parties are therefore in opposition. When one party blocks the means to a goal of another, a conflict state exists.

Differences between definitions tend to center around *intent* and whether conflict is a term limited only to *overt* acts. The intent issue is a debate over whether blockage behavior must be a determined action or whether it could occur as a result of fortuitous circumstances. As to whether conflict can only refer to overt acts, some definitions, for example, require signs of manifest fighting or open struggle as criteria for the existence of conflict.

Our definition of conflict acknowledges awareness (perception), opposition, scarcity, and blockage. Further, we assume it to be a determined action, which can exist at either the latent or overt level. We define conflict as *a process in which an effort is purposely made by A to offset the efforts of B by some form of blocking that will result in frustrating B in attaining his or her goals or furthering his or her interests.*

■ TRANSITIONS IN CONFLICT THOUGHT

It is entirely appropriate to say there has been conflict over the role of conflict in groups and organizations. One school of thought has argued conflict must be avoided, that it indicates a malfunction within the group. We call this the *traditional* view. Another school of thought, the *human relations* view, argues conflict is a natural and inevitable outcome in any group. It need not be evil, but rather has the potential to be a positive force in determining group performance. The third, and most recent, perspective proposes not only that conflict *can* be a positive force in a group, but explicitly argues that some conflict is *absolutely necessary* for a group to perform effectively. We label this third school the *interactionist* approach. Let us take a closer look at each of these views.

The Traditional View

The early approach to conflict assumed conflict was bad. Conflict was viewed negatively, and it was used synonymously with terms like violence, destruction, and irrationality in order to reinforce its negative connotation. Conflict, then, was to be avoided.

The traditional view was consistent with the attitudes that prevailed about group behavior in the 1930s and 1940s. From findings provided by studies like those done at Hawthorne, it was argued that conflict was a dysfunctional outcome resulting from poor communication, a lack of openness and trust between people, and the failure of managers to be responsive to the needs and aspirations of their employees.

The view that all conflict is bad certainly offers a simple approach to looking at the behavior of people who create conflict. Since all conflict is to be avoided, we need merely direct our attention to the causes of conflict and correct these malfunctionings in order to improve group and organizational performance. Although research studies now provide strong evidence to dispute that this approach to conflict reduction results in high group performance, most of us still evaluate conflict situations utilizing this outmoded standard.

The Human Relations View

The human relations position argued that conflict was a natural occurrence in all groups and organizations. Since conflict was inevitable, the human relations school advocated acceptance of conflict. They rationalized its existence: It cannot be eliminated, and there are even times when conflict may benefit a group's performance. The human relations view dominated conflict theory from the late 1940s through the mid-1970s.

The Interactionist View

The current view toward conflict is the interactionist perspective. While the human relations approach *accepted* conflict, the interactionist approach *encourages* conflict on the grounds that a harmonious, peaceful, tranquil, and cooperative group is likely to become static, apathetic, and nonresponsive to needs for change and innovation. The major contribution of the interactionist approach, therefore, is encouraging group leaders to maintain an ongoing minimal level of conflict—enough to keep the group alive, self-critical, and creative.

Given the interactionist view, which is the one we take in this chapter, it becomes evident that to say conflict is all good or all bad is inappropriate and naïve. Whether a conflict is good or bad depends on the type of conflict. Specifically, it's necessary to differentiate between functional and dysfunctional conflicts.

■ DIFFERENTIATING FUNCTIONAL FROM DYSFUNCTIONAL CONFLICTS

The interactionist view does not propose that *all* conflicts are good. Rather, some conflicts support the goals of the group and improve its performance; these are functional, constructive forms of conflict. There are also conflicts that hinder group performance; these are dysfunctional or destructive forms.

How does one tell if a conflict is functional or dysfunctional? The demarcation between functional and dysfunctional is neither clear nor precise. No one level of conflict can be adopted as acceptable or unacceptable under all conditions. The type and level of conflict that creates healthy and positive involvement toward one group's goals may, in another group or in the same group at another time, be highly dysfunctional.

The important criterion is group performance. Since groups exist to attain a goal or goals, it is the impact the conflict has on the group, rather than on any singular individual, that defines functionality. The impact of conflict on the individual and on the group is rarely mutually exclusive, so the ways individuals perceive a conflict may have an important influence on its effect on the group. However, this need not be the case and when it is not, our orientation will be to the group. In appraising the impact of conflict on group behavior—to consider its functional and dysfunctional effects—whether the individual group members perceive the conflict as good or bad is irrelevant. A group member may perceive an action as dysfunctional because the outcome is personally dissatisfying to him or her. However, for our analysis, it would be functional if it furthers the objectives of the group.

■ THE CONFLICT PROCESS

The conflict process can be thought of as progressing through four stages: potential opposition, cognition and personalization, behavior, and outcomes. The process is diagrammed in Exhibit 11–1.

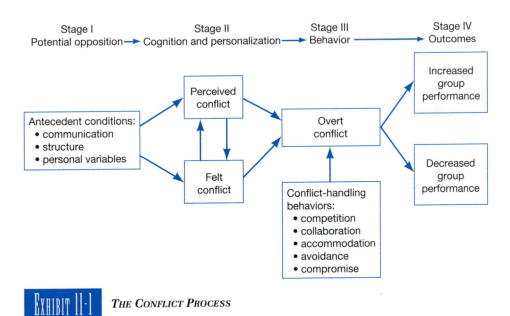

EXHIBIT 11-1   *THE CONFLICT PROCESS*

Stage I: Potential Opposition

The first step in the conflict process is the presence of conditions that create opportunities for conflict to arise. They *need not* lead directly to conflict, but one of these conditions is necessary if conflict is to arise. For simplicity's sake, these conditions (which also may be looked at as causes or sources of conflict) have been condensed into three general categories: communication, structure, and personal variables.

Communication. The communicative source represents those opposing forces that arise from semantic difficulties, misunderstandings, and "noise" in the communication channels. Much of this discussion can be related to our comments on communication and communication networks in Chapter 8.

One of the major myths that most of us carry around with us is that poor communication is the reason for conflicts. Such a conclusion is not unreasonable, given the amount of time each of us spends communicating. But, of course, poor communication is certainly not the source of *all* conflicts, though there is considerable evidence to suggest that problems in the communication process act to retard collaboration and stimulate misunderstanding.

A review of the research suggests that semantic difficulties, insufficient exchange of information, and noise in the communication channel are all barriers to communication and potential antecedent conditions to conflict. Specifically, evidence demonstrates that semantic difficulties arise as a result of differences in training, selective perception, and inadequate information about others. Research has further demonstrated a surprising finding: The potential for conflict increases when either too little or too much communication takes place. Apparently, an increase in communication is functional up to a point, whereupon it is possible to overcommunicate, resulting in an increase in the potential for conflict. Too much information as well as too little can lay the foundation for conflict. Further, the channel chosen for communicating can have an influence on stimulating opposition. The filtering process that occurs as information is passed between members, and the divergence of communications from formal or previously established channels, offer potential opportunities for conflict to arise.

Structure. The term *structure* is used, in this context, to include variables such as size; degree of routinization, specialization, and standardization in the tasks assigned to group members; heterogeneity of members; leadership styles; reward systems; and the degree of dependence between groups.

Research indicates that size and specialization act as forces to stimulate conflict. The larger the group and the more specialized its activities, the greater the likelihood of conflict. Tenure and conflict have been found to be inversely related. The potential for conflict tends to be greatest where group members are younger and where turnover is high.

There is some indication that a close style of leadership, that is, tight and continuous observation with restrictive control of the others' behaviors, increases conflict potential, but the evidence is not strong. Too much reliance on participation may also stimulate conflict. Research tends to confirm that participation and conflict are highly correlated, apparently because participation encourages the promotion of differences. Reward systems, too, are found to create conflict when one member's gain is at another's expense. Finally, if a group is dependent on another group (in contrast to the two being mutually independent) or if interdependence allows one group to gain at another's expense, opposing forces are stimulated.

Personal Variables. The most important personal variables are individual value systems and individual idiosyncracies and differences.

The evidence indicates that certain personality types—for example, individuals who are highly authoritarian, dogmatic, and who demonstrate low esteem—lead to potential conflict. Most important, and probably the most overlooked variable in the study of social conflict, is the notion of differing value systems. That is, people differ in the importance they give to values such as freedom, pleasure, hard work, self-respect, honesty, obedience, and equality. Value differences, for example, are the best explanation of such diverse issues as prejudice, disagreements over one's contribution to the group and the rewards one deserves, or assessments of whether this particular book is any good. The fact that John dislikes blacks and Dana believes John's position indicates his ignorance; that an employee thinks he is worth $30,000 a year but his boss believes him to be worth $24,000; and that Ann thinks this book is interesting to read while Jennifer views it as a "crock of . . .," are all value judgments. And differences in value systems are important sources for creating the potential for conflict.

Stage II: Cognition and Personalization

If the conditions cited in Stage I generate frustration, then the potential for opposition becomes realized in the second stage. The antecedent conditions can lead to conflict only when one or more of the parties are affected by, and cognizant of, the conflict.

As we noted in our definition of conflict, perception is required. Therefore, one or more of the parties must be aware of the existence of the antecedent conditions. But just because a conflict is perceived does not mean it is personalized. You may be aware that you and a co-worker are in disagreement. However, it may not make you tense or anxious and it may not influence your affection toward this co-worker. It is at the level where conflict is felt, when individuals become emotionally involved, that parties experience anxiety, tension, frustration, or hostility.

Stage III: Behavior

We are in the third stage of the conflict process when a member engages in action that frustrates the attainment of another's goals or prevents the furthering of the other's interests. This action must be intended; that is, there must be a known effort to frustrate another. At this juncture, the conflict is out in the open.

Overt conflict covers a full range of behaviors, from subtle, indirect, and highly controlled forms of interference to direct, aggressive, violent, and uncontrolled struggle. At the low range, this overt behavior is illustrated by the student who raises his or her hand in class and questions a point the instructor has made. At the high range, strikes, riots, and wars come to mind.

Stage III is also where most conflict-handling behaviors are initiated. Once the conflict is overt, the parties will develop a method for dealing with the conflict. This does not exclude conflict-handling behaviors from being initiated in Stage II, but in most cases, these techniques for reducing the frustration are used not as preventive measures but only when the conflict has become observable. Five conflict-handling approaches are typically available to the parties: competition, collaboration, avoidance, accommodation, and compromise.

Competition. When one party seeks to achieve certain goals or further personal interests, regardless of the impact on the parties to the conflict, he or she competes and dominates. These win-lose struggles, in formal groups or in an organization, frequently utilize the formal authority of a mutual superior as the dominant force, and the conflicting parties will each use his or her own power base in order to resolve a victory in his or her favor.

Collaboration. When each of the parties in conflict desires to satisfy fully the concern of all parties, we have cooperation and the search for a mutually beneficial outcome. In collaboration, the behavior of the parties is aimed at solving the problem and at clarifying the differences rather than accommodating various points of view. The participants consider the full range of alternatives; the similarities and differences in viewpoint become more clearly focused; and the causes or differences become outwardly evident. Because the solution sought is advantageous to all parties, collaboration is often thought of as a win-win approach to resolving conflicts. It is, for example, a tool used frequently by marriage counselors. Behavioral scientists, who value openness, trust, and spontaneity in relationships, are also strong advocates of a collaborative approach to resolving conflicts.

Avoidance. A party may recognize that a conflict exists but react by withdrawing, or suppressing the conflict. Indifference or the desire to evade overt demonstration of a disagreement can result in withdrawal: The parties acknowledge physical separation and each stakes out a territory that is distinct from the other's. If withdrawal is not possible or desirous, the parties may suppress, that is, withhold their differences. When group members are required to interact because of the interdependence of their tasks, suppression is a more probable outcome than withdrawal.

Accommodation. When the parties seek to appease their opponents, they may be willing to place their opponents' interests above their own. In order to maintain the relationship, one party is willing to be self-sacrificing. We refer to this behavior as accommodation. When husbands and wives have differences, it is not uncommon for one to accommodate the other by placing a spouse's interest above one's own.

Compromise. When each party to the conflict must give up something, sharing occurs, resulting in a compromised outcome. In compromising, there is no clear winner or loser. Rather, there is a rationing of the object of the conflict or, where the object is not divisible, one rewards the other by yielding something of substitute value. The distinguishing characteristic of compromise, therefore, is the requirement that each party give up something. In negotiations between unions and management, compromise is required in order to reach a settlement and agree upon a labor contract.

The Impact of National Culture on Conflict Behavior. Your approach to handling conflict will, to some degree, be influenced by your cultural roots. Americans, for example, have a reputation for being open, direct, and competitive. These characteristics are consistent with a society marked by relatively low uncertainty avoidance and high masculinity rankings.

As we discovered in Chapter 2, people in countries low in uncertainty avoidance feel secure and relatively free from threats of uncertainty. Their organizations, therefore, tend to be more open and flexible. Countries high in masculinity emphasize assertiveness. The cultural climate of low uncertainty avoidance and high masculinity tends to shape a society that is open, direct, and competitive. It would also tend to create individuals who favor such conflict-handling behaviors as competition and collaboration.

This suggests that uncertainty avoidance and masculinity-femininity rankings would be fairly good predictors of which conflict styles are preferred in different countries. It suggests, for instance, that when one is in a Scandinavian country—which tends to rate high on femininity—avoidance or accommodation behaviors should be emphasized. The same recommendation would apply in Japan, Greece, or other countries that rate high on uncertainty avoidance, because the extensive use of formal rules and employment guarantees tends to minimize conflicts and encourage cooperation.

Stage IV: Outcomes

The interplay between the overt conflict behavior and conflict-handling behaviors results in consequences. As Exhibit 11–1 demonstrates, they may be functional in that the conflict has resulted in an improvement in the group's performance. Conversely, group performance may be hindered and the outcome then would be dysfunctional.

Functional Outcomes. How might conflict increase group performance? It is hard to visualize a situation where open or violent aggression could be functional. But there are a number of instances where it is possible to envision how low or moderate levels of conflict could improve the effectiveness of a group. Because it is often difficult to think of instances where conflict can be constructive, let us consider some examples, and then look at the research evidence.

Conflict is constructive when it improves the quality of decisions, stimulates creativity and innovation, encourages interest and curiosity among group members, provides the medium through which problems can be aired and tensions released, and fosters an environment of self-evaluation and change. The evidence suggests that conflict can improve the quality of decision making by allowing all points, particularly the ones that are unusual or held by a minority, to be weighed in important decisions. Conflict is an antidote for groupthink. It does not allow the group to rubber-stamp decisions that may be based on weak assumptions, inadequate consideration to relevant alternatives, or other debilities. Conflict challenges the status quo and therefore furthers the creation of new ideas, promotes reassessment of group goals and activities, and increases the probability that the group will respond to change.

Research studies in diverse settings confirm the functionality of conflict. Consider the following findings.

A comparison of six major decisions during the administrations of four different U.S. presidents found that conflict reduced the chance that groupthink would overpower policy decisions. The comparisons demonstrated that conformity among presidential advisers was related to poor decisions, while an atmosphere of constructive conflict and critical thinking surrounded the well-developed decisions.

Not only do better and more innovative decisions result from situations where there is some conflict, there is evidence indicating that conflict can be related positively to productivity. It was demonstrated that, among established groups, performance tended to improve more when there was conflict among members than when there was fairly close agreement. The investigators observed that when groups analyzed decisions that had been made by the individual members of that group, the average improvement among the high-conflict groups was 73 percent greater than that of those groups characterized by low-conflict conditions.[1] Others have found similar results: Groups composed of members with different interests tend to produce higher-quality solutions to a variety of problems than do homogeneous groups.[2]

The preceding findings suggest that conflict in the group might be an indication of strength rather than, in the traditional view, of weakness.

---

[1] J. Hall and M.S. Williams, "A Comparison of Decision-Making Performances in Established and Ad-Hoc Groups," *Journal of Personality and Social Psychology* (February 1966), p. 217.

[2] Richard L. Hoffman, "Homogeneity of Member Personality and Its Effect on Group Problem Solving," *Journal of Abnormal and Social Psychology* (January 1959), pp. 27–32; Richard L. Hoffman and Norman R.F. Maier, "Quality and Acceptance of Problem Solutions by Members of Homogeneous and Heterogeneous Groups," *Journal of Abnormal and Social Psychology* (March 1961), pp. 401–7.

Dysfunctional Outcomes. The destructive consequences of conflict on a group or organization's performance are generally well known. A reasonable summary might state: Uncontrolled opposition breeds discontent, which acts to dissolve common ties, and eventually leads to destruction of the group. And, of course, there is a substantial body of literature to document how the dysfunctional varieties of conflict can reduce group effectiveness. Among the more undesirable consequences are a retarding of communication, reductions in group cohesiveness, and subordination of group goals to the primacy of infighting among members. At the extreme, conflict can bring group functioning to a halt and potentially threaten the group's survival.

This discussion has again returned us to the issue of what is functional and what is dysfunctional. Research on conflict has yet to identify those situations where conflict is more likely to be constructive than destructive. However, the difference between functional and dysfunctional conflict is important enough for us to go beyond the substantive evidence and propose at least two hypotheses. The first is that extreme levels of conflict, exemplified by overt struggle or violence, are rarely, if ever, functional. Functional conflict is probably most often characterized by low to moderate levels of subtle and controlled opposition. Second, the type of group activity should be another factor determining functionality. We hypothesize that the more creative or unprogrammed the decision making of the group, the greater the probability that internal conflict is constructive. Groups required to tackle problems demanding new and novel approaches—for example, in research or advertising—will benefit more from conflict than groups performing highly programmed activities, such as work teams on an automobile assembly line.

◼ NEGOTIATION

Negotiation permeates the interactions of almost everyone in groups and organizations. There's the obvious: Labor bargains with management. There's the not-so-obvious: Managers negotiate with subordinates, peers, and bosses; salespeople negotiate with customers; purchasing agents negotiate with suppliers. And there's the subtle: A worker agrees to answer a colleague's phone for a few minutes in exchange for some past or future benefit.

For definitional purposes, we define *negotiation* as a process in which two or more parties exchange goods or services and attempt to agree on the exchange rate for them. Additionally, we use the terms *negotiation* and *bargaining* interchangeably.

Bargaining Strategies

There are two general approaches to negotiation—*distributive bargaining* and *integrative bargaining*. These are compared in Exhibit 11–2.

EXHIBIT 11-2 *DISTRIBUTIVE VERSUS INTEGRATIVE BARGAINING*

Bargaining Characteristic	Distributive Bargaining	Integrative Bargaining
Available resources	Fixed amount of resources to be divided	Variable amount of resources to be divided
Primary motivations	I win, you lose	I win, you win
Primary interests	Opposed to each other	Convergent or congruent with each other
Focus of relationships	Short term	Long term

Source: Based on R.J. Lewicki and J.A. Litterer, *Negotiation* (Homewood, IL: Richard D. Irwin, 1985), p. 280.

Distributive Bargaining. You see a used car advertised for sale in the newspaper. It appears to be just what you've been looking for. You go out to see the car. It's great and you want it. The owner tells you the asking price. You don't want to pay that much. The two of you then negotiate over the price. The negotiating process you are engaging in is called distributive bargaining. Its most identifying feature is that it operates under zero-sum conditions. That is, any gain I make is at your expense, and vice versa. Referring back to the used car example, every dollar you can get the seller to cut from the car's price is a dollar you save. Conversely, every dollar more he can get from you comes at your expense. So the essence of distributive bargaining is negotiating over who gets what share of a fixed pie.

Probably the most widely cited example of distributive bargaining is in labor-management negotiations over wages. Typically, labor's representatives come to the bargaining table determined to get as much money as possible out of management. Since every cent more that labor negotiates increases management's costs, each party bargains aggressively and treats the other as an opponent who must be defeated.

Exhibit 11–3 depicts the distributive bargaining strategy. Parties A and B represent the two negotiators. Each has a *target point* that defines what he or should would like to achieve. Each also has a *resistance point*, which marks the lowest outcome that is acceptable—the point below which they would break off negotiations rather than accept a less favorable settlement. The area between their resistance points is the settlement range. As long as there is some overlap in their aspiration ranges, there exists a settlement area where each one's aspirations can be met.

When engaged in distributive bargaining, one's tactics focus on trying to get one's opponent to agree to one's specific target point or to get as close to it as possible. Examples of such tactics are persuading your opponent of the impossibility of getting to his or her target point and the advisability of

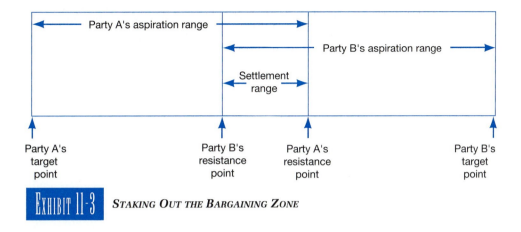

EXHIBIT 11-3 *STAKING OUT THE BARGAINING ZONE*

accepting a settlement near yours; arguing that your target is fair, while your opponent's isn't; and attempting to get your opponent to feel emotionally generous toward you and thus accepting an outcome close to your target point.

Integrative Bargaining. A sales representative for a women's sportswear manufacturer has just closed a $15,000 order from a small clothing retailer. The sales rep calls in the order to her firm's credit department. She is told the firm can't approve credit to this customer because of a past slow-pay record. The next day, the sales rep and the firm's credit manager meet to discuss the problem. The sales rep doesn't want to lose the business. Neither does the credit manager, but he also doesn't want to get stuck with an uncollectable debt. The two openly review their options. After considerable discussion, they agree on a solution that meets both their needs: The credit manager will approve the sale, but the clothing store's owner will provide a bank guarantee that will assure payment if the bill isn't paid within 60 days.

This sales-credit negotiation is an example of integrative bargaining. In contrast to distributive bargaining, integrative problem solving operates under the assumption that one or more settlements exist which can create a win-win solution.

All things being equal, integrative bargaining is preferable to distributive bargaining. Why? Because the former builds long-term relationships and facilitates working together in the future. It bonds negotiators and allows each to leave the bargaining table feeling he or she has achieved a victory. Distributive bargaining, on the other hand, leaves one party a loser. It tends to build animosities and deepen divisions when people have to work together on an ongoing basis.

Why, then, don't we see more integrative bargaining in organizations? The answer lies in the conditions necessary for this type of negotiation to succeed. These include parties who are open with information and candid about their concerns; a sensitivity by both parties to the other's needs; the ability to trust one another; and a willingness by both parties to maintain flexibility.

Since many organizational cultures and interorganizational relationships are not characterized by openness, trust, and flexibility, it isn't surprising that negotiations often take on a win-at-any-cost dynamic.

Decision-Making Biases That Hinder Effective Negotiations

All of us have had negotiating experiences where the results have been less than we had hoped for. Why? We tend to be blind to opportunities that prevent us from getting as much as possible out of a negotiation. The following identifies seven decision-making biases that can blind us.[3]

Irrational Escalation of Commitment. People tend to continue a previously selected course of action beyond what rational analysis would recommend. Such misdirected persistence can lead to wasting a great deal of time, energy, and money. Time and money already invested are "sunk costs." They *cannot* be recovered and should *not* be considered when selecting future courses of action.

The Mythical Fixed Pie. Bargainers assume their gain must come at the expense of the other party. As noted with integrative bargaining, that needn't be the case. There are often win-win solutions. But assuming a zero-sum game means missed opportunities for trade-offs that could benefit both sides.

Anchoring and Adjustments. People often have a tendency to anchor their judgments on irrelevant information, such as an initial offer. Many factors influence the initial positions people take when entering a negotiation. They are often meaningless. Effective negotiators don't let an initial anchor minimize the amount of information and the depth of thinking they use to evaluate a situation, and don't give too much weight to their opponent's initial offer too early in the negotiation.

Framing Negotiations. People tend to be overly affected by the way information is presented to them. For instance, in a labor-management contract negotiation, assume your employees are currently making $15 an hour but the union is seeking a $4 raise. You are prepared to go to $17. The union's response is likely to be different if you can successfully frame this as a $2 an hour gain (in comparison to the current wage) rather than a $2 an hour loss (when compared against the union's demand).

Availability of Information. Negotiators often rely too much on readily available information, while ignoring more relevant data. Things or events that people have encountered more often are usually easy to remember—they're more "available" in their memory. It's also easier to remember or imagine more vivid events. Information that is easily recalled because it's familiar or

---

[3] Max H. Bazerman and Margaret A. Neale, *Negotiating Rationally* (New York: Free Press, 1992).

vivid may be interpreted as being reliable when it's not. So effective negotiators learn to distinguish what's emotionally familiar to them from what's reliable and relevant.

The Winner's Curse. In most negotiations, one side (usually the seller) has much better information than the other. Yet people in a negotiation tend to act as if their opponent is inactive and ignore the valuable information that can be learned by thinking about the other side's decisions. The "winner's curse" reflects the regret one often feels after closing a negotiation. Your opponent has accepted your offer, which might suggest you offered too much. You can reduce the "curse" by gaining as much information as possible and putting yourself in your opponent's shoes.

Overconfidence. Many of the previous biases can combine to inflate a person's confidence in his or her judgment and choices. When people hold certain beliefs and expectations, they tend to ignore information that contradicts them. The result is that negotiators tend to be overconfident. This, in turn, lessens the incentive to compromise. Considering the suggestions of qualified advisers or seeking objective assessment about your position from a neutral party are two ways to temper this tendency.

■ IMPLICATIONS FOR MANAGERS

Managing Conflict

Many people assume conflict is related to lower group and organizational performance. This chapter has demonstrated that this assumption is often fallacious. Conflict can be either constructive or destructive to the functioning of a group or unit. When it's too high or too low, it hinders performance. An optimal level is one in which there is enough conflict to prevent stagnation, stimulate creativity, allow tensions to be released, and initiate the seeds for change, yet not so much as to be disruptive.

What advice can we give to managers faced with excessive conflict and the need to reduce it? Don't assume there's one conflict-handling approach that will always be best! You should select the resolution technique appropriate for each situation. The following provides some guidelines:[4]

Use *competition* when quick, decisive action is vital (in emergencies); on important issues, where unpopular actions need implementing (in cost cutting, enforcing unpopular rules, discipline); on issues vital to the organization's welfare when you know you're right; and against people who take advantage of noncompetitive behavior.

---

[4] Kenneth W. Thomas, "Toward Multidimensional Values in Teaching: The Example of Conflict Behaviors," *Academy of Management Review* (July 1977), p. 487.

Use *collaboration* to find an integrative solution when both sets of concerns are too important to be compromised; when your objective is to learn; to merge insights from people with different perspectives; to gain commitment by incorporating concerns into a consensus; and to work through feelings that have interfered with a relationship.

Use *avoidance* when an issue is trivial, or more important issues are pressing; when you perceive no chance of satisfying your concerns; when potential disruption outweighs the benefits of resolution; to let people cool down and regain perspective; when gathering information supersedes immediate decision; when others can resolve the conflict more effectively; and when issues seem tangential or symptomatic of other issues.

Use *accommodation* when you find you are wrong and to allow a better position to be heard, to learn, and to show your reasonableness; when issues are more important to others than yourself and to satisfy others and maintain cooperation; to build social credits for later issues; to minimize loss when you are outmatched and losing; when harmony and stability are especially important; and to allow subordinates to develop by learning from mistakes.

Use *compromise* when goals are important, but not worth the effort of potential disruption of more assertive approaches; when opponents with equal power are committed to mutually exclusive goals; to achieve temporary settlements to complex issues; to arrive at expedient solutions under time pressure; and as a backup when collaboration or competition is unsuccessful.

Toward Improving Negotiation Skills

The following recommendations should help improve your effectiveness at negotiating:[5]

Research Your Opponent. Acquire as much information as you can about your opponent's interests and goals. What constituencies must he or she appease? What is his or her strategy? This will help you to better understand your opponent's behavior, predict responses to your offers, and help you to frame solutions in terms of his or her interests.

Begin with a Positive Overture. Research shows that concessions tend to be reciprocated and lead to agreements. As a result, begin bargaining with a positive overture—perhaps a small concession—and then reciprocate your opponent's concessions.

Address the Problem, Not Personalities. Concentrate on the negotiation issues, not on the personal characteristics of your opponent. When negotiations get tough, avoid the tendency to attack your opponent. It's your oppo-

[5] Based on Roger Fisher and William Ury, *Getting to Yes: Negotiating Agreement without Giving In* (Boston: Houghton Mifflin, 1981); James A. Wall, Jr., and Michael W. Blum, "Negotiations," *Journal of Management* (June 1991), pp. 295–96; and Max H. Bazerman and Margaret A. Neale, *Negotiating Rationally*.

nent's ideas or position that you disagree with, not him or her personally. Separate the people from the problem, and don't personalize differences.

Pay Little Attention to Initial Offers. Treat initial offers as merely a point of departure. Everyone has to have an initial position. They tend to be extreme and idealistic. Treat them as such.

Emphasize Win-Win Solutions. If conditions are supportive, look for an integrative solution. Frame options in terms of your opponent's interests, and look for solutions that can allow your opponent to declare a victory as well as yourself.

Be Open to Accepting Third-Party Assistance. When stalemates are reached, consider the use of a neutral third party. *Mediators* can help parties come to an agreement, but they don't impose a settlement. *Arbitrators* hear both sides of the dispute, then impose a solution. *Conciliators* are more informal—acting as a communication conduit—passing information between the parties, interpreting messages, and clarifying misunderstandings.

$\mathcal{S}$UGGESTIONS FOR FURTHER READING

NEALE, MARGARET A., AND MAX H. BAZERMAN, "Negotiating Rationally: The Power and Impact of the Negotiator's Frame," *Academy of Management Executive*, August 1992, pp. 42–51.

PINKLEY, ROBIN L., "Dimensions of Conflict Frame: Disputant Interpretations of Conflict," *Journal of Applied Psychology*, April 1990, pp. 117–26.

RAHIM, M. AFZALUR, *Theory and Research in Conflict Management* (New York: Praeger, 1990).

SIMONS, TONY, "Speech Patterns and the Concept of Utility in Cognitive Maps: The Case of Integrative Bargaining," *Academy of Management Journal*, February 1993, pp. 139–56.

SITKIN, SIM B., AND ROBERT J. BIES, "Social Accounts in Conflict Situations: Using Explanations to Manage Conflict," *Human Relations*, March 1993, pp. 349–70.

THOMAS, KENNETH W., "Conflict and Negotiation Processes in Organizations," in M.D. Dunnette and L.M. Hough, eds., *Handbook of Industrial & Organizational Psychology*, 2nd ed., Vol. 3 (Palo Alto, CA: Consulting Psychologists Press, 1992), pp. 651–717.

TJOSVOLD, DEAN, *The Conflict Positive Organization* (Reading, MA: Addison-Wesley, 1991).

VAN DE VLIERT, EVERT, AND BORIS KABANOFF, "Toward Theory-Based Measures of Conflict Management," *Academy of Management Journal*, March 1990, pp. 199–209.

CHAPTER 12

FOUNDATIONS OF ORGANIZATION STRUCTURE

After reading this chapter, you should be able to:

1. Define *organization structure*
2. Identify the advantages and disadvantages to division of labor
3. Explain the reason for maintaining unity of command
4. Differentiate line from staff authority
5. List the ways an organization can departmentalize
6. Explain why wide spans of control increase organizational efficiency
7. Discuss the effects of structural variables on organizational behavior
8. Explain why structure may be a perception phenomenon

Jerry Nichols's job is pretty good. He's got an attractively furnished office on the top floor of a New York skyscraper, a nice view, his own secretary, the prestige that goes with being a marketing research analyst at a *Fortune* 100 company, and a salary and bonus package that earns him more than $100,000 a year—not bad for a 28-year-old guy who has been out of school for less than five years.

In contrast to a blue-collar assembly-line worker, Jerry Nichols has a lot of freedom on his job. But in absolute terms, Jerry and the more than 120 million other North Americans who go to work every Monday have a number of restrictions imposed on them by their organizations that limit and regulate their attitudes and behavior. Most employees have a job description that says what they are supposed to do. The organization has rules telling Jerry and the other employees like Jerry what they can and cannot do. An authority hierarchy defines who everyone's boss is and the formal channels through which communications are to pass. These are examples of the structural characteristics that most organizations have. In this chapter, we demonstrate how an organization's *structure* affects the attitudes and behavior of its members.

■ WHAT IS STRUCTURE?

An organization's structure is made up of three components. The first has to do with the amount of vertical, horizontal, and spatial differentiation. This is called *complexity*. Next is the degree to which rules and procedures are utilized. This is referred to as *formalization*. The third is *centralization*, which considers where decision-making authority lies. Let's briefly elaborate on each of these components.

Complexity

Complexity can be broken down into three parts. *Horizontal differentiation* considers the degree of horizontal separation between units. *Vertical differentiation* refers to the depth of the organizational hierarchy. *Spatial differentiation* encompasses the degree to which the location of an organization's facilities and personnel are geographically dispersed. The more an organization is differentiated along these dimensions, the more complex it is.

Horizontal Differentiation. Horizontal differentiation refers to the degree of differentiation between units based on the orientation of members, the nature of the tasks they perform, and their education and training. We can state that the larger the number of different occupations within an organization that require specialized knowledge and skills, the more horizontally complex that organization is. Why? Because diverse orientations make it more difficult for organizational members to communicate and more difficult for management to coordinate their activities. For instance, when organizations create specialized groups or expand departmental designations, they separate groups from each other, making interactions between those groups more complex. If the organization is staffed by people who have similar backgrounds, skills, and training, they are likely to see the world in more similar terms. Conversely, diversity increases the likelihood they will have different goal emphases, time orientations, and even a different work vocabulary. Job specialization reinforces differences—the chemical engineer's job is clearly different from that of the personnel recruitment interviewer. Their training is different. The language they use on their respective jobs is different. They are typically assigned to different departments, which further reinforces their diverse orientations.

Vertical Differentiation. Vertical differentiation refers to the depth of the structure. Differentiation increases, and so does complexity, as the number of hierarchical levels in the organization increases. The more levels that exist between top management and operatives, the greater the potential for communication distortion, the more difficult it is to coordinate the decisions of managerial personnel, and the more difficult it is for top management to oversee closely the actions of operatives.

Vertical and horizontal differentiation should not be construed as independent of each other. Vertical differentiation may be best understood as a response to an increase in horizontal differentiation. As work is divided into smaller parts, it becomes increasingly necessary to coordinate tasks. Since high horizontal differentiation means members will have diverse training and backgrounds, it may be difficult for the individual units to see how their tasks fit into the greater whole. The bricklayers on a large construction site may see themselves as merely laying bricks, not putting up a building. Someone must supervise their tasks to see they are done according to the architect's plan and consistent with the time schedule. The result is a need for increased coordination, which shows itself in the development of vertical differentiation.

Spatial Differentiation. An organization can perform the same activities with the same horizontal and vertical arrangement in multiple locations. Yet, this existence of multiple locations increases complexity. Therefore, the third element in complexity is spatial differentiation, or the degree to which the location of an organization's offices, plants, and personnel are geographically dispersed.

A manufacturing company horizontally differentiates when it separates the marketing function from production. Yet, if essentially identical marketing activities are carried on in six geographically dispersed sales offices—Seattle, Los Angeles, Atlanta, New York, Toronto, and Brussels—while all production is done in a large factory in Cleveland, this organization is more complex than if both the marketing and production activities were performed at the same facility in Cleveland. The spatial concept applies similarly to vertical differentiation. If an organization's senior executives reside in one city, middle managers in a half-dozen cities, and lower-level managers in a hundred different company offices around the world, complexity has increased. Why? Because communication, coordination, and control are easier where spatial differentiation is low.

A final point: Spatial differentiation considers distance as well as numbers. If the state of Delaware had two regional welfare offices located in Dover and Wilmington, these offices would be approximately 45 miles apart. If the state of Alaska had two comparably sized offices in Anchorage and Fairbanks, these offices would be separated by 350 miles. Although the number of offices is the same in both cases, the Delaware welfare organization would be less complex because the distance between the offices is smaller.

Formalization

Formalization refers to the degree to which jobs within the organization are standardized. If a job is highly formalized, then the job incumbent has a minimum amount of discretion over what is to be done, when it is to be done, and how he or she should do it. Employees can be expected always to handle the same input in exactly the same way, resulting in a consistent and uniform output. There are explicit job descriptions, lots of organizational rules, and clearly defined procedures covering work processes in organizations where there is high formalization. Where formalization is low, job behaviors are relatively nonprogrammed and employees have a great deal of freedom to exercise discretion in their work. Since an individual's discretion on the job is inversely related to the amount of behavior that is preprogrammed by the organization, the greater the standardization, the less input the employee has into how his or her work is to be done. Standardization not only eliminates the possibility of employees engaging in alternative behaviors, but even removes the need for employees to consider alternatives.

The degree of formalization can vary widely between organizations and within organizations. Certain jobs, for instance, are well known to have little formalization. College textbook representatives, who call on professors to inform them of new publications, have a great deal of freedom in their jobs. They have no standard sales pitch, and the extent that rules and procedures govern their behavior may be little more than the requirement that they submit a weekly sales report and some suggestions on what pluses to emphasize for the various new titles. At the other extreme, there are clerical and editorial positions in the same publishing houses where employees are required to clock in at their work stations by 8 A.M. or be docked a half-hour of pay and, once at that work station, to follow a set of precise procedures dictated by management.

It is generally true that the narrowest of unskilled jobs—those that are simplest and most repetitive in nature—are most amenable to high degrees of formalization. The greater the professionalization of a job, the less likely it is to be highly formalized. Yet, there are obvious exceptions. Public accountants and consultants, for instance, typically are required to keep detailed hour-by-hour records of their activities so their companies can appropriately bill clients for their services. In general, however, the relationship holds. The jobs of lawyers, engineers, social workers, librarians, and like professionals tend to rate low on formalization.

Formalization not only differs if the jobs are unskilled or professional, but also by level in the organization and by functional department. Employees higher in the organization are increasingly involved in activities that are less repetitive and require more complex solutions. The discretion that managers have increases as they move up the hierarchy so formalization is lowest at the highest levels of the organization.

The kind of work people are engaged in also influences the degree of formalization. Jobs in production are typically more formalized than those in sales or research. Why? Because production tends to be concerned with stable and repetitive activities. Such jobs lend themselves to standardization. In contrast, the sales department must be flexible in order to respond to changing needs of customers, and research must be flexible if it is to be innovative.

Centralization

Centralization is the degree to which decision making is concentrated at a single point in the organization. The concept includes only formal authority—that is, the rights inherent in one's position. Typically, it is said that if top management makes the organization's key decisions with little or no input from lower-level personnel, then the organization is centralized. In contrast, the more that lower-level personnel provide input or are given the discretion to make decisions, the more decentralized the organization. As we point out, an organization characterized by centralization is an inherently different structural animal from one where decision making has been pushed down to those individuals who are closest to the action.

■ BASIC ORGANIZATIONAL CONCEPTS

Both management practitioners and theorists have been concerned with developing organizational principles since before the turn of the century. For instance, Adam Smith wrote on the advantages of division of labor in his celebrated *The Wealth of Nations* in the late eighteenth century.[1] During the first half of this century, a group of management practitioners and academics postulated a set of principles to guide managers in making structural decisions. This group has come to be known as the *classical theorists* and their recommendations as the *classical principles*.

A number of decades have passed since most of these principles were originally proposed. Given the passing of that much time and all the changes that have taken place in our society, you might think these principles would be pretty worthless today. Surprisingly, they're not! For the most part, they still provide valuable insight into understanding the structure of organizations. Of course, we've also gained a great deal of knowledge over the years about the limitations of these principles. In this section, we discuss the five basic classical principles. We also present an updated analysis of how each has had to be modified to reflect the increasing complexity and changing nature of today's organizational activities.

Division of Labor

The Classical View. *Division of labor* means that, rather than an entire job being done by one individual, it is broken down into a number of steps, each step being completed by a separate individual. In essence, individuals specialize in doing part of an activity rather than the entire activity. Assembly-line production, in which each worker does the same standardized task over and over again, is an example of division of labor.

---

[1] Adam Smith, *An Inquiry into the Nature and Causes of the Wealth of Nations* (New York: Modern Library, 1937). Originally published in 1776.

The classical theorists were strong proponents of division of labor. They saw it as a way to significantly increase the economic efficiencies of organizations.

Division of labor makes efficient use of the diversity of skills that workers hold. In most organizations, some tasks require highly developed skills; others can be performed by the untrained. If all workers were engaged in each step of, say, an organization's manufacturing process, all must have the skills necessary to perform both the most demanding and the least demanding jobs. The result would be that, except when performing the most skilled or highly sophisticated tasks, employees would be working below their skill levels. And since skilled workers are paid more than unskilled workers and their wages tend to reflect their highest level of skill, it represents an inefficient usage of organizational resources to pay highly skilled workers to do easy tasks.

A number of other efficiencies are achieved through division of labor. One's skills at performing a task successfully increase through repetition. Less time is spent in changing tasks, in putting away one's tools and equipment from a prior step in the work process, and in getting ready for another. Equally important, training for specialization is more efficient from the organization's perspective. It is easier and less costly to find and train workers to do specific and repetitive tasks. This is especially true of highly sophisticated and complex operations. For example, could Lear produce one Lear Jet a year if one person had to build the entire plane alone? Finally, division of labor increases efficiency and productivity by encouraging the creation of special inventions and machinery.

The Contemporary View. The classical writers viewed division of labor as an unending source of increased productivity. At the turn of the century and earlier, this generalization was undoubtedly accurate. Because specialization was not widely practiced, its introduction almost always generated higher productivity. But a good thing can be carried too far. There is a point when the human diseconomies from division of labor—which surface as boredom, fatigue, stress, low productivity, poor quality, increased absenteeism, and high turnover—exceed the economic advantages (see Exhibit 12–1).

By the 1960s, it became clear that that point had been reached in a number of jobs. In such cases, productivity could be increased by enlarging, rather than narrowing, the scope of job activities. If you'll remember Chapter 5, where we discussed the motivational properties of jobs, we dealt with job characteristics and design. We demonstrated that when employees are given a variety of activities to do, allowed to do a whole and complete piece of work, and put together into teams, they often achieve higher productivity and satisfaction. But notice that increasing skill variety, task identity, and the like runs counter to the division of labor concept.

So where are we today? In spite of all the recent attention focused on expanding and enriching jobs, it is probably accurate to conclude that the division of labor concept is still alive and well in most organizations today. But it is not seen as a panacea nor as an unending source of increased produc-

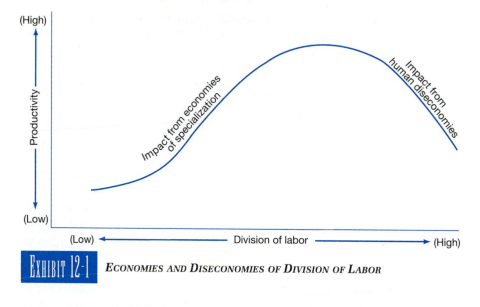

EXHIBIT 12-1 *ECONOMIES AND DISECONOMIES OF DIVISION OF LABOR*

tivity. Rather, managers recognize the economies it provides in certain types of jobs and also the problems it creates when it is carried too far.

Unity of Command

The Classical View. Classical theorists professing the *unity of command* principle argued that a subordinate should have one and only one superior to whom he or she is directly responsible. No person should report to two or more bosses. Otherwise, a subordinate might have to cope with conflicting demands or priorities from several superiors. In those rare instances when the unity of command principle had to be violated, the classical viewpoint always explicitly designated that there be a clear separation of activities and a supervisor responsible for each.

The Contemporary View. The unity of command concept was logical when organizations were comparatively simple in nature. Under most circumstances, it is still sound advice. Most organizations today closely adhere to this principle. Yet there are instances—and we introduce them in the next chapter—when strict adherence to the unity of command creates a degree of inflexibility that hinders an organization's performance.

Authority and Responsibility

The Classical View. *Authority* refers to the rights inherent in a managerial position to give orders and expect the orders to be obeyed. It was a major tenet of the classical theorists, in that authority was viewed as the glue which held the organization together. It was to be delegated downward to subordinate managers, giving them both certain rights and certain prescribed limits within which they could operate.

Each management position has specific inherent rights that incumbents acquire from the position's rank or title. Authority relates, therefore, to one's position within an organization and ignores the personal characteristics of the individual manager. It has nothing directly to do with the individual. The expression "The king is dead; long live the king" illustrates the concept. Whoever is king acquires the rights inherent in the king's position. When a position of authority is vacated, the person who has left the position no longer has any authority. The authority remains with the position and the new incumbent.

When we delegate authority, the classicists argued, we must allocate commensurate *responsibility*. That is, when one is given *rights*, one also assumes a corresponding *obligation* to perform. To allocate authority without responsibility creates opportunities for abuse, and no one should be held responsible for what he or she has no authority over.

Classical theorists recognized the importance of equating authority and responsibility. Additionally, they stated that responsibility cannot be delegated. They supported this contention by noting that the delegator was held responsible for the actions of his or her delegates. But how it is possible to have equal authority and responsibility, if responsibility cannot be delegated?

The classicists' answer was to recognize two forms of responsibility: *operating* responsibility and *ultimate* responsibility. Managers pass on operating responsibility, which in turn may be passed on further. But there is an aspect of responsibility—its ultimate component—that must be retained. A manager is ultimately responsible for the actions of his or her subordinates to whom the operating responsibility has been passed. Therefore, managers should delegate operating responsibility equal to the delegated authority; however, ultimate responsibility can never be delegated.

The classical theorists also distinguished between two forms of authority relations: line authority and staff authority. *Line authority* is the authority that entitles a manager to direct the work of a subordinate. It is the superior-subordinate authority relationship that extends from the top of the organization to the lowest echelon, following what is called the *chain of command*. As a link in the chain of command, a manager with line authority has the right to direct the work of subordinates and to make certain decisions without consulting others. Of course, in the chain of command, every manager is also subject to the direction of his or her superior.

Sometimes the term *line* is used to differentiate *line* managers from *staff* managers. In this context, line emphasizes those managers whose organizational function contributes directly to the achievement of the organizational objectives. In a manufacturing firm, line managers are typically in the production function, whereas executives in personnel or accounting are considered staff managers. But whether a manager's function is classified as line or staff depends on the organization's objectives. At a firm like Kelly Services, which is a temporary personnel placement organization, personnel interviewers have a line function. Similarly, at the accounting firm of Price Waterhouse, accounting is a line function.

The preceding definitions are not contradictory but, rather, represent two ways of looking at the term *line*. Every manager has line authority over his or her subordinates, but not every manager is in a line function or position. This latter determination depends on whether or not the function directly contributes to the organization's objectives.

As organizations get larger and more complex, line managers find they do not have the time, expertise, or resources to get their jobs done effectively. In response, they create *staff authority* functions to support, assist, advise, and in general reduce some of their informational burdens. The hospital administrator can't effectively handle all the purchasing of supplies the hospital needs, so she creates a purchasing department. The purchasing department is a staff department. Of course, the head of the purchasing department has line authority over her subordinate purchasing agents. The hospital administrator may also find she is overburdened and needs an assistant. In creating the position of assistant to the hospital administrator, she has created a staff position.

Exhibit 12–2 illustrates line and staff authority.

The Contemporary View. The classical theorists were enamored with authority. They naively assumed that the rights inherent in one's formal position in an organization were the sole source of influence. They believed managers were all-powerful.

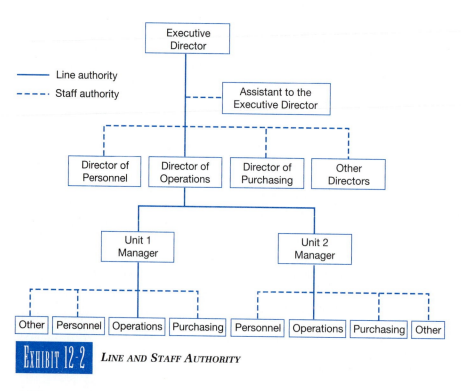

EXHIBIT 12-2 *LINE AND STAFF AUTHORITY*

This may have been true 50 or more years ago. Organizations were simpler. Staff was less important. Managers were only minimally dependent on technical specialists. Under such conditions, influence is the same as authority; and the higher a manager's position in the organization, the more influence he or she had. But, as we described in Chapter 10, those conditions no longer hold. Researchers and practitioners of management now recognize that you don't have to be a manager to have power, nor is power perfectly correlated to one's level in the organization. Authority is an important concept in organizations, but an exclusive focus on it produces a narrow and unrealistic view of influence in organizations. Today we recognize that authority is but one element in the larger concept of power.

Moreover, organizations today have increasingly turned to participation, teams, and other devices to downplay authoritative superior-subordinate relationships. Managers are increasingly viewing their jobs as liberating and enabling their employees rather than directly supervising them.

Span of Control

The Classical View. How many subordinates can a manager efficiently and effectively direct? This question of *span of control* received a great deal of attention from the classicists. While there is no consensus on a specific number, the classical theorists favored small spans—typically no more than six—in order to maintain close control. Several, however, did acknowledge level in the organization as a contingency variable. They argued that as a manager rises in an organization, he or she has to deal with a greater number of ill-structured problems, so top executives need a smaller span than middle managers, and middle managers require a smaller span than supervisors.

The span of control concept was important to the classical theorists because, to a large degree, it determines the number of levels and managers an organization has. All things being equal, the wider or larger the span, the more efficient the organization. An example can illustrate the validity of this statement.

Assume we have two organizations, both of which have approximately 4,100 operative-level employees. As Exhibit 12–3 illustrates, if one has a uniform span of four and the other a span of eight, the wider span would have two fewer levels and approximately 800 fewer managers. If the average manager made $40,000 a year, the wider span would save $32 million a year in management salaries! Obviously, wider spans are more *efficient* in terms of cost. However, at some point wider spans reduce *effectiveness*.

The Contemporary View. A few years back, management guru Tom Peters correctly predicted that Wal-Mart would pass Sears, Roebuck to become the number one retailer in the United States: "Sears doesn't have a chance!" he said. "A twelve-layer company can't compete with a three-layer company."[2]

---

[2] Tom Peters quoted in J. Braham, "Money Talks," *Industry Week* (April 17, 1989), p. 23.

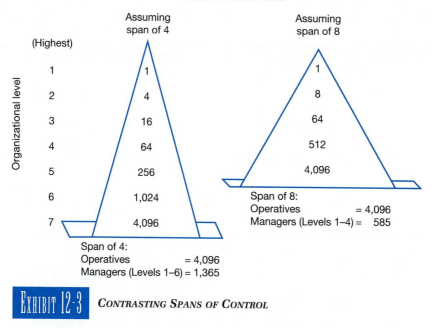

Members at each level

Span of 4:
Operatives = 4,096
Managers (Levels 1–6) = 1,365

Span of 8:
Operatives = 4,096
Managers (Levels 1–4) = 585

EXHIBIT 12-3   *CONTRASTING SPANS OF CONTROL*

Peters may have exaggerated the point a bit, but it clearly reflects the fact that the pendulum has swung in recent years toward creating flat structures with wide spans of control.

More and more organizations today are increasing their spans of control. For example, the span for managers at companies such as General Electric and Reynolds Metals has expanded to ten or twelve subordinates—twice the number of a dozen years ago. The span of control is increasingly being determined by looking at contingency variables. For instance, it's obvious that the more training and experience subordinates have, the less direct supervision they need. This is fully consistent with the research findings on the path-goal theory of leadership presented in Chapter 9. So managers who have well-trained and experienced employees can function with a wider span. Other contingency variables that will determine the appropriate span include similarity of subordinate tasks, the complexity of those tasks, the physical proximity of subordinates, the degree to which standardized procedures are in place, and the preferred style of the manager.

Departmentalization

The Classical View. The classical theorists argued that activities in an organization should be specialized and grouped into departments. Division of labor creates specialists who need coordination. This coordination is facilitated by putting specialists together in departments under the direction of a manager.

Creation of these departments is typically based on the work functions being performed, the product or service being offered, the target customer or client, the geographic territory being covered, or the process being used to turn inputs into outputs. No single method of departmentalization was advocated by the classical theorists. The method or methods used should reflect the grouping that would best contribute to the attainment of the organization's objectives and the goals of individual units.

One of the most popular ways to group activities is by functions performed—*functional departmentalization.* A manufacturing manager might organize his or her plant by separating engineering, accounting, manufacturing, personnel, and purchasing specialists into common departments. Of course, departmentalization by function can be used in all types of organizations. Only the functions change to reflect the organization's objectives and activities. A hospital might have departments devoted to research, patient care, accounting, and so forth. A professional football franchise might have departments entitled Player Personnel, Ticket Sales, and Travel and Accommodations. The major advantage to this type of grouping is obtaining efficiencies from putting like specialists together. Functional departmentalization seeks to achieve economies of scale by placing people with common skills and orientations into common units.

Sun Petroleum Products uses *product departmentalization.* Each major product area in the corporation is placed under the authority of a vice president who is a specialist in, and responsible for, everything having to do with his or her product line. In contrast to functional departmentalization, manufacturing and other major activities are divided up to give the product managers considerable autonomy and control. The major advantage to this type of grouping is that it provides increased accountability for product performance.

If an organization's activities are service rather than product related, each service would be autonomously grouped. For instance, an accounting firm would have departments for tax, management consulting, auditing, and the like. Each would offer a common array of services under the direction of a product or service manager.

The particular type of customer the organization seeks to reach can also be used to group employees. The sales activities in an office supply firm, for instance, can be broken down into three departments to service retail, wholesale, and government customers. A large law office can segment its staff on the basis of whether they service corporate or individual clients. The assumption underlying *customer departmentalization* is that customers in each department have a common set of problems and needs that can best be met by having specialists for each.

Another way to departmentalize is on the basis of geography or territory—*geographic departmentalization.* The sales function may have western, southern, midwestern, and eastern regions. A large school district may have six high schools to provide for each of the major geographical territories within the district. If an organization's customers are scattered over a large geographic area, then this form of departmentalization can be valuable.

Reynolds Metals uses *process departmentalization* in one of its aluminum plants. Each department specializes in one specific phase in the production of aluminum tubing. The metal is cast in huge furnaces; sent to the press department, where it is extruded into aluminum pipe; transferred to the tube mill, where it is stretched into various sizes and shapes of tubing; moved to the finishing department, where it is cut and cleaned; and finally arrives in the inspect, pack, and ship department. Since each process requires different skills, this method offers a basis for the homogeneous categorizing of activities.

Process departmentalization can be used for processing customers as well as products. If you have ever been to a state motor vehicle office to get a driver's license, you probably went through several departments before receiving your license. In one state, applicants must go through three steps, each handled by a separate department: (1) validation, by motor vehicles division; (2) processing, by the licensing department; and (3) payment collection, by the treasury department.

The Contemporary View. Most large organizations continue to use most or all of the departmental groupings suggested by the classical theorists. A major electronics firm, for instance, organizes each of its divisions along functional lines and its manufacturing units around processes; departmentalizes sales around four geographic regions; and divides each sales region into three customer groupings. But two recent trends need to be mentioned. First, customer departmentalization has become increasingly emphasized. Second, rigid departmentalization is being complemented by the use of teams that cross over traditional departmental lines.

Today's competitive environment has refocused management's attention on its customers. In order to better monitor the needs of customers and to be able to respond to changes in those needs, many organizations have given greater emphasis to customer departmentalization. Xerox, for example, has eliminated its corporate marketing staff and placed marketing specialists out in the field. This allows the company to better understand who their customers are and to respond faster to their requirements.

As discussed previously in this book, you see a great deal more use of teams today as a device for accomplishing organizational objectives. As tasks have become more complex and more diverse skills are needed to accomplish them, management has introduced the use of teams and task forces. For example, a large part of Chrysler Corporation's success in the 1990s is due to revamping its design process around teams that cross the company's traditional departmental lines. The LH team—which encompasses the Intrepid-Vision-Concorde nameplates—brought together people from engineering, manufacturing, sales, marketing, and other departments to create the first all-new sedan out of Chrysler in 11 years. The LH cars have been called "world class" by car magazines and are selling briskly in dealer showrooms.

■ STRUCTURAL VARIABLES
AND ORGANIZATIONAL BEHAVIOR

We opened this chapter by implying that an organization's structure can have profound effects on its members. In this section we want to directly assess just what those effects might be. Let's look again at each of the five basic organizational concepts we've just reviewed, but this time consider their implications on organizational behavior.

Division of Labor

Generalizing across the population, the evidence indicates that division of labor contributes to higher employee productivity but at the price of reduced job satisfaction. However, this generalization ignores individual differences.

As we noted previously, division of labor is not an unending source of higher productivity. Problems start to surface, and productivity begins to suffer, when the human diseconomies of doing repetitive and narrow tasks overtake the economies of specialization. As the work force has become more highly educated and desirous of jobs that are intrinsically rewarding, the point where productivity begins to decline seems to be reached more quickly than in decades past.

While more people today are undoubtedly turned off by overly specialized jobs than were their parents or grandparents, it would be naïve to ignore the reality that there is still a segment of the work force that prefers the routine and repetitiveness of highly specialized jobs. Some individuals want work that makes minimal intellectual demands and provides the security of routine. For these people, high division of labor is a source of job satisfaction. The empirical question, of course, is whether this represents 2 percent of the work force or 52 percent.

Given that there is some self-selection operating in the choice of careers, we might conclude that negative behavioral outcomes from high division of labor are most likely to surface in professional jobs occupied by individuals with high needs for personal growth and diversity.

Unity of Command

There is little evidence to indicate that any significant segment of the work force actually *prefers* jobs where they must live under the rule of multiple bosses. It's hard—sometimes impossible—to serve two masters. The exception is when those bosses coordinate their actions so as not to place unrealistic or conflicting demands on their mutual subordinates.

From the worker's perspective, organizations that closely apply the unity of command concept reduce ambiguity and hence lessen employee stress. But not without a price! The clarity and predictability that the unity of command concept provides also tend to contribute toward making organizations hierarchically obsessed. Everything has to go through channels. Communication becomes highly formalized. The result is that employees can become frustrated from a feeling of being boxed in.

Combine strict adherence to the unity of command with high division of labor and you have the probable explanation for some of your worst personal experiences in dealing with large corporations or government agencies. For example, have you ever been frustrated when trying to return merchandise to a big department store or in seeking clarification on a tax matter with the Internal Revenue Service? Well, the frustration works both ways. Organizations that divide jobs up into narrow tasks and require employees to closely follow the unity of command create an impersonal climate for their employees. Just as this can frustrate you as a customer or client, it can also frustrate those people who have to work in such places.

Authority and Responsibility

Authority provides employees with clarity and minimizes ambiguity because people know whose directives they are expected to follow.

While the classical theorists may have viewed authority as the glue that held organizations together, an overreliance by managers on their formal authority is likely to cause problems in organizations today. The might makes right thesis was effective, for the most part, when people in organizations had minimal levels of education and supervisors could do their subordinates' jobs as well or better than the subordinates could. Nowadays, as jobs have become more technical and specialized, those in authority often don't know exactly what their people do or how they do it. As a result, they are more dependent on their employees. An overreliance on formal authority, in such situations, is likely to alienate employees.

Competence and respect are not necessarily perfectly correlated with authority. When managers rely on authority rather than on knowledge, persuasive skills, or other bases of power, they can lose credibility among their followers. Managers who hide behind their formal rights are likely to have less productive and less satisfied employees than those who develop additional sources of power.

Span of Control

A review of the research indicates that it is probably safe to say there is no evidence to support a relationship between span of control and employee performance. While it is intuitively attractive to argue that large spans might lead to higher employee performance because they provide more distant supervision and more opportunity for personal initiative, the research fails to support this notion. At this point it is impossible to state that any particular span of control is best for producing high performance or high satisfaction among subordinates. The reason is probably individual differences. That is, some people like to be left alone, while others prefer the security of a boss who is quickly available at all times. Consistent with several of the contingency theories of leadership, we would expect factors such as employees' experiences and abilities and the degree of structure in their tasks to explain when wide or narrow spans of control are likely to contribute to their performance and job satisfaction. However, there is evidence indicating that a *manager's* job satisfaction increases as the number of subordinates he or she supervises increases.

Departmentalization

Organizations departmentalize in order to increase efficiency and effectiveness. But what effect does it have on the people in the organization?

From an employee's perspective, putting together people who share similar interests, skills, concerns for a product, or the like facilitates *intra*departmental communication. For instance, in functional departmentalization, marketing people get to work closely with other marketing people and design engineers get to do the same. In product departmentalization, all the members of a department can put their individual efforts into developing, making, and selling a common product and can experience the common feeling of accomplishment when the product succeeds.

As with all the other structural variables we've discussed, there is a downside to departmentalization. It develops a narrow perspective among its department members. In some cases, especially in the functional and process varieties, jobs can become repetitious and boring. Additionally, rigid departmentalization tends to create barriers to effective *inter*departmental communication and to cross-fertilization of ideas. These barriers, then, can contribute to reducing employee productivity and satisfaction.

■ ARE ORGANIZATIONAL STRUCTURES REAL OR IN PEOPLE'S MINDS?

Complexity, formalization, and centralization are objective structural components that can be measured by organizational researchers. Every organization can be evaluated on the degree to which it is high or low in all three. But employees don't objectively measure these components. They observe things around them in an unscientific fashion and then form their own implicit models of what the organization's structure is like. How many different people did they have to interview with before they were offered their jobs? How many people work in their departments and buildings? How visible is the organization's policy manual, if one exists? Is everyone given a copy? If not, is one readily available? Is it referred to frequently? How are the organization and its top management described in newspapers and periodicals? Answers to questions such as these, when combined with an employee's past experiences and comments made by peers, lead members to form an overall subjective image of what their organization's structure is like. This image, though, may in no way resemble the organization's actual objective structural characteristics.

The importance of implicit models of organization structure should not be overlooked. As we noted in Chapter 3, people respond to their perceptions rather than to objective reality. The research, for instance, on the relationship between many structural variables and subsequent levels of performance or job satisfaction are inconsistent. Some of this is explained as being attributable to individual differences. Some employees, for instance, prefer narrowly defined and routine jobs; others abhor such characteristics. Additionally, however, a contributing cause to these inconsistent findings may be diverse perceptions of the objective characteristics. Researchers have focused on actual levels of the various structural components, but these may be irrelevant if people interpret similar components differently. The bottom line, therefore, is to understand how employees interpret their organization's structure. That should prove a more meaningful predictor of their behavior than the objective characteristics themselves.

■ IMPLICATIONS FOR MANAGERS

This chapters has demonstrated that, in addition to individual differences and group factors, the structural relationships in which people work have an important bearing on employee attitudes and behavior.

What is the basis for the argument that structure has an impact on both attitudes and behavior? To the degree that an organization's structure reduces ambiguity for employees and clarifies such concerns as "What am I supposed to do?" "How am I supposed to do it?" "Who do I report to?" and "Who do I go to if I have a problem?", it shapes their attitudes and facilitates and motivates them to higher levels of performance.

Of course, structure also constrains employees to the extent that it limits and controls what they do. For example, organizations structured around high levels of formalization and division of labor, strict adherence to the unity of command, limited delegation of authority, and narrow spans of control give employees little autonomy. Controls in such organizations are tight and behavior will tend to vary within a narrow range. In contrast, organizations that are structured around limited division of labor, low formalization, wide spans of control, and the like provide employees greater freedom and, thus, will be characterized by greater behavioral diversity. As we pointed out previously, the effect of these structural variables on employee performance and satisfaction will be substantially a function of an employee's preferences and how he or she cognitively interprets the actual structure.

𝒮UGGESTIONS FOR FURTHER READING

BENNETT, AMANDA, *The Death of the Organization Man* (New York: William Morrow, 1990).

BOYETT, JOSEPH H., AND HENRY P. CONN, *Workplace 2000: The Revolution Reshaping American Business* (New York: Dutton, 1991).

CHANDLER, ALFRED D., JR., "Origins of the Organization Chart," *Harvard Business Review*, March-April 1989, pp. 81–87.

DAFT, RICHARD L., *Organization Theory and Design*, 4th ed. (St. Paul, MN: West, 1992).

HUBER, GEORGE P., C. CHET MILLER, AND WILLIAM H. GLICK, "Developing More Encompassing Theories about Organizations: The Centralization-Effectiveness Relationship as an Example," *Organization Science*, February 1990, pp. 11–40.

JAQUES, ELIOT, "In Praise of Hierarchy," *Harvard Business Review*, January-February 1990, pp. 127–33.

ROBBINS, STEPHEN P., *Organization Theory: Structure, Design, and Applications*, 3rd ed. (Englewood Cliffs, NJ: Prentice Hall, 1990).

ROBEY, DANIEL, *Designing Organizations*, 3rd ed. (Homewood, IL: Richard D. Irwin, 1991).

CHAPTER 13

ORGANIZATION DESIGN

After reading this chapter, you should be able to:

1. Differentiate between mechanistic and organic structures
2. List the factors that favor different organization structures
3. Explain how these factors affect an organization's structure
4. Describe the simple structure
5. Summarize the strengths and weaknesses of the matrix structure
6. Explain why organizations would use the network structure

W. L. Gore & Associates is a company with sales of nearly $700 million a year. The firm is best known for producing the highly successful Gore-Tex fabric. Impervious to sunlight, heat, cold, or water, the fiber is used in high-quality tents, sleeping bags, gloves, ski clothes, boots, and other outdoor products. But the most fascinating fact about this company is that it employs 5,300 people but has *no formal hierarchy or structure*. There are no titles, no bosses, no chains of command. Everyone is an "associate," with equal authority. Instead of bosses, "leaders" head teams in plants and staff departments. But these leaders can't give orders and must share the power to hire, discipline, or fire associates with peer committees and personnel staffers. To keep this hierarchy-free organization running smoothly, plants are limited to 200 people. The result is 41 small plants operating in six different countries. While this family-held company doesn't reveal profits, it does acknowledge that it ranks in the top 5 percent of major companies in return on assets and equity.

Contrast W. L. Gore & Associates with the typical firm that employs 5,000 or more people. As described in the previous chapter, its workers probably perform specialized activities in departments. Departments will have supervisors who report to middle managers who, in turn, report to top-level managers. And this pyramid-shaped hierarchy is justified as necessary to achieve efficiency, to establish clear lines of responsibility, and to maintain control. Yet, as W. L. Gore & Associates illustrates, there is more than one way to structure a successful organization. Moreover, the different structural designs that organizations use do not emerge at random. They are chosen by management for certain reasons. In this chapter, we build on concepts introduced in Chapter 12. More specifically, we review the factors that influence management's choice of an organization design and present a number of organization design options.

■ MECHANISTIC VERSUS ORGANIC STRUCTURES

Before we begin reviewing the factors that influence management's choice of an organization design, we need to introduce a simple designation device for generalizing about organization structures.

Management can mix and match the three structural components of complexity, formalization, and centralization in many ways. However, an organization's overall structure generally falls into one of two designs.[1] One is the *mechanistic structure*, which is characterized by high complexity (especially a great deal of horizontal differentiation), high formalization, a limited information network (mostly downward communication), and little participation by low-level members in decision making. The mechanistic structure is synonymous with the rigid pyramid-shaped organization. At the other extreme is the *organic structure*. It is low in complexity and formalization, it possesses a comprehensive information network (utilizing lateral and upward communication as well as downward), and it involves high participation in decision making. W. L. Gore & Associates has many of the characteristics associated with the organic structure.

As Exhibit 13–1 depicts, mechanistic structures are rigid, relying on authority and a well-defined hierarchy to facilitate coordination. The organic structure, on the other hand, is flexible and adaptive. Coordination is achieved through constant communication and adjustment.

■ WHY DO STRUCTURES DIFFER?

Why are some organizations structured along more mechanistic lines while others follow organic characteristics? What are the forces that influence the form that is chosen? In the following pages, we present the major forces that have been identified as causes or determinants of an organization's structure.

---

1 Tom Burns and G. M. Stalker, *The Management of Innovation* (London: Tavistock, 1961).

Mechanistic
structure

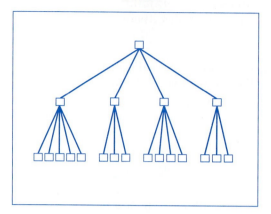

Organic
structure

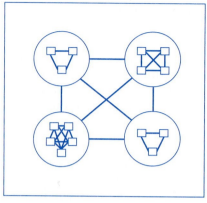

- High horizontal differentiation
- Rigid hierarchical relationships
- Fixed duties
- High formalization
- Formalized communication channels
- Centralized decision authority

- Low horizontal differentiation
- Collaboration (both vertical and horizontal)
- Adaptable duties
- Low formalization
- Informal communication
- Decentralized decision authority

 MECHANISTIC VERSUS ORGANIC STRUCTURES

Strategy

An organization's structure is a means to help management achieve its objectives. Since objectives are derived from the organization's overall strategy, it is only logical that strategy and structure should be closely linked. More specifically, structure should follow strategy. If management makes a significant change in its organization's strategy, the structure will need to be modified to accommodate and support this change.

Chandler's Strategy-Structure Thesis. The classic research supporting this strategy-structure relationship was a study of close to one hundred large U.S. companies conducted by Alfred Chandler and published in the early 1960s.[2] Tracing the development of these organizations over a period of 50 years, and compiling extensive case histories of companies such as DuPont, General Motors, Standard Oil of New Jersey, and Sears, Roebuck, Chandler concluded that changes in corporate strategy precede and lead to changes in an organization's structure. Chandler found that organizations usually begin with a single product or line. They do only one thing, like manufacturing, sales, or warehousing. The simplicity of the strategy requires only a simple, or loose, form of structure to execute it. Decisions can be centralized in the hands of a single senior manager, while complexity and formalization will be low.

---

[2] Alfred D. Chandler, Jr., *Strategy and Structure: Chapters in the History of the Industrial Enterprise* (Cambridge, MA: MIT Press, 1962).

As organizations grow, their strategies become more ambitious and elaborated. From the single product line, companies often expand their activities within their industry. This vertical integration strategy makes for increased interdependence between organizational units and creates the need for a more complex coordination device. This is achieved by redesigning the structure to form specialized units based on functions performed.

Finally, if growth proceeds further into product diversification, structure needs to be adjusted again to gain efficiency. A product diversification strategy demands a structural form that allows for the efficient allocation of resources, accountability for performance, and coordination between units. This can be achieved best by creating many independent divisions, each responsible for a specified product line.

In summary, Chandler's thesis argued that as strategies move from single product through vertical integration to product diversification, management will need to develop more elaborate structures to maintain effectiveness. That is, they will begin with an organic structure and, over time, move to a more mechanistic structure.

Contemporary Research on the Strategy-Structure Thesis. More recent research confirms the strategy-structure thesis, but the notion of strategy has been rethought from Chandler's original framework. Most strategy frameworks now focus on three strategy dimensions—innovation, cost minimization, and imitation—and the structural design that works best with each.

To what degree does an organization introduce major new products or services? An *innovation strategy* does not mean a strategy merely for simple or cosmetic changes from previous offerings but rather one for meaningful and unique innovations. Obviously, not all firms pursue innovation. This strategy may appropriately characterize 3M Company, but it certainly is not a strategy pursued by *Reader's Digest*.

An organization that is pursuing a *cost-minimization strategy* tightly controls costs, refrains from incurring unnecessary innovation or marketing expenses, and cuts prices in selling a basic product. This would describe the strategy pursued by Wal-Mart or the sellers of generic grocery products.

Organizations following an *imitation strategy* try to capitalize on the best of both of the previous strategies. They seek to minimize risk and maximize opportunity for profit. Their strategy is to move into new products or new markets only after viability has been proven by innovators. They take the successful ideas of innovators and copy them. Manufacturers of mass-marketed fashion goods that are copies of designer styles follow the imitation strategy. This label also probably characterizes such well-known firms as IBM and Caterpillar. They essentially follow their smaller and more innovative competitors with superior products, but only after their competitors have demonstrated that the market is there.

Exhibit 13–2 describes the structural option that best matches each strategy. Innovators need the flexibility of the organic structure, while cost minimizers seek the efficiency and stability of the mechanistic structure. Imitators

Strategy	Structural Option
Innovation	Organic. A loose structure, low division of labor, low formalization, decentralized
Cost minimization	Mechanistic. Tight control, extensive division of labor, high formalization, high centralization
Imitation	Mechanistic and organic. Mix of loose with tight properties. Tight controls over current activities and looser controls for new undertakings

combine the two structures. They use a mechanistic structure in order to maintain tight controls and low costs in their current activities while at the same time they create organic subunits in which to pursue new undertakings.

Organization Size

A quick glance at the organizations we deal with regularly in our lives would lead most of us to conclude that *size* would have some bearing on an organization's structure. The more than 800,000 employees of the U.S. Postal Service, for example, do not neatly fit into one building, or into several departments supervised by a couple of managers. It's pretty hard to envision 800,000 people being organized in any manner other than one that contains a great deal of horizontal, vertical, and spatial differentiation, uses a large number of procedures and regulations to ensure uniform practices, and follows a high degree of decentralized decision making. On the other hand, a local messenger service that employs ten people and generates less than $300,000 a year in service fees is not likely to need decentralized decision making or formalized procedures and regulations.

A little more thought suggests that the same conclusion—size influences structure—can be arrived at through a more sophisticated reasoning process. As an organization hires more operative employees, it will attempt to take advantage of the economic benefits of specialization. The result will be increased horizontal differentiation. Grouping like functions together will facilitate intragroup efficiencies, but will cause intergroup relations to suffer as each performs its different activities. Management, therefore, will need to increase vertical differentiation to coordinate the horizontally differentiated units. This expansion in size is also likely to result in spatial differentiation. All of this increase in complexity will reduce top management's ability to directly supervise the activities within the organization. The control achieved through direct surveillance, therefore, will be replaced by the implementation of formal rules and regulations. This increase in formalization may also be accompanied by still greater vertical differentiation as management creates new units to coordinate the expanding and diverse activities of organizational members. Finally, with top management further removed from the operating level, it becomes difficult for senior executives to make rapid and informative decisions. The solution is to substitute decentralized decision making for centralization. Following this reasoning, we see changes in size leading to major structural changes.

But does it actually happen this way? Does structure change directly as a result in a change in the total number of employees? A review of the evidence indicates that size has a significant influence on some but not all elements of structure.

Size appears to have a decreasing rate of impact on complexity. That is, increases in organization size are accompanied by initially rapid and subsequently more gradual increases in differentiation. The biggest effect, however, is on vertical differentiation. As organizations increase their number of employees, more levels are added, but at a decreasing rate.

The evidence linking size and formalization is quite strong. There is a logical connection between the two. Management seeks to control the behavior of its employees. This can be achieved by direct surveillance or by the use of formalized regulations. While not perfect substitutes for each other, as one increases the need for the other should decrease. Because surveillance costs should increase very rapidly as an organization expands in size, it seems reasonable to expect that it would be less expensive for management to substitute formalization for direct surveillance as size increases.

There is also a strong inverse relationship between size and centralization. In small organizations, it's possible for management to exercise control by keeping decisions centralized. As size increases, management is physically unable to maintain control in this manner and, therefore, is forced to decentralize.

Technology

The term *technology* refers to how an organization transfers its inputs to outputs. Every organization has at least one technology for converting financial, human, and physical resources into products or services. The Ford Motor Company, for instance, predominantly uses an assembly-line process to make its products. On the other hand, colleges may use a number of instruction technologies—the ever-popular formal lecture method, the case analysis method, the experiential exercise method, the programmed learning method, and so forth.

The central theme in this section is that organization structures adapt to their technology. That is, the technology is a major determinant of an organization's structure.

Joan Woodward. The initial interest in technology as a determinant of structure can be traced to the work of Joan Woodward.[3] She studied nearly one hundred small manufacturing firms in the south of England to determine the extent to which classical principles such as unity of command and span of control were related to firm success. She was unable to derive any consistent

---

[3] Joan Woodward, *Industrial Organization: Theory and Practice* (London: Oxford University Press, 1965).

pattern from her data until she segmented her firms into three categories based on the size of their production runs. The three categories, representing three distinct technologies, had increasing levels of complexity and sophistication. The first category, *unit production*, was comprised of unit or small-batch producers that manufactured such custom products as tailormade suits and turbines for hydroelectric dams. The second category, *mass production*, included large-batch or mass-production manufacturers that made items like refrigerators and automobiles. The third and most complex group, *process production*, included continuous-process producers like oil and chemical refiners.

Woodward found that (1) distinct relationships existed between these technology classifications and the subsequent structure of the firms, and (2) the effectiveness of the organizations was related to the "fit" between technology and structure.

For example, the degree of vertical differentiation increased with technical complexity. The median levels for firms in the unit, mass, and process categories were three, four, and six, respectively. More important, from an effectiveness standpoint, the more successful firms in each category clustered around the median for their production group. But not all the relationships were linear. As a case in point, the mass-production firms scored high in terms of overall complexity and formalization, whereas the unit and process firms rated low on these structural dimensions. Imposing rules and regulations, for instance, was impossible with the nonroutine technology of unit production and unnecessary in the highly standardized process technology.

After carefully analyzing her findings, Woodward concluded that specific structures were associated with each of the three categories and that successful firms met the requirements of their technology by adopting the proper structural arrangements. Within each category, the firms that most nearly conformed to the median figure for each structural component were the most effective. She found there was no one best way to organize a manufacturing firm. Unit and process production are most effective when matched with an organic structure; mass production is most effective when matched with a mechanistic structure. A summary of Woodward's findings is shown in Exhibit 13–3.

 EXHIBIT 13-3   *WOODWARD'S FINDINGS ON TECHNOLOGY, STRUCTURE, AND EFFECTIVENESS*

	Unit Production	Mass Production	Process Production
Structural characteristics	Low vertical differentiation	Moderate vertical differentiation	High vertical differentiation
	Low horizontal differentiation	High horizontal differentiation	Low horizontal differentiation
	Low formalization	High formalization	Low formalization
Most effective structure	Organic	Mechanistic	Organic

Charles Perrow. One of the major limitations of Woodward's technological classification scheme was that it applied only to manufacturing organizations. Since manufacturing firms represent less than half of all organizations, technology needed to be operationalized in a more generic way if the concept was to have meaning across all organizations. Charles Perrow suggested such an alternative.[4]

Perrow directed his attention to knowledge technology rather than production technology. He proposed that technology be viewed in terms of two dimensions: (1) the number of exceptions individuals encountered in their work, and (2) the type of search procedures followed to find successful methods for responding adequately to these exceptions. The first dimension he termed *task variability;* the second he called *problem analyzability*.

The exceptions in task variability are few when the job is high in routineness. Examples of jobs that normally have few exceptions in their day-to-day practice include a worker on a manufacturing assembly line or a fry cook at McDonald's. At the other end of the spectrum, if a job has a great deal of variety, it will have a large number of exceptions. This would characterize top management positions, consulting jobs, or jobs such as putting out fires on offshore oil platforms.

The second dimension, problem analyzability, assesses search procedures. The search can, at one extreme, be described as well defined. An individual can use logical and analytical reasoning in the search for a solution. If you're basically a high B student and you suddenly fail the first exam in a course, you logically analyze the problem and find a solution. Did you spend enough time studying for the exam? Did you study the right material? Was the exam fair? How did other good students do? Using this kind of logic, you can find the source of the problem and rectify it. At the other extreme are ill-defined problems. If you're an architect given an assignment to design a building to conform to standards and constraints that you've never encountered or read about before, you won't have any formal search technique to use. You will have to rely on your prior experience, judgment, and intuition to find a solution. Through guesswork and trial and error you might find an acceptable choice.

Perrow used these two dimensions, task variability and problem analyzability, to construct a two-by-two matrix, shown in Exhibit 13–4. The four cells in this matrix represent four types of technology: routine, engineering, craft, and nonroutine.

Routine technologies (cell 1) have few exceptions and have easy-to-analyze problems. The mass-production processes used to make steel and automobiles or to refine petroleum belong in this category. Engineering technologies (cell 2) have a large number of exceptions, but they can be handled in a rational and systemized manner. The construction of bridges falls in this category. Craft technologies (cell 3) deal with relatively difficult

---

[4] Charles Perrow, "A Framework for the Comparative Analysis of Organizations," *American Sociological Review* (April 1967), pp. 194–208.

Task variability

Few exceptions   Many exceptions

Well-defined	Routine 1	2 Engineering
Ill-defined	3 Craft	4 Nonroutine

Problem analyzability

PERROW'S TECHNOLOGY CLASSIFICATION

problems, but with a limited set of exceptions. Shoemaking or furniture restoring fits in this category. Finally, nonroutine technologies (cell 4) are characterized by many exceptions and by difficult-to-analyze problems. This technology describes many aerospace operations, such as Rockwell International's initial development of the space shuttle.

In summary, Perrow argued that if problems can be systematically analyzed, cells 1 and 2 are appropriate. Problems that can be handled only by intuition, guesswork, or unanalyzed experience require the technology of cells 3 or 4. Similarly, if new, unusual, or unfamiliar problems appear regularly, they would be in either cells 2 or 4. If problems are familiar, then cells 1 or 3 are appropriate. Using our mechanistic-organic classification, Perrow would suggest that cells 1 and 2 fit with mechanistic structures and cells 3 and 4 align with organic structures.

James Thompson.   Another approach to technology was proposed by James D. Thompson.[5] His technology categories, which he argued could be used to classify all organizations, are long linked, mediating, and intensive.

If tasks or operations are sequentially interdependent, Thompson called them long linked. This technology is characterized by a fixed sequence of repetitive steps, as shown in Exhibit 13–5A. That is, activity A must be performed before activity B, activity B before activity C, and so forth. Examples of *long-linked technology* include mass-production assembly lines and most school cafeterias.

Thompson identified *mediating technology* as one that links clients on both the input and output side of the organization. Banks, telephone utilities, security brokerage firms, most large retail stores, computer dating services, employment and welfare agencies, and post offices are examples. As shown in

---

5 James D. Thompson, *Organizations in Action* (New York: McGraw-Hill, 1967).

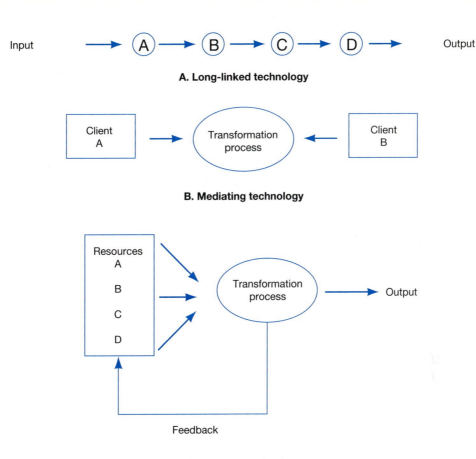

Input → (A) → (B) → (C) → (D) → Output

A. Long-linked technology

Client A → Transformation process ← Client B

B. Mediating technology

Resources A, B, C, D → Transformation process → Output

Feedback

C. Intensive technology

EXHIBIT 13-5 *THOMPSON'S TECHNOLOGY CLASSIFICATION*

Exhibit 13–5B, mediators perform an interchange function, linking units that are otherwise independent. The linking unit responds by standardizing the organization's transactions and establishing conformity in clients' behavior. Banks, for instance, bring together those who want to save (depositors) with those who want to borrow. They don't know each other, but the bank's success depends on attracting both.

Thompson's third category—*intensive technology*—represents a customized response to a diverse set of contingencies. The exact response depends on the nature of the problem and the variety of problems, which cannot be predicted accurately. (See Exhibit 13–5C). This includes technologies dominant in hospitals, universities, research labs, full-service management-consulting firms, and military combat teams.

The intensive technology is most dramatically illustrated by the general hospital. At any moment an emergency admission may require some combination of dietary, X-ray, laboratory, and housekeeping or hotel services, together with the various medical specialties, pharmaceutical services, occupational therapies, social work services, and spiritual or religious services. Which of these, and when, can be determined only from evidence about the state of the patient.[6]

Thompson was not directly concerned with demonstrating a link between his technology categories and structural options. Rather, he is most recognized for suggesting that organizations arrange themselves to protect their technology from uncertainty. He proposed that technology determines the selection of a strategy for reducing uncertainty and that specific structural arrangements can facilitate uncertainty reduction. So, for example, organizations using long-linked technology might vertically integrate to ensure the availability of inputs and the ability to dispose of its outputs.

While Thompson didn't directly address structural options, it is not difficult to make the connection. It seems logical that long-linked and mediating technologies tend to fit best with mechanistic structures, while intensive technology is best matched to the organic form.

Synthesis. If there is a common denominator among the various classification schemes it is the *degree of routineness.* By this we mean that technologies tend toward either routine or nonroutine activities. The former are characterized by automated and standardized operations. This essentially encompasses mass, process, engineering, long-linked, and mediating technologies. Nonroutine activities are customized. They include such varied operations as furniture restoring, custom shoemaking, and genetic research. Nonroutine technologies include unit, craft, and intensive.

What relationships have been found between technology and the three components in our definition of structure? Although the relationship is not overwhelmingly strong, we do find that routine tasks are associated with high complexity. Repetition essentially encourages increased horizontal and vertical differentiation, which leads to taller and more complex structures.

The technology-formalization relationship is stronger. Studies consistently show routineness to be associated with the presence of rule manuals, job descriptions, and other formalized documentation.

Finally, the technology-centralization relationship is less straightforward. It seems logical that routine technologies would be associated with a centralized structure, whereas nonroutine technologies, which rely more heavily on the knowledge of specialists, would be characterized by delegated decision authority. This position has met with some support. However, a more generalizable conclusion is that the technology-centralization relationship is moderated by the degree of formalization. Formal regulations and centralized decision making are both control mechanisms and management can

---

[6] Ibid., p. 17.

substitute them for each other. Routine technologies should be associated with centralized control if there is a minimum of rules and regulations. However, if formalization is high, routine technology can be accompanied by decentralization. So, we would predict that routine technology would lead to centralization, but only if formalization is low.

Environment

An organization's *environment* represents anything outside the organization itself. The problem of defining an organization's environment, however, is often quite difficult. "Nature has neatly packaged people into skins, animals into hides, and allowed trees to enclose themselves with bark. It is easy to see where the unit is and where the environment is. Not so for social organizations."[7] We define the environment as composed of those institutions or forces that affect the performance of the organization, but over which the organization has little control. These typically include suppliers, customers, government regulatory agencies, and the like. But keep in mind that it is not always clear who or what is included in any specific organization's relevant environment.

Why should an organization's structure be affected by its environment? Because of environmental uncertainty. Some organizations face relatively static environments—few forces in their environment are changing. There are, for example, no new competitors, no new technological breakthroughs by current competitors, or little activity by public pressure groups to influence the organization. Other organizations face very dynamic environments—rapidly changing government regulations affecting their business, new competitors, difficulties in acquiring raw materials, continually changing product preferences by customers, and so on. Static environments create significantly less uncertainty for managers than do dynamic ones. And since uncertainty is a threat to an organization's effectiveness, management will try to minimize it. One way to reduce environmental uncertainty is through adjustments in the organization's structure.

Emery and Trist. Fred Emery and Eric Trist identified four kinds of environments that an organization might confront: (1) placid-randomized, (2) placid-clustered, (3) disturbed-reactive, and (4) turbulent field.[8] Emery and Trist described each as increasingly more complex than the previous one.

1. The placid-randomized environment is relatively unchanging and therefore poses the least threat to an organization. Demands are randomly distributed, and changes take place slowly over time. Environmental uncertainty is low. Although not many organizations are fortunate enough to find themselves in a

---

[7] Jeffrey Pfeffer and Gerald R. Salancik, *The External Control of Organizations: A Resource Dependence Perspective* (New York: Harper & Row, 1978), p. 29.

[8] F. E. Emery and Eric Trist, "The Causal Texture of Organizational Environments," *Human Relations* (February 1965), pp. 21–32.

placid-randomized environment, many state workers' compensation agencies enjoy this type of environment. Their environment is relatively stable, and no single client can have a significant impact on their operation.

2. The placid-clustered environment also changes slowly, but presents clusters of threats to the organization. Thus an organization must be more aware of such an environment than it would of one in which threats occurred at random. For instance, suppliers or customers may join forces to form a powerful coalition. This would describe a public utility like Consolidated Edison. If Con Ed seeks a large rate hike, it faces a potential unified action by a mass of consumers. So organizations in a placid-clustered environment are motivated to engage in long-range, strategic planning, and to centralize their decision making.

3. The disturbed-reactive environment is more complex than the previous two. Here many competitors seek similar ends. One or more organizations may be large enough to exert influence over their own environment and over other organizations. Two or three large companies in an industry can dominate it. A couple of large firms, for instance, can exert price leadership in such industries as computer software, automobiles, and tobacco. Lotus Development and Novell cannot afford to ignore the future plans or current actions of Microsoft. Organizations facing a disturbed-reactive environment need to be able to develop a series of tactical maneuvers, calculate reactions by others to their tactics, and evolve counteractions. In other words, they need to maintain a relative degree of flexibility.

4. The turbulent-field environment is the most dynamic and has the highest degree of uncertainty. Change is ever present, and elements in the environment are increasingly interrelated. In a turbulent-field environment, the organization may be required to consistently develop new products or services in order to survive. Also, it may have to reevaluate continually its relationship to government agencies, customers, and suppliers. Two obvious examples of organizations currently facing this type of environment are manufacturers of microchips and providers of health-care services.

Although Emery and Trist offered no specific suggestions concerning which type of structure best suited each environment, organizations having the first two environments will respond with more mechanistic structures, whereas the dynamic environments will require a structure that offers the advantages of the organic form.

Lawrence and Lorsch. Paul Lawrence and Jay Lorsch, both of the Harvard Business School, went beyond Emery and Trist. They undertook a study of ten firms in three industries to test empirically the relationship between environmental differences and effective organization structures.[9]

Lawrence and Lorsch chose to do their research on firms in the plastics, food, and container industries. (These were selected because, at the time, they operated in what the researchers believed to be diverse environments.) The plastics industry was highly competitive. The life cycle of any product was historically short, and firms were characterized by considerable new product and process development. The container industry, on the other hand, was

---

[9] Paul Lawrence and J. W. Lorsch, *Organization and Environment: Managing Differentiation and Integration* (Boston: Harvard Business School, Division of Research, 1967).

quite different. There had been no significant new products in two decades. Sales growth had kept pace with population growth, but nothing more. Lawrence and Lorsch described the container firms as operating in a relatively certain environment, with no real threats to consider. The food industry was midway between the two. There was heavy innovation, but new product generation and sales growth were less than in the plastics industry and more than in the container industry.

Lawrence and Lorsch measured two dimensions of structure: what they called differentiation and integration. *Differentiation* refers to the degree to which managers of different functional departments vary in their goal and value orientations. *Integration* refers to the degree to which members of various departments achieve unity of effort.

First, they proposed that different departments within a firm face different environments. Therefore, they expected to find that the more successful firms in each industry would structure their departments to align with their specific subenvironments. That is, the same organization might have different structures across its departments. The research and development department, because it faces a turbulent environment, might use an organic structure, whereas production, if it had a stable environment, would be organized along mechanistic lines. Second, they hypothesized that the degree of differentiation within firms in the three industries was related to the environments they face, and that the more diverse the environments, the more differentiated the organization's structure. They expected the plastics firms to be the most differentiated, followed by food and container firms, in that order. Third, Lawrence and Lorsch proposed that, inside the organization, the more successful firms have achieved a higher degree of integration than the less successful firms. By that they meant that the successful firms would have devised more effective mechanisms for coordinating the various departments toward achieving the organization's overall goals.

Lawrence and Lorsch's research confirmed their expectations. Their firms did not all have uniform internal structures. It depended on whether or not the organizations faced a homogeneous environment. When they divided the firms within each industry into high, moderate, and low performers, they found that the high-performing firms had a structure that best fit their environmental demands. In the turbulent plastics industry, this meant high differentiation. In the stable container industry, this meant low differentiation. Firms in the food industry were midway in terms of differentiation. In addition, the most successful firms in all three industries had a higher degree of integration than their low-performing counterparts.

What are the implications of Lawrence and Lorsch's research? First, environments are not uniformly stable or turbulent. Organizations face multiple specific environments with different degrees of uncertainty. Second, successful organizations' departments or subunits meet the demands of their subenvironments. Because differentiation and integration represent opposing forces, the key is to appropriately match the two. An organization needs to differentiate enough to deal with the specific problems and tasks it faces; but the more differentiation, the more difficult it is to get people to integrate and work as a cohesive team toward the organization's goals. Successful organizations have more nearly solved the dilemma of providing both differentiation and integration by matching their internal subunits to the demands of the subenvironments. Finally, Lawrence and Lorsch presented evidence confirming that environment is critically important in determining the structure of successful organizations.

Synthesis. Recent research has synthesized much of the discussion on environmental uncertainty. It has been found that there are three key dimensions to any organization's environment. They are labeled capacity, volatility, and complexity.

The *capacity* of an environment refers to the degree to which it can support growth. Rich and growing environments generate excess resources, which can buffer the organization in times of relative scarcity. Abundant capacity, for example, leaves room for an organization to make mistakes, while scarce capacity does not. In 1993, firms operating in the cellular telephone business had relatively abundant environments, whereas those in the commercial airline industry faced relative scarcity.

The degree of instability in an environment is captured in the *volatility* dimension. Where there is a high degree of unpredictable change, the environment is dynamic. This makes it difficult for management to predict accurately the probabilities associated with various decision alternatives. At the other extreme is a stable environment. The accelerated changes in Eastern Europe and the demise of the Cold War had dramatic effects on the defense industry in the early 1990s. This moved the environment of major defense contractors like McDonnell-Douglas, General Dynamics, and Northrop from relatively stable to dynamic.

Finally, the environment needs to be assessed in terms of *complexity*, that is, the degree of heterogeneity and concentration among environmental elements. Simple environments are homogeneous and concentrated. This might describe the tobacco industry, since there are relatively few players. It's easy for firms in this industry to keep a close eye on the competition. In contrast, environments characterized by heterogeneity and dispersion are called complex. This is essentially the current environment in the cable television network industry. Every week there is another "new kid on the block" with whom established cable stations have to deal.

Exhibit 13–6 summarizes our definition of the environment along its three dimensions. The arrows in this figure are meant to indicate movement toward higher uncertainty. So organizations that operate in environments characterized as scarce, dynamic, and complex face the greatest degree of uncertainty. Why? Because they have little room for error, high unpredictability, and a diverse set of elements in the environment to constantly monitor.

Given this three-dimensional definition of environment, we can offer general conclusions. There is evidence that relates the degrees of environmental uncertainty to different structural arrangements. Specifically, the more

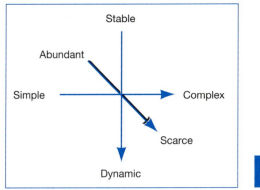

EXHIBIT 13-6   **THREE-DIMENSIONAL MODEL OF THE ENVIRONMENT**

scarce, dynamic, and complex the environment, the more organic a structure should be. The more abundant, stable, and simple the environment, the more the mechanistic structure will be preferred.

Power-Control

An increasingly popular and insightful approach to the question of what causes structure is to look to a political explanation. Strategy, size, technology, and environment—even when combined—can at best explain only 50 to 60 percent of the variability in structure. A growing body of evidence suggests that power and control can explain a good portion of the residual variance. More specifically, the *power-control* explanation states that an organization's structure is the result of a power struggle by internal constituencies who are seeking to further their interests. Like all decisions in an organization, the structural decision is not fully rational. Managers do not necessarily choose those alternatives that will maximize the organization's interest. They choose criteria and weight them so the "best choice" will meet the minimal demands of the organization, and also satisfy or enhance the interests of the decision maker. Strategy, size, technology, and environmental uncertainty act as constraints by establishing parameters and defining how much discretion is available. Almost always, within the parameters, there is a great deal of room for the decision maker to maneuver. The power-control position, therefore, argues that those in power will choose a structure that will maintain or enhance their control. Consistent with this perspective, we should expect structures to change very slowly, if at all. Significant changes would occur only as a result of a political struggle in which new power relations evolve. But this rarely occurs. Transitions in the executive suite are usually peaceful. They are evolutionary rather than revolutionary. However, major shake-ups in top management occasionally do occur. Not surprisingly, they are typically followed by major structural changes.

Predictions based on the power-control viewpoint differ from those based on the four previous approaches in that those approaches were basically contingency models: Structures change to reflect changes in strategy, size, technology, or environmental uncertainty. The power-control approach, however, is essentially noncontingent. It assumes little change within the organization's power coalition. Hence, it would propose that structures are relatively stable over time. More important, power-control advocates would predict that after taking into consideration strategy, size, technology, and environmental factors, those in power would choose a structure that would best serve their personal interests. What type of structure would that be? Obviously one that would be low in complexity, high in formalization, and centralized. These structural dimensions will most likely maximize control in the hands of senior management. A structure with these properties becomes the single "one best way" to organize. Of course, *best* in this context refers to "maintenance of control" rather than enhancement of organizational performance.

Is the power-control position an accurate description? The evidence suggests that it explains a great deal of why organizations are structured the way they are. The dominant structural forms in organizations today are essentially mechanistic. Organic structures have received a great deal of attention by academicians, but the vast majority of real organizations, especially those of moderate and large size, are mechanistic.

Applying the Contingency Factors

Under what conditions would each of the contingency factors we've introduced—strategy, organization size, technology, and environment—be the dominant determinant of an organization's structure? More specifically, when should we expect to find mechanistic structures and when should organic structures be most prevalent?

Strategy. The strategy-determines-structure thesis argues that managers change their organization's structure to align with changes in strategy. Organizations that seek innovation demand a flexible structure. Organizations that attempt to be low-cost operators must maximize efficiency, and the mechanistic structure helps achieve that. Those organizations that pursue an imitation strategy need structures that contain elements of both the mechanistic and the organic forms.

Studies generally support that strategy influences structure at the top levels of business firms. But strategy undoubtedly has less impact on the structure of subunits within the overall organization. Additionally, it is not clear how the strategy-structure relationship operates in service businesses or among not-for-profit organizations such as hospitals, educational institutions, and government agencies.

Organization Size. The larger an organization's size, in terms of the number of members it employs, the more likely it is to use the mechanistic structure. The creation of extensive rules and regulations only makes sense when there is a large number of people to be coordinated. Similarly, given the fact that a manager's ability to supervise a set of subordinates directly has some outside limit, as more people are hired to do the work, more managers will be needed to oversee these people. This creates increased complexity.

We should not, however, expect the size-structure relationship to be linear over a wide range. This is because once the organization becomes relatively large—with 1,500 to 2,000 employees or more—it will tend to have already acquired most of the properties of a mechanistic structure. So the addition of 500 employees to an organization that has only 100 employees is likely to lead to significantly increased levels of complexity and formalization. Yet adding 500 employees to an organization that already employs 10,000 is likely to have little or no impact on that organization's structure.

Technology. The evidence demonstrates that routine technologies are associated with mechanistic structures, whereas organic structures are best for dealing with the uncertainties inherent with nonroutine technologies. But we shouldn't expect technology to affect all parts of the organization equally.

The closer a department or unit within the organization is to the operating core, the more it will be affected by technology and, hence, the more technology will act to define structure. The primary activities of the organization take place at the operating core. State motor vehicle divisions, for example, process driver's license applications, distribute vehicle license plates, and monitor the ownership of vehicles within their state. Those departments within the motor vehicle division that are at the operating core—giving out driver's tests, collecting fees for plates, and so on—will be significantly affected by technology. But as units become removed from this core, technology will play a less important role. The structure of the executive offices at the motor vehicle division, for instance, are not likely to be affected much by technology. So, to continue with the motor vehicle example, the use of routine technology at the operating core should result in the units at the core being high in both complexity and formalization. As units within the division move farther away from activities at the operating core, technology will become less of a constraint on structural choices.

Environment. Will a dynamic and uncertain environment always lead to an organic structure? Not necessarily. Whether environment is a major determinant of an organization's structure depends on the degree of dependence of the organization on its environment.

A drug company like Merck operates in a highly dynamic environment—the result of a continual stream of competitors introducing new products to compete against theirs. But Merck's size, reputation, research capabilities, and marketing expertise act as potent forces to lessen the impact of this uncertain environment on Merck's performance. Merck's ability to lessen its dependence on its environment results in a structure that is much more mechanistic in design than would be expected given the uncertain environment within which it exists. In contrast, firms like Amgen and Genentech have been far less successful in managing their dependence on their environment. Environment, therefore, is a much stronger influence on Amgen and Genentech's structure than at Merck.

What About the Computer's Effect on Organization Structure?

The contingency approach to organization design has tended to underemphasize the increasing role that computers and management information systems (MIS) are playing in the design of organization structures. Computer-based management information systems are redefining what we mean by organization structure and are allowing management to make organizations more organic with almost no loss in control.

Remember that in the last chapter we defined an organization structure as made up of three components—complexity, formalization, and centralization. Certainly at least two of these components are being reshaped by computer-based information systems. Increased vertical and spatial differentiation, for instance, need no longer create increased complexity. When a senior executive can monitor what's happening on the operating floor at a plant 2,000 miles away or review the status of payments in the accounts payable department by merely pushing a few keys on his or her desktop terminal, differentiation created by multiple levels or distance no longer make communication and coordination more difficult. Similarly, the historic definition of centralization and decentralization assumed that decentralization of authority required upper-level managers to give up control. That's not true with a sophisticated computer-based information system. Decisions can be decentralized, yet those very decisions can also be closely watched by top management through the monitoring capability of its computer system.

Computer-based information systems allow managers to handle more subordinates because computer control substitutes for personal supervision. As a result, managers can effectively oversee more people and the organization will require fewer managers and, hence, there will be fewer levels in the hierarchy. The need for staff support is also reduced with a computer-based information system. Managers can tap information directly, which makes large staff-support groups redundant. Both forces—wider spans of control and reduced staff—lead to flatter organizations.

Maybe the most interesting phenomena created by sophisticated information systems is that they have allowed management to make organizations more organic without any loss in control. Management can lessen formalization and become more decentralized—thus making their organizations more organic—without giving up control. This is because an MIS substitutes computer control for rules and decision discretion. Computer technology rapidly apprises top managers of the consequences of any lower-level decision and allows them to take corrective action if the decision is not to their liking. Thus there's the appearance of decentralization without any commensurate loss of control.

■ ORGANIZATION DESIGN APPLICATIONS

Now it's time to move from the general to the specific. While up to this point we've used the terms *mechanistic* and *organic* to classify organizations, let's go beyond these generic labels to specific, real-world applications of both categories.

The Simple Structure

One of the most widely used organic designs, especially among small business firms, seems to be almost absent of structure. This is the *simple structure*. It is low in complexity, has little formalization, and has its authority centralized in a single person. The simple structure is a "flat" organization—typically one with only two or three vertical levels, with a loose body of employees, and with almost everyone reporting to the one individual in whom the decision-making authority is centralized.

The strengths of the simple structure are obvious. It's flexible, inexpensive to maintain, and accountability is clear. One of its major weaknesses is that it is really applicable only to small organizations. When confronted with increased size, the simple structure is generally inadequate. Its low formalization and high centralization result in information overload at the top. As size increases, decision making becomes slower and may eventually come to a standstill as the single executive tries to continue making all decisions.

The Functional Structure

The popular mechanistic counterpart of the simple structure is the *functional structure*. It is structural design for large organizations, essentially built around functional departmentalization. That is, it groups similar and related occupational specialties together.

Bethlehem Steel is an example of an organization that uses the functional structure. Reporting to its chief executive officer are vice presidents for operations, legal and governmental affairs, finance, marketing and sales, human resources, union relations, state and community affairs, and materials and transportation.

Consistent with our discussion of functional departmentalization in the previous chapter, the strength of the functional structure is in the advantages that accrue from specialization. Putting similar specialties together results in economies of scale, minimizes the duplication of personnel and equipment, and allows comfortable and satisfied employees to have the opportunity to talk "the same language" among their peers.

The functional structure's major weakness is that the best interests of the organization are frequently lost in the pursuit of functional goals. Members within individual functions become insulated and have little understanding of what people in other functions are doing. The diversity of interests and perspectives that exist between functions can result in continual conflict as each function tries to assert its importance.

The Divisional Structure

The *divisional structure* creates self-contained and autonomous units. Each unit or division is headed by a division manager who is responsible for performance and who holds complete strategic and operating decision-making authority. For instance, at General Motors, which uses the divisional form, there are division managers to head up groups such as Hughes Electronics, EDS operations, the truck and bus unit, and the various car divisions (Saturn, Chevrolet, Pontiac, and so on).

Typically, divisional structures are composed of functional subsets. That is, each divisional unit has its own autonomous functional structure. So it is essentially a mechanistic structure. In the divisional form, a central headquarters provides support services to the divisions. This usually includes financial and legal services, but can include any activity in which there are economies to providing centralized operations. Of course, the headquarters also acts as an external overseer to coordinate and control the various divisions. Divisions, therefore, are autonomous within given parameters. Division managers are usually free to direct their divisions any way they see fit, as long as it is within the overall guidelines set down by headquarters.

What primary advantage does the divisional structure offer? It focuses on results. Division managers have full responsibility for a product or service. Its major disadvantage is duplication of activities and resources. Each division, for instance, may have a marketing research department. In the absence of autonomous divisions, all of the organization's marketing research might be centralized and done for a fraction of the cost that divisionalization requires. So the divisional form's duplication of functions increases the organization's costs and reduces efficiency.

The Matrix Structure

The *matrix structure* combines functional and product departmentalization in order to try to gain the advantages and minimize the disadvantages of each.

The strength of functional departmentalization lies in putting like specialists together, which minimizes the number necessary, while it allows the pooling and sharing of specialized resources across products. Its major disadvantage is the difficulty of coordinating the tasks of diverse functional specialists so their activities are completed on time and within budget. Product departmentalization, on the other hand, has exactly the opposite benefits and disadvantages. It facilitates coordination among specialties to achieve on-time completion and meet budget targets. Further, it provides clear responsibility for all activities related to a product, but with duplication of activities and costs. The matrix attempts to gain the strengths of each, while avoiding their weaknesses.

The matrix structure is created by superimposing products over functions. Functional units are used to gain the economies from specialization. But overlaid on the functional departments is a set of managers who are responsible for specific products, projects, or programs within the organization. So the most obvious structural feature of the matrix is that it breaks the unity of command concept. Employees in the matrix have two bosses—their functional department manager and their product managers. Therefore, the matrix has a dual chain of command.

It's the matrix's ability to be adaptive and flexible that places it in the organic category. It can, for example, permit an aerospace firm or advertising agency to work on dozens of projects, adding new ones and dropping completed ones as needed. The success or failure of any project can be directly linked to its project manager. Meanwhile, specialists are grouped by function, which minimizes the number necessary and allows for specialized resources to be shared and pooled across projects. Of course, these advantages don't come without costs. The matrix is a complex structure that is difficult to coordinate and can be frustrating to employees when their multiple bosses make conflicting demands on them.

The Task-Force Structure

The *task force* is not an independent structure. It is essentially an organic appendage designed to be used with a mechanistic structure to gain flexibility.

The task force is a temporary structure created to accomplish a specific, well-defined, and complex task involving personnel from various organization subunits. Members serve on the task force until its goal is achieved. They then disband to move on to a new task force, return to their permanent functional department, or leave the organization.

Because the task force is temporary, it can be used to attack problems that cut across functional lines with only minimal disturbance to the organization's mechanistic mainframe. It allows the organization the best of organic and mechanistic structures—flexibility and efficiency.

The Network Structure

The search by managers for high flexibility has resulted in the creation of a new form of organization design called the *network structure*. It's been made possible as a result of recent advances in connecting interorganizational computers.

The essence of the network structure is a small central organization that relies on other organizations to perform manufacturing, distribution, marketing, or other crucial business functions on a contract basis. It is a viable option for both small and large organizations. For instance, Nike, Esprit, Emerson Radio, Exabyte, and Lewis Galoob Toys are large companies that have found they can sell hundreds of millions of dollars of products every year and earn a very competitive return with few or no manufacturing facilities of their own and only a limited number of employees. What these firms have done is create an organization of relationships. They connect with independent designers, manufacturers, commissioned sales representatives, and the like to perform the functions they need on a contract basis.

The network stands in sharp contrast to divisional structures that have many vertical levels of management and in which organizations seek to control their destiny through ownership. In such organizations, research and development is done in-house, production occurs in company-owned manufacturing plants, and sales and marketing are performed by their own employees. To support all this, management has to employ extra personnel such as accountants, human resource specialists, and lawyers. In the network structure, most of these functions are bought outside the organization and coordinated through interfacing computer networks. This gives management a high degree of flexibility and allows the organization to concentrate on what it does best. For most North American firms, that means focusing on design or marketing and buying manufacturing capability outside. Emerson Radio Corporation, for example, designs and engineers its televisions, stereos, and other consumer electronic products, but contracts out their manufacture to Asian suppliers.

The network organization is not appropriate for all endeavors. It fits industrial companies like toy and apparel firms, which require very high flexibility in order to respond quickly to fashion changes. It also fits firms whose manufacturing operations require low-cost labor that is available only outside North America and can best be utilized by contracting with foreign suppliers. On the negative side, management in network structures lacks the close control of manufacturing operations that exists in more traditional organizations. Reliability of supply is also less predictable. Finally, any innovation in design that a network organization acquires is susceptible to being ripped off. It is very difficult, if not impossible, to closely guard innovations that are under the direction of management in another organization.

■ IMPLICATIONS FOR MANAGERS

Exhibit 13–7 integrates the key issues introduced in this and the preceding chapter. Strategy, size, technology, environment, and power-control determine the type of structure an organization will have. Complexity, formalization, and centralization represent the structural components that can be mixed and matched to form various structural designs. For the most part, structural designs fall into one of two categories: mechanistic or organic. Finally, different structural designs have different effects on employees.

From a managerial perspective, it is important to emphasize that managers have some discretion in the structural decision. Even though the organization's strategy, size, technology, and environment constrain structural options, managers still have considerable influence on which structure is implemented. Given this discretion and the fact that structural configurations

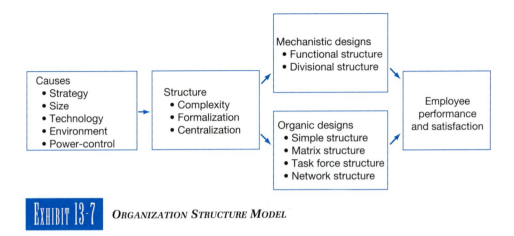

EXHIBIT 13-7 *ORGANIZATION STRUCTURE MODEL*

appear to influence employee performance and satisfaction, managers should consider carefully the behavioral implications when they make structural decisions. Let's now consider some general thoughts.

For a large proportion of the population, high structure—that is, high complexity, high formalization, and centralization—leads to reduced job satisfaction. High vertical differentiation tends to alienate lower-level employees because vertical communication becomes more difficult and one can feel like the low person on the totem pole. On the other hand, upper management undoubtedly finds that the rewards accompanying their positions enhance job satisfaction.

Specialization also tends to be inversely related to satisfaction, especially where jobs have been divided into minute tasks. This conclusion would have to be moderated to reflect individual differences among employees. While most prefer autonomy, not *all* do.

For individuals who value autonomy and self-actualization, large size, when accompanied by high centralization, results in lower satisfaction. As we have noted, there are fewer opportunities to participate in decision making, less proximity and identification with organizational goals, and less feeling that individual effort is linked to an identifiable outcome. In other words, the larger the organization, the more difficult it is for the individual to see the impact of his or her contribution to the final goods or service produced.

For certain types of activities, the organic structure will result in more effective performance. For instance, if tasks are nonroutine and there exists a great deal of environmental uncertainty, the organization can be more responsive when structured along organic rather than mechanistic lines. But this more responsive structure provides both advantages and disadvantages to employees. There are rarely restrictive job descriptions or excessive rules and regulations; and the structure does not require workers to obey commands that are issued by distant executives. But there are usually overlapping layers of responsibility and this wreaks havoc with individuals who need the security of standardized tasks. To maximize employee performance and satisfaction, individual differences should be taken into account. Individuals with a high degree of bureaucratic orientation tend to place a heavy reliance on higher authority, prefer formalized and specific rules, and prefer formal relationships with others on the job. These people are better suited to mechanistic structures. Individuals with a low degree of bureaucratic orientation are better suited to organic structures.

SUGGESTIONS FOR FURTHER READING

ASTLEY, W. GRAHAM, AND EDWARD J. ZAJAC, "Intraorganizational Power and Organizational Design: Reconciling Rational and Coalitional Models of Organization," *Organization Science*, November 1991, pp. 399–411.

BOSCHKEN, HERMAN L., "Strategy and Structure: Reconceiving the Relationship," *Journal of Management*, March 1990, pp. 135–50.

BURNS, LAWTON R., AND DOUGLAS R. WHOLEY, "Adoption and Abandonment of Matrix Management Programs: Effects of Organizational Characteristics and Interorganizational Networks," *Academy of Management Journal*, February 1993, pp. 106–38.

BYRNE, JOHN A., "The Virtual Corporation," *Business Week*, February 8, 1993, pp. 98–102.

COURTRIGHT, JOHN A., GAIL T. FAIRHURST, AND L. EDNA ROGERS, "Interaction Patterns in Organic and Mechanistic Systems," *Academy of Management Journal*, December 1989, pp. 773–802.

PENNINGS, JOHANNES M., "Structural Contingency Theory: A Reappraisal," in B.M. Staw and L.L. Cummings, eds., *Research in Organizational Behavior*, Vol. 14 (Greenwich, CT: JAI Press, 1992), pp. 267–309.

SNOW, CHARLES C., RAYMOND E. MILES, AND HENRY J. COLEMAN, JR., "Managing 21st Century Network Organizations," *Organizational Dynamics*, Winter 1992, pp. 5–20.

TULLY, SHAWN, "The Modular Corporation," *Fortune*, February 8, 1993, pp. 106–16.

CHAPTER 14

PERFORMANCE APPRAISAL AND REWARD SYSTEMS

After reading this chapter, you should be able to:

1. Explain the purposes of performance appraisal

2. Identify the advantages of using behaviors rather than traits in appraising performance

3. Describe the potential problems in performance appraisal and actions that can correct these problems

4. Explain why managers often dislike giving performance reviews

5. Outline the various types of rewards

6. Explain the links between performance appraisals, rewards, and employee behavior

Would you study differently for a course if your goal was *to learn as much as you could about the subject* rather than *to make a high grade on the tests in the course*? When I ask that question of students, I frequently get an affirmative answer. When I inquire further, I am typically told that making a high grade is only partially determined by knowledge of the material. You also need to know what the instructor thinks is important. I have been told by many a student that, "If you want to do well in a course, you do best to study what the instructor tests for." In some cases, that approach will also result in learning as much as you can about the subject. But in many courses, studying to make a high grade means studying much differently than if you were studying for general knowledge.

Let me propose another question. Assume you are taking two similar classes, both with enrollments of about 20. In one class, the grade is determined totally by your scores on the midterm and final. In the other class, the midterm and final each count only 25 percent, with the remaining 50 percent being allocated for class participation. Would your in-class behavior be different in the two classes? I would predict that most students would talk more—ask questions, answer questions, offer examples, elaborate on points made by the instructor—in the class where participation was so highly weighted.

The previous paragraphs are meant to illustrate how the system's appraisal and reward practices influence behavior. Studying and in-class behavior are modified to take into consideration the criteria that the instructor appraises and the linking of those appraisals to desirable rewards (high grades). It's not unusual, in fact, for the more experienced student to behave five different ways in five different classes in order to obtain five high grades. The reason studying and in-class behaviors vary is certainly in large measure directly attributable to the different performance appraisal and reward systems that instructors use.

What applies in the school context also applies to employees at work. In this chapter, we show how performance appraisal and reward systems influence the attitudes and behaviors of people in organizations.

■ PERFORMANCE APPRAISAL

Why do organizations appraise the performance of their employees? *How* do they appraise? *What* potential problems can arise to subvert the intentions of objective appraisals? *How* can managers overcome these problems? These are the key questions addressed in this section.

Purposes of Performance Appraisal

Performance appraisal serves a number of purposes in organizations. First, management uses appraisals for general personnel decisions. Appraisals provide information for such important decisions as promotions, transfers, and terminations. Second, appraisals identify training and development needs. They pinpoint employee skills and competencies that are currently inadequate, but for which programs can be developed to remedy. Third, performance appraisals can be used as a criterion against which selection and development programs are validated. Newly hired employees who perform poorly can be identified through performance appraisal. Similarly, the effectiveness of training and development programs can be determined by assessing how well those employees who have participated do on their performance appraisals. Fourth, appraisals also fulfill the purpose of providing feedback to employees on how the organization views their performance. Finally, performance appraisals are used as the basis for reward allocations. Decisions about who gets merit pay increases and other rewards are determined by performance appraisals.

Each of these functions of performance appraisal is important. Yet their importance to us depends on the perspective we're taking. Several are clearly most relevant to personnel management decisions. But our interest is in organizational behavior. As a result, we emphasize performance appraisal in its role as a determinant of reward allocations.

Performance Appraisal and Motivation

In Chapter 4, considerable attention was given to the expectancy model of motivation. We argued that this model currently offers the best explanation of what conditions the amount of effort an individual will exert on his or her job. A vital component of this model is performance, specifically the effort-performance and performance-reward linkages. Do people see effort leading to performance, and performance to the rewards that they value? Clearly, they have to know what is expected of them. They need to know how their performance will be measured. Further, they must feel confident that if they exert an effort within their capabilities it will result in a satisfactory performance as defined by the criteria by which they are being measured. Finally, they must feel confident that if they perform as they are being asked, they will achieve the rewards they value.

In brief, if the objectives that employees are seeking are unclear, if the criteria for measuring those objectives are vague, and if the employees lack confidence that their efforts will lead to a satisfactory appraisal of their performance, or believe there will be an unsatisfactory payoff by the organization when their performance objectives are achieved, we can expect individuals to work considerably below their potential.

Performance Appraisal Methods

Obviously, performance appraisals are important. But how do you evaluate an employee's performance? That is, what are the specific techniques for appraisal? The following reviews the major performance appraisal methods.

Written Essays. Probably the simplest method of appraisal is to write a narrative describing an employee's strengths, weaknesses, past performance, potential, and suggestions for improvement. The written essay requires no complex forms or extensive training to complete. But the results often reflect the ability of the writer. A good or bad appraisal may be determined as much by the evaluator's writing skill as by the employee's actual level of performance.

Critical Incidents. Critical incidents focus the evaluator's attention on those behaviors that are key in making the difference between executing a job effectively or ineffectively. That is, the appraiser writes down anecdotes that describe what the employee did that was especially effective or ineffective. The key here is that only specific behaviors, and not vaguely defined personality traits, are cited. A list of critical incidents provides a rich set of examples from which the employee can be shown those behaviors that are desirable and those that call for improvement.

Graphic Rating Scales. One of the oldest and most popular methods of appraisal is the use of graphic rating scales. In this method, a set of performance factors, such as quantity and quality of work, depth of knowledge, cooperation, loyalty, attendance, honesty, and initiative, are listed. The evaluator then goes down the list and rates each on incremental scales. The scales typically specify five points, so a factor like *job knowledge* might be rated 1 ("poorly informed about work duties") to 5 ("has complete mastery of all phases of the job").

Why are graphic rating scales so popular? Though they don't provide the depth of information that essays or critical incidents do, they are less time consuming to develop and administer. They also allow for quantitative analysis and comparison.

Behaviorally Anchored Rating Scales. Behaviorally anchored rating scales have received a great deal of attention in recent years. These scales combine major elements from the critical incident and graphic rating scale approaches: The appraiser rates the employees based on items along a continuum, but the points are examples of actual behavior on the given job rather than general descriptions or traits.

Behaviorally anchored rating scales specify definite, observable, and measurable job behavior. Examples of job-related behavior and performance dimensions are found by asking participants to give specific illustrations of effective and ineffective behavior regarding each performance dimension. These behavioral examples are then translated into a set of performance dimensions, each dimension having varying levels of performance. The results of this process are behavioral descriptions, such as anticipates, plans, executes, solves immediate problems, carries out orders, and handles emergency situations.

Multiperson Comparisons. Multiperson comparisons evaluate one individual's performance against one or more others. It is a relative rather than an absolute measuring device. The three most popular comparisons are group order ranking, individual ranking, and paired comparisons.

The group order ranking requires the evaluator to place employees into a particular classification, such as top one-fifth or second one-fifth. This method is often used in recommending students to graduate schools. Evaluators are asked to rank the student in the top 5 percent, the next 5 percent, the next 15 percent, and so forth. But when used by managers to appraise employees, managers deal with all their subordinates. Therefore, if a rater has 20 subordinates, only 4 can be in the top fifth and, of course, 4 must also be relegated to the bottom fifth.

The individual ranking approach rank orders employees from best to worst. If the manager is required to appraise 30 subordinates, this approach assumes that the difference between the first and second employee is the same as that between the 21st and 22nd. Even though some of the employees may be closely grouped, this approach allows for no ties. The result is a clear ordering of employees, from the highest performer down to the lowest.

The paired comparison approach compares each employee with every other employee and rates each as either the superior or the weaker member of the pair. After all paired comparisons are made, each employee is assigned a summary ranking based on the number of superior scores he or she achieved. This approach ensures that each employee is compared against every other, but it can obviously become unwieldy when many employees are being compared.

Multiperson comparisons can be combined with one of the other methods to blend the best from both absolute and relative standards. For example, a college might use the graphic rating scale and the individual ranking method to provide more accurate information about its students' performance. The student's relative rank in the class could be noted next to an absolute grade of A,B,C,D, or F. A prospective employer or graduate school could then look at two students who each got a "B" in their different financial accounting courses and draw considerably different conclusions about each where next to one grade it says "ranked 4th out of 26," while the other says "ranked 17th out of 30." Obviously, the latter instructor gives out a lot more high grades!

Potential Problems

While organizations may seek to make the performance appraisal process free from personal biases, prejudices, or idiosyncracies, a number of potential problems can creep into the process. To the degree that the following factors are prevalent, an employee's evaluation is likely to be distorted.

Single Criterion. The typical employee's job is made up of a number of tasks. An airline flight attendant's job, for example, includes welcoming passengers, seeing to their comfort, serving meals, and offering safety advice. If performance on this job were assessed by a single criterion measure—for example, the time it took to provide food and beverages to a hundred passengers—the result would be a limited evaluation of that job. More important, flight attendants whose performance appraisal included assessment on only this single criterion would be motivated to ignore those other tasks composing the job. Similarly, if a football quarterback were appraised only on his percentage of completed passes, he would be likely to throw short passes and only in situations where he felt assured they would be caught. Our point is that when employees are appraised on a single job criterion, even though successful performance on that job requires good performance on a number of criteria, employees will emphasize the single criterion to the exclusion of other relevant factors.

Leniency Error. Every appraiser has his or her own value system that acts as a standard against which appraisals are made. Relative to the true or actual performance of an individual, some evaluators mark high and others low. The former is referred to as positive leniency error, and the latter as negative leniency error. When evaluators are positively lenient in their appraisal, an individual's performance becomes overstated, that is, rated higher than it actually should. Similarly, a negative leniency error understates performance, giving the individual a lower appraisal.

If all individuals in an organization were appraised by the same person, there would be no problem. Although there would be an error factor, it would be applied equally to everyone. The difficulty arises when we have different raters with different leniency errors making judgments. For example, Jones and Smith are performing the same job for different supervisors, but they have absolutely identical job performance. If Jones's supervisor tends to err toward positive leniency, while Smith's supervisor errs toward negative leniency, we might be confronted with two dramatically different evaluations.

Halo Error. The halo error is the tendency for an evaluator to let the assessment of an individual on one trait influence his or her appraisal of that person on other traits. For example, if an employee tends to be dependable, we might become biased toward that individual and rate him or her high on many other desirable attributes.

People who design teaching appraisal forms for college students to fill out in evaluating the effectiveness of their instructors each semester must confront the halo effect. Students tend to rate a faculty member as outstanding on all criteria when they are particularly appreciative of a few things he or she does in the classroom. Similarly, a few bad habits like showing up late for lectures or being slow in returning papers might result in students' appraising the instructor as lousy across the board.

Similarity Error. When evaluators rate other people by giving special consideration to those qualities that they perceive in themselves they are making a similarity error. For example, evaluators who perceive themselves as aggressive may appraise others by looking for aggressiveness. Those who demonstrate this characteristic tend to benefit, while others are penalized.

Again, this error would tend to be cancelled out if the same evaluator appraised all the people in the organization. However, interrater reliability obviously suffers when various evaluators are utilizing their own similarity criteria.

Low Differentiation. It is possible that, regardless of whom the appraiser evaluates and what traits are used, the pattern of evaluation remains the same. It is possible that the evaluator's ability to appraise objectively and accurately has been impeded by social differentiation, that is, by the evaluator's style of rating behavior.

It has been suggested that evaluators may be classified as either high differentiators, who use all or most of the scale, or low differentiators, who use a limited range of the scale.

Low differentiators tend to ignore or suppress differences, perceiving the universe as more uniform than it really is. High differentiators, on the other hand, tend to utilize all available information to the utmost extent and thus are better able to perceive anomalies and contradictions.

This finding tells us that evaluations made by low differentiators need to be carefully inspected and that the people working for a low differentiator have a high probability of being appraised as significantly more homogeneous than they really are.

Forcing Information to Match Nonperformance Criteria. While rarely advocated, it is not an infrequent practice to find the formal appraisal taking place *following* the decision about the individual's performance! This may sound illogical, but it shows that subjective, yet formal, decisions are often arrived at prior to the gathering of objective information to support that decision. For example, if the evaluator believes the appraisal should not be based on performance, but rather seniority, he or she may be unknowingly adjusting each performance appraisal to bring it into line with the employee's seniority rank. In this and other cases, the evaluator is increasing or decreasing performance appraisals to align with the nonperformance criteria actually being utilized.

Overcoming the Problems

The fact that organizations can encounter problems with performance appraisals should not lead managers to give up on the process. Steps can be taken to overcome most of the problems we have identified.

Use Multiple Criteria. Since successful performance on most jobs requires doing a number of things well, all those things should be identified and evaluated. The more complex the job, the more criteria that will need to be identified and evaluated. But everything need not be assessed. The critical activities that lead to effective or ineffective performance are the ones that need to be appraised.

Deemphasize Traits. Many traits often considered to be related to good performance may, in fact, have little or no performance relationship. Traits like loyalty, initiative, courage, reliability, and self-expression are intuitively appealing characteristics in employees. But the relevant question is, Are individuals who are appraised as high on those traits better performers than those who rate low? We can't answer this question. We know there are employees who rate high on these characteristics and are poor performers. We can find others who are excellent performers but do not score well on traits like these. Our conclusion is that traits like loyalty and initiative may be prized by managers, but there is no evidence to support that certain traits will be adequate synonyms for performance in a large cross section of jobs.

Another weakness in traits is the judgment itself. What is "loyalty"? When is an employee "reliable"? What one considers "loyalty," another may not. So traits suffer from weak agreement among evaluators.

Emphasize Behavior. Whenever possible, it is better to use measures based on behavior rather than traits for appraisals. Why? They can deal with the two major objections to traits. First, because measures based on behavior focus on specific examples—both good and bad—of performance, we avoid the problem of using inappropriate substitutes for actual performance. Second, because we are appraising specific examples of behavior, we increase the likelihood that two or more evaluators will see the same thing. You might consider a given employee as friendly, while I rate her standoffish. But when asked to rate her in terms of specific behaviors, we might both agree that she "frequently says 'Good morning' to customers," "rarely gives advice or assistance to co-workers," and "almost always avoids idle chatter with co-workers."

Use Multiple Evaluators. As the number of evaluators increases, the probability of attaining more accurate information increases. If rater error tends to follow a normal curve, an increase in the number of appraisers will tend to show the majority congregating about the middle. You see this approach being used in athletic competitions in such sports as diving and gymnastics. A multiple set of evaluators judge a performance, the highest and lowest scores are dropped, and the final performance appraisal is derived from the cumulative scores of those remaining. The logic of multiple evaluators applies to organizations as well.

If an employee has had ten supervisors, nine having rated her excellent and one poor, we can discount the value of the one poor appraisal. Therefore, by moving employees about within the organization to gain a number of evaluations, we increase the probability of achieving more valid and reliable appraisals.

Appraise Selectively. Appraisers should evaluate in only those areas in which they have some expertise. If raters make appraisals on *only* those dimensions on which they are in a good position to rate, we increase inter-rater agreement and make the evaluation a more valid process. This approach also recognizes that different organizational levels often have different orientations toward ratees and observe them in different settings. In general, therefore, we would recommend that appraisers should be as close as possible, in terms of organizational level, to the individual being evaluated. Conversely, the more levels that separate the evaluator and evaluatee, the less opportunity the evaluator has to observe the individual's behavior and, not surprisingly, the greater the possibility for inaccuracies.

The specific application of these concepts would result in having immediate supervisors or co-workers as the major contributors to the appraisal and having them evaluate those factors that they are best qualified to judge. For example, when professors are evaluating secretaries within a university, they could use criteria like judgment, technical competence, and conscientiousness, whereas peers (other secretaries) could use criteria like job knowledge, organization, cooperation with co-workers, and responsibility. Such an approach is both logical and more reliable, since people are appraising only those dimensions about which they are in a good position to make judgments.

Train Appraisers. If you can't *find* good appraisers, the alternative is to *make* good appraisers. By training appraisers, we can make them more accurate raters.

Common errors such as halo and leniency have been minimized or eliminated in workshops where managers can practice observing and rating behaviors. These workshops would typically run from one to three days, but allocating many hours to training may not always be necessary. One case has been cited where both halo and leniency errors were decreased immediately after exposing evaluators to explanatory training sessions lasting only five minutes.[1] But the effects of training do appear to diminish over time. This suggests the need for regular training refresher sessions.

Don't Forget Performance Feedback!

A few years back, a nationwide motel chain advertised that when it came to motel rooms, "the best surprise is no surprise." This logic also holds for performance appraisals. Employees like to know how they are doing. They expect feedback. This is typically done in the annual review. But this review frequently creates problems. In some cases, it's a problem merely because managers put off such reviews. This is particularly likely if the appraisal is negative. But the annual review is additionally troublesome if the manager saves up information related to performance and unloads it during the appraisal review. In such instances, it is not surprising the manager may try to avoid addressing stressful issues that, even if confronted, may only be denied or rationalized by the employee. Much of this problem can be avoided by giving feedback to employees on an ongoing basis, for example, providing daily output reports with comparative data on actual units produced and the goal for the day, or bringing up problems as they occur rather than allowing them to accumulate for the annual review.

Regardless of whether feedback is provided annually or on an ongoing basis, management needs to offer performance feedback to employees. Yet, appraising another person's performance is one of the most emotionally charged of all management activities. The impression subordinates receive about their assessment has a strong impact on their self-esteem and, importantly, on their subsequent performance. Of course, conveying good news is considerably less difficult for both the manager and the subordinate than revealing that performance has been below expectations. In this context, the discussion of the evaluation can have negative as well as positive motivational consequences. Statistically speaking, half of all employees are below the median, yet evidence tells us that the average employee's estimate of his or her own performance level generally falls around the 75th percentile.[2] A

---

[1] H. John Bernardin, "The Effects of Rater Training on Leniency and Halo Errors in Student Rating of Instructors," *Journal of Applied Psychology* (June 1978), pp. 301–8.

[2] Ronald J. Burke, "Why Performance Appraisal Systems Fail," *Personnel Administration* (June 1972), pp. 32–40.

A MANAGER'S GUIDE TOWARD MORE EFFECTIVE PERFORMANCE APPRAISAL REVIEWS

1. Don't let problems fester until the annual review. Give daily or weekly feedback. The annual review is *not* the place to spring surprises.

2. Separate performance feedback reviews from pay reviews. In their eagerness to find out how much of a pay increase they are to receive, employees tend to tune out appraisals of their performance when combined.

3. Allow employees to engage in self-evaluation. Ask them how they are doing, how you and the organization can help them perform better, and how much co-operation they get from their peers.

4. When you have to be critical, focus the criticism on specific examples of behavior rather than on the individual personally.

5. Treat the review as only a point in an ongoing process. Use it to achieve agreement about what constitutes satisfactory performance in the future.

Source: Based on Beth Brophy, "The Rite of Annual Reviews," *U.S. News & World Report*, February 2, 1986, p. 59.

survey of over 800,000 high school seniors also found that people seem to see themselves as better than average. Seventy percent rated themselves above average on leadership, and when asked to rate themselves on "ability to get along with others," none rated himself or herself below average. Sixty percent rated themselves in the top 10 percent, and 25 percent saw themselves among the top 1 percent! Similarly, a survey of 500 clerical and technical employees found that 58 percent rated their own performance as falling in the top 10 percent of their peers doing comparable jobs and a total of 81 percent placed themselves in the top 20 percent.[3]

The inevitable conclusion is that employees tend to be unrealistic and inflate the assessment of their own performance. This puts the manager in the uncomfortable position of recognizing that even good news may not be good enough! Suggestions for making the best of a tough situation are listed in Exhibit 14–1.

Performance Appraisal in a Global Context

We previously examined the role that performance appraisal plays in motivation and in affecting behavior. Caution must be used, however, in generalizing across cultures. Why? Because many cultures are not particularly concerned with performance appraisal or, if they are, they don't look at it the same way as they do in the United States or Canada.

To illustrate these points let's look at three cultural dimensions discussed in Chapter 2: a person's relationship to the environment, time orientation, and focus of responsibility.

---

[3] "How Do I Love Me? Let Me Count the Ways," *Psychology Today* (May 1980), p. 16.

American and Canadian organizations hold people responsible for their actions because people in these countries believe they can dominate their environment. In Middle Eastern countries, on the other hand, performance appraisals aren't likely to be widely used, since managers in these countries tend to see people as subjugated to their environment.

Some countries, such as the United States, have a short-term time orientation. Performance appraisals are likely to be frequent in such a culture, conducted at least once a year. In Japan, however, where people hold a long-term time frame, performance appraisals may occur only at five- or ten-year intervals.

Israel's culture values group activities much more than does the United States or Canada. So, while North American managers focus on the individual in performance appraisals, their counterparts in Israel are much more likely to emphasize group contributions and performance.

■ REWARD SYSTEMS

Our knowledge of motivation tells us that people do what they do to satisfy needs. Before they do anything, they look for the payoff or reward. Because many of these rewards—salary increases, promotions, and preferred job assignments, to name a few—are organizationally controlled, we should consider rewards as an important force influencing the behavior of employees.

Determinants of Rewards

Most organizations believe their reward systems are designed to reward merit. The problem is that we find differing definitions of merit. Some define merit as being "deserving," while to others merit is being "excellent." One person's merit is another person's favoritism. A consideration of "deserving" may take into account such factors as intelligence, effort, or seniority. The problem is that what is deserving may differ from what is excellent—a problem that is exacerbated by the difficulty of defining excellence. If excellence refers to performance, we concede how unsatisfactory our efforts have been to measure performance. Creation of quantifiable and meaningful performance measures of most white-collar and service jobs, and many blue-collar jobs, have eluded us. Thus, while few disagree with the viewpoint that rewards should be based on merit, what constitutes merit is highly debatable.

In the next several pages we briefly assess the role of performance as a prerequisite for rewards and then discuss other popular criteria by which rewards are distributed. In Chapter 4, we argued that motivation will be highest when performance and rewards are closely linked. But, in reality, performance is only *one* of many criteria on which organizational rewards are based.

Performance. Performance is the measurement of results. It asks the simple question: Did you get the job done? To reward people in the organization, therefore, requires some agreed-upon criterion for defining their performance.

Whether this criterion is valid or not in representing performance is not relevant to our definition; as long as rewards are allocated based on factors that are directly linked to doing the job successfully, we are using performance as the determinant. For many jobs, productivity is used as a single criterion. But as jobs become less standardized and routine, productivity becomes more difficult to measure, and hence, defining performance becomes increasingly complex.

Yet, for senior managers in corporations or those who oversee distinct business units, there is increased attention being paid to linking rewards (particularly pay) to performance. Companies as diverse as American Broadcasting, Security Pacific National Bank, Sears, Roebuck, and Dow Chemical are measuring the economic performance of their business units, comparing the results against the competition, and awarding rewards accordingly.

Effort. It is not uncommon for a report card in grammar school to include effort as one of the categories used in grading students. Organizations rarely make their rewarding of effort that explicit, yet it is certainly a major determinant in the reward distribution.

The rewarding of effort represents the classical example of rewarding means rather than ends. In organizations where performance is generally of low caliber, rewarding effort may be the only criterion by which to differentiate rewards. For example, a major eastern university was attempting to increase its research efforts and had designated obtaining funded research grants as a critical benchmark toward this end. Upon selection of this objective, all faculty members were informed that rewards for the coming year were going to be based on performance in obtaining grants. Unfortunately, after the first year of the program, even though approximately 20 percent of the faculty had made grant applications, none were approved. When the time came for performance evaluation and the distribution of rewards, the dean chose to give the majority of the funds available for pay raises to those faculty members who had applied for grants. Here is a case where performance, defined in terms of obtaining funded research grants, was zero, so the dean chose to allocate rewards based on effort.

This practice is more common than you might think. Effort can count *more than* actual performance when it is believed those who try should be encouraged. The employee who is clearly perceived by her superiors to be working less than her optimum can often expect to be rewarded less than some other employee who, while producing less, is giving out a greater effort. Even where it is clearly stated that performance is what will be rewarded, people who make evaluations and distribute rewards are only human. Therefore, they are not immune to sympathizing with those who try hard, but with minimal success, and allowing this to influence their evaluation and reward decisions.

Seniority. Seniority, job rights, and tenure dominate most civil service systems in the United States, and while they do not play as important a role in business corporations, the length of time on the job is still a major factor in determining the allocation of rewards. Seniority's greatest virtue is that, relative to other criteria, it is easy to determine. We may disagree whether the quality of Smith's work is higher or lower than that of Jones, but we would probably not have much debate over who has been with the organization longer. So seniority represents an easily quantifiable criterion that can be substituted for performance.

Skills Held. Another practice not uncommon in organizations is to allocate rewards based on the skills of the employee. Regardless of whether the skills are used, those individuals who possess the highest levels of skill or talent will be rewarded commensurately.

When individuals enter an organization, their skill level is usually a major determinant of the compensation they will receive. In such cases, the marketplace or competition has acted to make skills a major element in the reward package. These externally imposed standards can evolve from the community or from occupational categories themselves. In other words, the relationship of demand and supply for particular skills in the community can significantly influence the rewards the organization must expend to acquire those skills. Also, the demand-supply relationship for an entire occupational category throughout the country can affect rewards.

Job Difficulty. The complexity of the job can be a criterion by which rewards are distributed. For example, those jobs that are highly repetitive and quickly learned may be viewed as less deserving of rewards than those that are more complex and sophisticated. Jobs that are difficult to perform or are undesirable due to stress or unpleasant working conditions may have to carry with them higher rewards in order to attract workers to them.

Discretionary Time. The greater the discretion called for on a job, the greater the impact of mistakes and the greater the need for good judgment. In a job that has been completely programmed—that is, where each step has been accorded a procedure and there is no room for decision making by the incumbent—there is little discretionary time. Such jobs require less judgment, and lower rewards can be offered to attract people to take these positions. As discretionary time increases, greater judgmental abilities are needed, and rewards must commensurately be expanded.

Types of Rewards

The types of rewards that an organization can allocate are more complex than is generally thought. Obviously, there is direct compensation. But there are also indirect compensation and nonfinancial rewards. Each of these types of rewards can be distributed on an individual, group, or organization-wide basis. Exhibit 14–2 presents a structure for looking at rewards.

Intrinsic rewards are those that individuals receive for themselves. They are largely a result of the worker's satisfaction with his or her job. As noted in

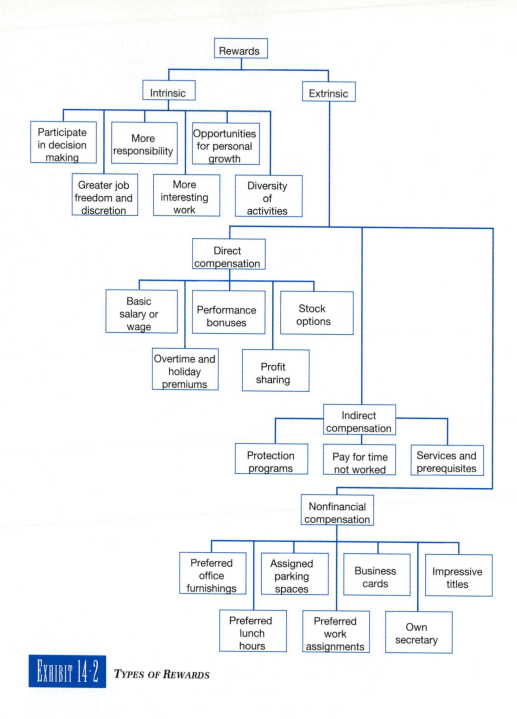

Exhibit 14-2 *Types of Rewards*

Chapter 5, techniques like job enrichment or any efforts to redesign or restructure work to increase its personal worth to the employee may make his or her job more intrinsically rewarding.

As previously noted, extrinsic rewards include direct compensation, indirect compensation, and nonfinancial rewards. Of course, an employee expects some form of direct compensation: a basic wage or salary, overtime and holiday premium pay, bonuses based on performance, profit sharing, and/or possibly opportunities to receive stock options. Employees expect their direct compensation generally to align with their assessment of their contribution to the organization and, additionally, expect it to be relatively comparable with the direct compensation given to other employees with similar abilities, responsibilities, and performance.

The organization will provide employees with indirect compensation: insurance, paid holidays and vacations, services, and perquisites. Inasmuch as these are generally made uniformly available to all employees at a given job level, regardless of performance, they are really not motivating rewards. However, where indirect compensation is controllable by management and is used to reward performance, then it clearly needs to be considered as a motivating reward. To illustrate, if a company-paid membership in a country club is not available to all middle- and upper-level executives, but only to those who have shown particular performance ratings, then it is a motivating reward. Similarly, if company-owned automobiles and aircraft are made available to certain employees based on their performance rather than their "entitlement," we should view these indirect compensations as motivating rewards for those who might deem these forms of compensation as attractive.

As with direct compensation, indirect compensation may be viewed in an individual, group, or organizational context. However, if rewards are to be linked closely with performance, we should expect individual rewards to be emphasized. On the other hand, if a certain group of managers within the organization has made a significant contribution to the effective performance of the organization, a blanket reward like a membership in a social club might be appropriate.

The classification of nonfinancial rewards tends to be a smorgasbord of desirable "things" that are potentially at the disposal of the organization. The creation of nonfinancial rewards is limited only by managers' ingenuity and ability to assess "payoffs" that individuals in the organization find desirable and that are within the managers' discretion.

The old saying "One man's food is another man's poison" certainly applies to rewards. What one employee views as highly desirable, another finds superfluous. Therefore *any* reward may not get the desired result; however, where selection has been done assiduously, the benefits to the organization by way of higher worker performance should be impressive.

Some workers are very status conscious. A paneled office, a carpeted floor, a large walnut desk, or a private bathroom may be just the office furnishings that stimulate an employee toward top performance. Status-oriented employees may also value an impressive job title, their own business cards, their own secretary, or a well-located parking space with their name clearly painted underneath the "Reserved" sign.

Some employees value having their lunch at, say, 1 P.M. to 2 P.M. If lunch is normally from 11 A.M. to 12 noon, the benefit of being able to take their lunch at another, more desirable time can be viewed as a reward. Having a chance to work with congenial colleagues or getting a desired work assignment are rewards that are within the discretion of management and, when carefully aligned to individual needs, can provide stimulus for improved performance.

■ IMPLICATIONS FOR MANAGERS

Managers choose how employees are appraised and rewarded. Because these decisions affect the behavior of employees, care should be taken to ensure that the organization's appraisal and reward systems encourage the kinds of behaviors that management desires.

People do not work gratis. They expect payoffs: salary, benefits, promotion opportunities, recognition, social contact, and so forth. If employees perceive that their efforts are accurately appraised, and if they further perceive that the rewards they value are closely linked to their appraisals, management will have optimized the motivational properties from the organization's appraisal and reward procedures and policies. More specifically, based on the contents of this chapter and our discussion of motivation in Chapter 4, we can conclude that rewards are likely to lead to effective performance and satisfaction when they are (1) perceived as equitable by the employee, (2) tied to performance, and (3) tailored to the needs of the individual. These conditions should foster a minimum of dissatisfaction among employees, reduced withdrawal patterns, and increased organizational commitment. If these conditions don't exist, the probability of withdrawal behavior increases, and the prevalence of marginal or barely adequate performance increases. If workers perceive that their efforts are not recognized or rewarded, and if they view their alternatives as limited, they may continue working but perform at a level considerably below their capabilities.

$\mathcal{S}$UGGESTIONS FOR FURTHER READING

CASCIO, WAYNE F., *Applied Psychology in Personnel Management*, 4th ed. (Englewood Cliffs, NJ: Prentice Hall, 1991).

CLEVELAND, JEANETTE N., K. R. MURPHY, AND R. E. WILLIAMS, "Multiple Uses of Performance Appraisal: Prevalence and Correlates," *Journal of Applied Psychology*, February 1989, pp. 130–35.

DALEY, DENNIS M., "Great Expectations, or a Tale of Two Systems: Employee Attitudes toward Graphic Rating Scales and MBO-Based Performance Appraisal," *Public Administration Quarterly*, Summer 1991, pp. 188–201.

DECENZO, DAVID A., AND STEPHEN P. ROBBINS, *Human Resource Management*, 4th ed. (New York: Wiley, 1994).

FARH, JIING-LIB, ALBERT A. CANNELLA, AND ARTHUR G. BEDIAN, "Peer Ratings: The Impact of Purpose on Rating Quality Acceptance," *Group and Organization Studies*, December 1991, pp. 367–86.

FERRIS, GERALD R., AND KENNETH M. ROWLAND, eds., *Performance Evaluation, Goal Setting, and Feedback* (Greenwich, CT: JAI Press, 1990).

MEYER, HERBERT H., "A Solution to the Performance Appraisal Feedback Enigma," *Academy of Management Executive*, February 1991, pp. 68–76.

O'NEAL, SANDRA, AND MADONNA PALLADINO, "Revamp Ineffective Performance Management," *Personnel Journal*, February 1992, pp. 93–102.

CHAPTER 15

ORGANIZATIONAL CULTURE

After reading this chapter, you should be able to:

1. Define the common characteristics making up organizational culture
2. Contrast strong and weak cultures
3. Identify the functional and dysfunctional effects of organizational culture on people
4. List the factors that maintain an organization's culture
5. Clarify how culture is transmitted to employees
6. Contrast organizational culture with national culture
7. Explain the paradox of diversity

Just as individuals have personalities, so too do organizations. In Chapter 3, we found that individuals have relatively enduring and stable traits that help us to predict their attitudes and behaviors. In this chapter, we propose that organizations, like people, can be characterized in terms like rigid, friendly, warm, innovative, or conservative. These traits, in turn, can then be used to predict attitudes and behaviors of the people within these organizations.

The theme of this chapter is that there is a systems variable in organizations that, while hard to define or describe precisely, nevertheless exists and which employees generally describe in common terms. We call this variable *organizational culture*. Just as tribal cultures have totems and taboos that dictate how each member will act toward fellow members and outsiders, organizations have cultures that govern how members behave. Just what organizational culture is, how it has an impact on employee attitudes and behavior, where it comes from, and whether or not it can be changed are discussed in the following pages.

■ DEFINING ORGANIZATIONAL CULTURE

There seems to be wide agreement that organizational culture refers to a system of shared meaning held by members that distinguishes the organization from other organizations. This system of shared meaning is, on closer analysis, a set of key characteristics that the organization values. There appear to be ten characteristics that, when mixed and matched, expose the essence of an organization's culture:

1. **Individual initiative**: the degree of responsibility, freedom, and independence that individuals have
2. **Risk tolerance**: the degree to which employees are encouraged to be aggressive, innovative, and risk seeking
3. **Direction**: the degree to which the organization creates clear objectives and performance expectations
4. **Integration**: the degree to which units within the organization are encouraged to operate in a coordinated manner
5. **Management support**: the degree to which managers provide clear communication, assistance, and support to their subordinates
6. **Control**: the number of rules and regulations, and the amount of direct supervision that is used to oversee and control employee behavior
7. **Identity**: the degree to which members identify with the organization as a whole rather than with their particular work group or field of professional expertise
8. **Reward system**: the degree to which reward allocations (that is, salary increases, promotions) are based on employee performance criteria in contrast to seniority, favoritism, and so on
9. **Conflict tolerance**: the degree to which employees are encouraged to air conflicts and criticisms openly
10. **Communication patterns**: the degree to which organizational communications are restricted to the formal hierarchy of authority

Each of these characteristics exists on a continuum from low to high. By appraising the organization on these ten characteristics, then, a composite picture of the organization's culture is formed. This picture becomes the basis for feelings of shared understanding that members have about the organization, how things are done in it, and the way members are supposed to behave. Exhibit 15–1 demonstrates how these characteristics can be mixed to create highly diverse organizations.

Culture Is a Descriptive Term

Organizational culture is concerned with how employees perceive the ten characteristics, not whether they like them or not. That is, it is a descriptive term. This is important because it differentiates this concept from that of job satisfaction.

EXHIBIT 15-1   *TWO HIGHLY DIVERSE ORGANIZATIONAL CULTURES*

Organization A	Organization B
This organization is a manufacturing firm. There are extensive rules and regulations that employees are required to follow. Every employee has specific objectives to achieve in his or her job. Managers supervise employees closely to ensure there are no deviations. People are allowed little discretion on their jobs. Employees are instructed to bring any unusual problem to their superior, who will then determine the solution. All employees are required to communicate through formal channels. Because management has no confidence in the honesty or integrity of its employees, it imposes tight controls. Managers and employees alike tend to be hired by the organization early in their careers, rotated into and out of various departments on a regular basis, and are generalists rather than specialists. Effort, loyalty, cooperation, and avoidance of errors are highly valued and rewarded.	This organization is also a manufacturing firm. Here, however, there are few rules and regulations. Employees are seen as hardworking and trustworthy, thus supervision is loose. Employees are encouraged to solve problems themselves, but to feel free to consult with their supervisors when they need assistance. Top management downplays authority differences. Employees are also encouraged to develop their unique specialized skills. Interpersonal and interdepartmental differences are seen as natural occurrences. Managers are evaluated not only on their department's performance but on how well their department coordinates its activities with other departments in the organization. Promotions and other valuable rewards go to employees who make the greatest contribution to the organization, even when those employees have strange ideas, unusual personal mannerisms, or unconventional work habits.

Research on organizational culture has sought to measure how employees see their organization: Are there clear objectives and performance expectations? Does the organization reward innovation? Does it stifle conflict?

In contrast, job satisfaction seeks to measure affective responses to the work environment. It is concerned with how employees feel about the organization's expectations, reward practices, methods for handling conflict, and the like. Although the two terms undoubtedly have characteristics that overlap, keep in mind that the term *organizational culture* is descriptive, while job satisfaction is evaluative.

Do Organizations Have Uniform Cultures?

Organizational culture represents a common perception held by the organization's members. This was made explicit when we defined culture as a system of *shared* meaning. We should expect, therefore, that individuals with different backgrounds or at different levels in the organization will tend to describe the organization's culture in similar terms.

Acknowledgment that organizational culture has common properties does not mean, however, that there cannot be subcultures within any given culture. Most large organizations have a dominant culture and numerous sets of subcultures.

A *dominant culture* expresses the core values that are shared by a majority of the organization's members. When we talk about an *organization's* culture, we are referring to its dominant culture. It is this macro view of culture that gives an organization its distinct personality. *Subcultures* tend to develop in large organizations to reflect common problems, situations, or experiences that members face. These subcultures are likely to be defined by department designations and geographical separation. The purchasing department, for example, can have a subculture that is uniquely shared by members of that department. It will include the core values of the dominant culture plus additional values unique to members of the purchasing department. Similarly, an office or unit of the organization that is physically separated from the organization's main operations may take on a different personality. Again, the core values are essentially retained but modified to reflect the separated unit's distinct situation.

If organizations had no dominant culture and were composed only of numerous subcultures, the value of organizational culture as an independent variable would be significantly lessened. Why? Because there would be no uniform interpretation of what represented appropriate or inappropriate behavior. It is the shared meaning aspect of culture that makes it such a potent device for guiding and shaping behavior. But we cannot ignore the reality that many organizations also have subcultures that can influence the behavior of members.

Strong versus Weak Cultures

It has become increasingly popular to differentiate between strong and weak cultures. The argument here is that strong cultures have a greater impact on employee behavior and are more directly related to reduced turnover.

A *strong culture* is characterized by the organization's core values being both intensely held and widely shared. The more members that accept the core values and the greater their commitment to those values, the stronger the culture is. Consistent with this definition, a strong culture will obviously have a greater influence on the behavior of its members. Religious organizations, cults, and Japanese companies are examples of organizations that have very strong cultures. When a David Koresh can entice dozens of his Branch Davidian members in Waco, Texas, to voluntarily die in flames, we see a behavioral influence considerably greater than that typically attributed to leadership. The culture of the Branch Davidians had a degree of sharedness and intensity that allowed for extremely high behavioral control. Of course, the same strong cultural influence that led to the tragedy in Waco can be directed positively to create immensely successful organizations like Microsoft, Mary Kay Cosmetics, and Sony.

A specific result of a strong culture should be lower employee turnover. A strong culture demonstrates high agreement among members about what the organization stands for. Such unanimity of purpose builds cohesiveness, loyalty, and organizational commitment. These, in turn, lessen the propensity for employees to leave the organization.

Culture versus Formalization

A strong organizational culture increases behavioral consistency. In this sense, we should recognize that a strong culture can act as a substitute for formalization.

In Chapter 12, we discussed how formalization's rules and regulations act to regulate employee behavior. High formalization in an organization creates predictability, orderliness, and consistency. Our point is that a strong culture achieves the same end without the need for written documentation. Therefore, we should view formalization and culture as two different roads to a common destination. The stronger an organization's culture, the less management need be concerned with developing formal rules and regulations to guide employee behavior. Those guides will have been internalized in employees when they accept the organization's culture.

■ WHAT DOES CULTURE DO?

We've alluded to organizational culture's impact on behavior. We've also explicitly argued that a strong culture should be associated with reduced turnover. In this section, we more carefully review the functions that culture performs and assess whether culture can be a liability for an organization.

Culture's Functions

Culture performs a number of functions within an organization. First, it has a boundary defining role; that is, it creates distinctions between one organization and others. Second, it conveys a sense of identity for organization members. Third, culture facilitates the generation of commitment to something larger than one's individual self-interest. Fourth, it enhances social system stability. Culture is the social glue that helps hold the organization together by providing appropriate standards for what employees should say and do. Finally, culture serves as a sense-making and control mechanism that guides and shapes the attitudes and behavior of employees. It is this last function that is of particular interest to us. As the following quote makes clear, culture defines the rules of the game:

> Culture by definition is elusive, intangible, implicit, and taken for granted. But every organization develops a core set of assumptions, understandings, and implicit rules that govern day-to-day behavior in the workplace. . . . Until newcomers learn the rules, they are not accepted as full-fledged members of the

organization. Transgressions of the rules on the part of high-level executives or front-line employees result in universal disapproval and powerful penalties. Conformity to the rules becomes the primary basis for reward and upward mobility.[1]

As we show later in this chapter, who is made job offers to join the organization, who is appraised as a high performer, and who gets the promotions are strongly influenced by the individual-organization fit, that is, whether the applicant or employee's attitudes and behavior are compatible with the culture. It is not a coincidence that employees at Disneyland and Disney World appear to be almost universally attractive, clean, wholesome, with bright smiles. That's the image Disney seeks. The company selects employees who will maintain that image. And once on the job, both the informal norms and formal rules and regulations ensure that Disney employees will act in a relatively uniform and predictable way.

Culture as a Liability

We are treating culture in a nonjudgmental manner. We haven't said that it's good or bad, only that it exists. Many of its functions, as outlined, are valuable for both the organization and the employee. Culture enhances organizational commitment and increases the consistency of employee behavior. These are clearly benefits to an organization. From an employee's standpoint, culture is valuable because it reduces ambiguity. It tells employees how things are done and what's important. But we shouldn't ignore the potentially dysfunctional aspects of culture, especially a strong one, on an organization's effectiveness.

Culture is a liability where the shared values are not in agreement with those that will further the organization's effectiveness. This is most likely to occur when the organization's environment is dynamic. When the environment is undergoing rapid change, the organization's entrenched culture may no longer be appropriate. So consistency of behavior is an asset to an organization when it faces a stable environment. It may, however, burden the organization and make it difficult to respond to changes in the environment.

■ CREATING AND SUSTAINING CULTURE

An organization's culture doesn't pop out of thin air. Once established, it rarely fades away. What forces influence the creation of a culture? What reinforces and sustains these forces once they are in place? We answer both of these questions in this section.

---

[1] Terrence E. Deal and Allan A. Kennedy, "Culture: A New Look through Old Lenses," *Journal of Applied Behavioral Science* (November 1983), p. 501.

How a Culture Begins

An organization's current customs, traditions, and general way of doing things are largely due to what it has done before and the degree of success it had with those endeavors. This leads us to the ultimate source of an organization's culture: its founders!

The founders of an organization traditionally have a major impact in establishing the early culture. They have a vision of what the organization should be. They are unconstrained by previous customs of doing things or ideologies. The small size that typically characterizes any new organization further facilitates the founders' imposing their vision on all organizational members. Because the founders have the original idea, they also typically have biases on how to get the idea fulfilled. The organization's culture results from the interaction between the founders' biases and assumptions and what the original members learn subsequently from their own experiences.

Henry Ford at the Ford Motor Company, Thomas Watson at IBM, J. Edgar Hoover at the FBI, Thomas Jefferson at the University of Virginia, Walt Disney at Walt Disney Company, Sam Walton at Wal-Mart, and David Packard at Hewlett-Packard are just a few obvious examples of individuals who have had immeasurable impact in shaping their organization's culture. For instance, Watson's views on research and development, product innovation, employee dress attire, and compensation policies are still evident at IBM, though he died in 1956. The Walt Disney Company continues to focus on Walt Disney's original vision of a company that created fantasy entertainment. Wal-Mart's commitment to frugality, simplicity, and value come directly from the late Sam Walton's persona. The formality found today at the University of Virginia is due, in large part, to the original culture created by its founder, Thomas Jefferson.

Keeping a Culture Alive

Once a culture is in place, practices within the organization act to maintain it by exposing employees to a set of similar experiences. For example, many of an organization's human resource practices reinforce its culture. The selection process, performance evaluation criteria, reward practices, training and career development activities, and promotion procedures ensure that those hired fit in with the culture, reward those who support it, and penalize (and even expel) those who challenge it. Three forces play a particularly important part in sustaining a culture—selection practices, the actions of top management, and socialization methods. Let's take a closer look at each.

Selection. The explicit goal of the selection process is to identify and hire individuals who have the knowledge, skills, and abilities to perform the jobs within the organization successfully. But, typically, more than one candidate will be found who meets any given job's requirements. When that point is reached, it would be naive to ignore that the final decision about who is hired will be significantly influenced by the decision maker's judgment of how well the candidates will fit into the organization. This attempt to ensure a proper match, whether purposely or inadvertently, results in the hiring of people who have common values (ones essentially consistent with those of the organization) or at least a good portion of those values. Additionally, the selection process provides information to applicants about the organization. Candidates learn about the organization, and, if they perceive a conflict between their values and those of the organization, they can self-select themselves out of the applicant pool. Selection, therefore, becomes a two-way street, allowing either employer or applicant to abrogate a marriage if there appears to be a mismatch. In this way, the selection process sustains an organization's culture by selecting out those individuals who might attack or undermine its core values.

Applicants for entry-level positions in brand management at Procter & Gamble (P&G) experience an exhaustive application and screening process. Their interviewers are part of an elite cadre who have been selected and trained extensively via lectures, videotapes, films, practice interviews, and role plays to identify applicants who will successfully fit in at P&G. Applicants are interviewed in depth for such qualities as their ability to "turn out high volumes of excellent work," "identify and understand problems," and "reach thoroughly substantiated and well-reasoned conclusions that lead to action." P&G values rationality and seeks applicants who think that way. College applicants receive two interviews and a general knowledge test on campus, before being flown back to Cincinnati for three more one-on-one interviews and a group interview at lunch. Each encounter seeks corroborating evidence of the traits that the firm believes correlate highly with "what counts" for success at P&G. Applicants for positions at Compaq Computer are carefully chosen for their ability to fit into the company's teamwork-oriented culture. As one executive put it, "We can find lots of people who are competent . . . The No. 1 issue is whether they fit into the way we do business."[2] At Compaq, that means job candidates who are easy to get along with and who feel comfortable with the company's consensus management style. To increase the likelihood that loners and those with big egos get screened out, it's not unusual for a new hire to be interviewed by 15 people who represent all departments of the company and a variety of seniority levels.

Top Management. The actions of top management also have a major impact on the organization's culture. Through what they say and how they behave, senior executives establish norms that filter down through the organization as to whether risk taking is desirable, how much freedom managers should give their subordinates, what is appropriate dress, what actions will pay off in terms of pay raises, promotions, and other rewards, and the like.

For example, look at Xerox Corp. Its chief executive from 1961 to 1968 was Joseph C. Wilson. An aggressive, entrepreneurial type, he oversaw Xerox's staggering growth on the basis of its 914 copier, one of the most successful products in American history. Under Wilson, Xerox had an entrepre-

---

2 "Who's Afraid of IBM?" *Business Week* (June 29, 1987) p. 72.

neurial environment, with an informal, high-camaraderie, innovative, bold, risk-taking culture. Wilson's replacement as CEO was C. Peter McColough, a Harvard MBA with a formal management style. He instituted bureaucratic controls and a major change in Xerox's culture. When McColough stepped down in 1982, Xerox had become stodgy and formal, with lots of politics and turf battles and layers of watchdog managers. His replacement was David T. Kearns. He believed the culture he inherited hindered Xerox's ability to compete. To increase the company's competitiveness, Kearns trimmed Xerox down by cutting fifteen thousand jobs, delegated decision making downward, and refocused the organization's culture around a simple theme: boosting the quality of Xerox products and services. By his actions and those of his senior managerial cadre, Kearns conveyed to everyone at Xerox that the company valued and rewarded quality and efficiency. When Kearns retired in 1990, Xerox still had its problems. The copier business was mature and Xerox had fared badly in developing computerized office systems. The new CEO, Paul Allaire, has again sought to reshape Xerox's culture. Specifically, he has reorganized the corporation around a worldwide marketing department, has unified product development and manufacturing divisions, and has replaced half of the company's top management team with outsiders. Allaire seeks to reshape Xerox's culture to focus on innovative thinking and outhustling the competition.

Socialization. No matter how good a job the organization does in recruiting and selection, new employees are not fully indoctrinated in the organization's culture. Maybe most important, because they are least familiar with the organization's culture, new employees are potentially most likely to disturb the beliefs and customs that are in place. The organization will, therefore, want to help new employees adapt to its culture. This adaptation process is called *socialization.*

All Marines must go through boot camp, where they prove their commitment. Of course, at the same time, the Marine trainers are indoctrinating new recruits in the "Marine way." The success of any cult depends on effective socialization. New Moonies undergo a "brainwashing" ritual that substitutes group loyalty and commitment in place of family. New Disneyland employees spend their first two full days of work watching films and listening to lectures on how Disney employees are expected to look and act.

As we discuss socialization, keep in mind that the most critical socialization stage is at the time of entry into the organization. This is when the organization seeks to mold the outsider into an employee in "good standing." Those employees who fail to learn the essential or pivotal role behaviors risk being labeled nonconformists or rebels, which often leads to expulsion. But the organization will be socializing every employee, though maybe not as explicitly, throughout his or her entire career in the organization. This further contributes to sustaining the culture.

Socialization can be conceptualized as a process made up of three stages: prearrival, encounter, and metamorphosis. The first stage encompasses all the

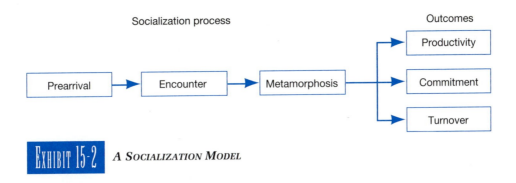

Socialization process   Outcomes

Prearrival	→	Encounter	→	Metamorphosis	→	Productivity

EXHIBIT 15-2   *A SOCIALIZATION MODEL*

learning that occurs before a new member joins the organization. In the second stage, the new employee sees what the organization is really like and confronts the likelihood that expectations and reality may diverge. In the third stage, the relatively long-lasting changes take place. The new employee masters the skills required for his or her job, successfully performs his or her new roles, and makes the adjustments to his or her work group's values and norms. This three-stage process has an impact on the new employee's work productivity, commitment to the organization's objectives, and his or her decision to stay with the organization. Exhibit 15–2 depicts this process.

The *prearrival stage* occurs before the employee joins the organization, so that he or she arrives with an established set of values, attitudes, and expectations. These cover both the work to be done and the organization. For instance, in many jobs, particularly professional work, new members will have undergone a considerable degree of prior socialization in training and in school. One major purpose of a business school, for example, is to socialize business students into the attitudes and behaviors that business firms want. If business executives believe successful employees value the profit ethic, are loyal, will work hard, want to achieve, and willingly accept directions from their superiors, they can hire individuals out of business schools who have been premolded in this pattern. But prearrival socialization goes beyond the specific job. The selection process is used in most organizations to inform prospective employees about the organization as a whole. In addition, as noted previously, the selection process also acts to ensure the inclusion of the right type—those who will fit in. "Indeed, the ability of the individual to present the appropriate face during the selection process determines his ability to move into the organization in the first place. Thus, success depends on the degree to which the aspiring member has correctly anticipated the expectations and desires of those in the organization in charge of selection."[3]

Upon entry into the organization, the new members enter the *encounter stage*. Here the individuals confront the possible dichotomy between their expectations about their job, co-workers, their boss, and the organization in

---

[3] John Van Maanen and Edgar H. Schein, "Career Development," in *Improving Life at Work*, eds. J. Richard Hackman and J.L. Suttle (Santa Monica, CA: Goodyear, 1977), p. 59.

general, and reality. If expectations prove to have been more or less accurate, the encounter stage merely provides a reaffirmation of the perceptions gained earlier. However, this is often not the case. Where expectations and reality differ, new employees must undergo socialization that will detach them from previous assumptions and replace these with another set the organization deems desirable. At the extreme, new members may become totally disillusioned with the actualities of their job and resign. Proper selection should significantly reduce the probability of the latter occurrence.

Finally, new members must work out any problems discovered during the encounter stage. This may mean going through changes; hence, we call this the *metamorphosis stage*. The choices presented in Exhibit 15–3 are alternatives designed to bring about the desired metamorphosis. But what is a desirable metamorphosis? We can say that metamorphosis, and the entry socialization process, are complete when new members have become comfortable with the organization and their job. They have internalized the norms of the organization and work group, and they understand and accept these norms. New members feel accepted by their peers as trusted and valued individuals. They

Exhibit 15-3   *ENTRY SOCIALIZATION OPTIONS*

Formal vs. Informal   The more a new employee is segregated from the ongoing work setting and differentiated in some way to make explicit his or her newcomer's role, the more formal socialization is. Specific orientation and training programs are examples. Informal socialization puts the new employee directly into his or her job, with little or no special attention.

Individual or Collective   New members can be socialized individually. This describes how it's done in many professional offices. They can also be grouped together and processed through an identical set of experiences, as in military boot camp.

Fixed vs. Variable   This refers to the time schedule in which newcomers make the transition from outsider to insider. A fixed schedule establishes standardized stages of transition. This characterizes rotational training programs. It also includes probationary periods, such as the six-year "tenure or out" procedure commonly used with new assistant professors in colleges. Variable schedules give no advanced notice of their transition timetable. This describes the typical promotion system, where one is not advanced to the next stage until he or she is "ready."

Serial vs. Random   Serial socialization is characterized by the use of role models who train and encourage the newcomer. Apprenticeship and mentoring programs are examples. In random socialization, role models are deliberately withheld. The new employee is left on his or her own to figure things out.

Investiture vs. Divestiture   Investiture socialization assumes that the newcomer's qualities and qualifications are the necessary ingredients for job success, so these qualities and qualifications are confirmed and supported. Divestiture socialization tries to strip away certain characteristics of the recruit. Fraternity and sorority "pledges" go through divestiture socialization to shape them into the proper role.

Source: Based on John Van Maanen, "People Processing: Strategies of Organizational Socialization," *Organizational Dynamics* (Summer 1978), pp. 19–36; and E.H. Schein, "Organizational Culture," *American Psychologist* (February 1990), p. 116.

EXHIBIT 15-4 *HOW ORGANIZATION CULTURES FORM*

are self-confident that they have the competence to complete the job successfully. They understand the system—not only their own tasks, but the rules, procedures, and informally accepted practices as well. Finally, they know how they will be evaluated, that is, what criteria will be used to measure and appraise their work. They know what is expected of them and what constitutes a job well done. As Exhibit 15–2 shows, successful metamorphosis should have a positive impact on the new employees' productivity and their commitment to the organization and reduce their propensity to leave the organization.

Summary: How Cultures Form

Exhibit 15–4 summarizes how an organization's culture is established and sustained. The original culture is derived from the founder's philosophy. This, in turn, strongly influences the criteria used in hiring. The actions of the current top management set the general climate of what is acceptable behavior and what is not. How employees are to be socialized will depend on the degree of success achieved in matching new employees' values to those of the organization in the selection process and top management's preference for socialization methods.

■ HOW EMPLOYEES LEARN CULTURE

Culture is transmitted to employees in a number of forms, the most potent being stories, rituals, material symbols, and language.

Stories

During the days when Henry Ford II was chairman of the Ford Motor Company, one would have been hard pressed to find a manager who hadn't heard the story about Henry Ford II reminding his executives, when they got too arrogant, that "it's *my* name that's on the building." The message was clear: Henry Ford II ran the company!

IBM employees tell the story of a plant security supervisor who challenged Thomas Watson, Jr., the all-powerful chairman of IBM's board. The supervisor, a 22-year-old woman, was required to make certain that people entering security areas wore the correct clearance identification. One day, surrounded by his usual entourage, Watson approached the doorway to an area where the supervisor was on guard. He wore an orange badge acceptable elsewhere in the plant, but not a green badge, which alone permitted entrance at her door. Although she knew who Watson was, she told him what she had been instructed to say to anyone without proper clearance: "You cannot enter. Your admittance is not recognized." The men accompanying Watson were taken back. Would this young security guard be fired on the spot? "Don't you know who he is?" someone asked. Watson raised his hand for silence while one of the party strode off and returned with the appropriate badge. The message to IBM employees: No matter who you are, you obey the rules.

Stories like these circulate through many organizations. They contain a narrative of events about the organization's founders, the present top management, and key decisions that affect the organization's future course. They anchor the present in the past and provide explanations and legitimacy for current practices.

Rituals

Rituals are repetitive sequences of activities that express and reinforce the key values of the organization, what goals are most important, which people are important and which are expendable.

College faculty members undergo a lengthy ritual in their quest for permanent employment, or tenure. Typically, the faculty member is on probation for six years. At the end of that period, the member's colleagues must make one of two choices: extend a tenured appointment or issue a one-year terminal contract. What does it take to obtain tenure? It usually requires satisfactory teaching performance, service to the department and university, and scholarly activity. But, of course, what satisfies the requirements for tenure in one department at one university may be appraised as inadequate in another. The key is that the tenure decision, in essence, asks those who are tenured to assess whether the candidate has demonstrated, based on six years of performance, whether he or she fits in. Colleagues who have been socialized properly will have proved themselves worthy of being granted tenure. Every year, hundreds of faculty members at colleges and universities are denied tenure. In some cases, this action is a result of poor performance across the board. More often, however, the decision can be traced to the faculty member not doing well in those areas that the tenured faculty believe are important. The instructor who spends dozens of hours each week preparing for class, achieves outstanding evaluations by students, but neglects his or her research and publication activities, may be passed over for tenure. What has happened, simply, is that the instructor has failed to adapt to the norms set by the department. The astute faculty member will assess early in the probationary period what attitudes and behaviors his or her colleagues want and will then proceed to give it to them. And, of course, by doing so the tenured faculty have made significant strides toward standardizing tenure candidates.

One of the best-known corporate rituals is Mary Kay Cosmetics' annual award meeting. Looking like a cross between a circus and a Miss America pageant, the meeting takes place over a couple of days in a large auditorium, on a stage in front of a large cheering audience, with all the participants dressed in glamorous evening clothes. Saleswomen are rewarded with an array of flashy gifts—gold and diamond pins, fur stoles, pink Cadillacs—based on success in achieving sales quota. This "show" acts as a motivator by publicly recognizing outstanding sales performance. In addition, the ritual aspect reinforces Mary Kay's personal determination and optimism, which enabled her to overcome personal hardships, found her own company, and achieve material success. It conveys to her salespeople that reaching their sales quota is important and that through hard work and encouragement they too can achieve success.

Material Symbols

Tandem Computers' headquarters in Cupertino, California, doesn't look like your typical head-office operation. It has jogging trails, a basketball court, space for dance and yoga classes, and a large swimming pool—all for its employees' enjoyment. Every Friday afternoon at 4:30, employees partake in the weekly beer bust, courtesy of the company. This informal corporate headquarters conveys to employees that Tandem values openness and equality.

Some corporations provide their top executives with chauffeur-driven limousines and, when they travel by air, unlimited use of the corporate jet. Others may not get to ride in limousines or private jets but they might still get a car and air transportation paid for by the company. Only, the car is a Chevrolet (with no driver) and the jet seat is in the economy section of a commercial airliner.

The layout of corporate headquarters, the types of automobiles top executives are given, and the presence or absence of corporate aircraft are a few examples of material symbols. Others include the size and layout of offices, the elegance of furnishings, executive perks, and dress attire. These material symbols convey to employees who is important, the degree of egalitarianism desired by top management, and the kinds of behavior (for example, risk taking, conservative, authoritarian, participative, individualistic, social) that are appropriate.

Language

Many organizations and units within organizations use language as a way to identify members of a culture or subculture. By learning this language, members attest to their acceptance of the culture and, in so doing, help to preserve it.

The following are examples of terminology used by employees at Dialog, a California-based data redistributor: *accession number* (a number assigned each individual record in a data base); *KWIC* (a set of key-words-in-context); and *relational operator* (searching a data base for names or key terms in some order). Librarians are a rich source of terminology foreign to people outside their profession. They sprinkle their conversations liberally with acronyms like *ARL* (Association for Research Libraries), *OCLC* (a center in Ohio that does cooperative cataloging), and *OPAC* (for on-line patron accessing catalog).

Organizations, over time, often develop unique terms to describe equipment, offices, key personnel, suppliers, customers, or products that relate to its business. New employees are frequently overwhelmed with acronyms and jargon that, after six months on the job, have become fully part of their language. But once assimilated, this terminology acts as a common denominator that unites members of a given culture or subculture.

■ DOES AN ORGANIZATION'S CULTURE OVERIDE A COUNTRY'S NATIONAL CULTURE?

In a number of places throughout this book we've argued that national differences—that is, national culture—must be taken into account if accurate predictions are to be made about organizational behavior in different countries. But does national culture override an organization's culture? Is an IBM facility in Germany, for example, more likely to reflect German ethnicity or IBM's corporate culture?

The research indicates that national culture has a greater impact on employees than does their organization's culture. German employees at an IBM facility in Munich, therefore, will be influenced more by German culture than by IBM's culture. This means that as influential as organizational culture is to understanding the behavior of people at work, national culture is even more so.

The preceding conclusion has to be qualified to reflect the self-selection that goes on at the hiring stage. IBM, for example, may be less concerned with hiring the "typical Italian" for its Italian operations than in hiring an Italian who fits within the IBM way of doing things. Italians who have a high need for autonomy are more likely to go to Olivetti than IBM. Why? Because Olivetti's organizational culture is informal and nonstructured. It allows employees considerably more freedom than IBM. In fact, Olivetti seeks to hire individuals who are impatient, risk taking, and innovative—qualities in job candidates that IBM's Italian operations would purposely seek to exclude in new hires.

■ ORGANIZATIONAL CULTURE AND THE PARADOX OF DIVERSITY

Before we conclude this chapter with a discussion of organizational culture's implications for managers, we want to briefly mention a contemporary challenge for managers. Socializing new employees who, because of race, gender, ethnic, or other differences, are not like the majority of the organization's members, creates what we call the *paradox of diversity.*

Management wants new employees to accept the organization's core cultural values. Otherwise, these employees are unlikely to fit in or be accepted. But at the same time, management wants to openly acknowledge and demonstrate support for the differences that these employees bring to the workplace.

Strong cultures put considerable pressure on employees to conform. They limit the range of values and styles that are acceptable. Obviously, this creates a dilemma. Organizations hire diverse individuals because of the alternative strengths these people bring to the workplace. Yet these diverse behaviors and strengths are likely to diminish in strong cultures as people attempt to fit in.

Management's challenge in this paradox of diversity is to balance two conflicting goals: get employees to accept the organizations' dominant values and encourage the acceptance of differences. Too much attention to investiture rites is likely to create employees who are misfits. On the other hand, too much emphasis on divestiture rites may eliminate those unique strengths that people of different backgrounds bring to the organization.

■ IMPLICATIONS FOR MANAGERS

There seems to be little doubt that culture has a strong influence on employee behavior. But what can management do to design a culture that molds employees in the way management wants?

When an organization is just being established, management has a great deal of influence. There are no established traditions. The organization is small. There are few, if any, subcultures. Everyone knows the founder and is directly touched by his or her vision of what the organization is. Not surprisingly, under these conditions management has the opportunity to create a culture that will best facilitate the achievement of the organization's goals.

However, when the organization is well established, so too is its dominant culture. Given that this culture is made up of relatively stable and permanent characteristics, it becomes very resistant to change. It took time to form; and once established, it tends to become entrenched. Strong cultures are particularly resistant to change because employees become so committed to them. So, if a given culture, over time, becomes inappropriate to an organization and a handicap to management, there may be little management can do to change it. This is especially true in the short run. Under the most favorable conditions, cultural changes have to be measured in years, not weeks or months.

What would those "favorable conditions" be that *might* facilitate changing a culture? The evidence suggests that cultural change is most likely to take place when most or all of the following conditions exist:

A dramatic crisis. This can be the shock that undermines the status quo and calls into question the relevance of the current culture. Examples of these crises might be a surprising financial setback, the loss of a major customer, or a dramatic technological breakthrough by a competitor.

Turnover in leadership. New top leadership, who can provide an alternative set of key values, may be perceived as more capable of responding to the crisis. This would definitely encompass the organization's chief executive but also might need to include all senior management positions.

Young and small organization. The younger the organization is, the less entrenched will be its culture. Similarly, it's easier for management to communicate its new values when the organization is small.

Weak culture. The more widely held a culture is and the higher the agreement among members on its values, the more difficult it will be to change. Conversely, weak cultures are more amenable to change than strong ones.

Keep in mind that even if these conditions exist, there is no assurance that the culture will change. Moreover, any significant change will take a long time. So, especially in the short and intermediate term, an organization's culture should be treated as an important influence on employee behavior and something that management has little influence over.

SUGGESTIONS FOR FURTHER READING

BOWEN, DAVID E., GERALD E. LEDFORD, JR., AND BARRY R. NATHAN, "Hiring for the Organization, Not the Job," *Academy of Management Executive*, November 1991, pp. 35–51.

CARTWRIGHT, SUSAN, AND CARY L. COOPER, "The Role of Culture Compatibility in Successful Organizational Marriage," *Academy of Management Executive*, May 1993, pp. 57–70.

GORDON, GEORGE G., "Industry Determinants of Organizational Culture," *Academy of Management Review*, April 1991, pp. 396–415.

GORDON, GEORGE G., AND NANCY DITOMASO, "Predicting Corporate Performance from Organizational Culture," *Journal of Management Studies*, November 1992, pp. 784–98.

HARRISON, J. RICHARD, AND GLENN R. CARROLL, "Keeping the Faith: A Model of Cultural Transmission in Formal Organizations," *Administrative Science Quarterly*, December 1991, pp. 552–82.

SACKMANN, SONJA A., "Culture and Subcultures: An Analysis of Organizational Knowledge," *Administrative Science Quarterly*, March 1992, pp. 140–61.

SHERIDAN, JOHN E., "Organizational Culture and Employee Retention," *Academy of Management Journal*, December 1992, pp. 1036–56.

TRICE, HARRISON M., AND JANICE M. BEYER, *The Cultures of Work Organizations* (Englewood Cliffs, NJ: Prentice Hall, 1993).

CHAPTER 16

ORGANIZATIONAL CHANGE AND DEVELOPMENT

After reading this chapter, you should be able to:

1. Describe forces that act as stimulants to change
2. Define *planned change*
3. Summarize Lewin's three-step change model
4. Explain sources of resistance to change
5. List techniques for overcoming resistance to change
6. Define organizational development (OD)
7. Identify symptoms of work stress
8. Describe specific actions that will facilitate empowering employees
9. Summarize sources of innovation

More and more organizations today face a dynamic and changing environment that requires these organizations to adapt. Let's begin our look at organizational change by looking at specific forces that are acting as stimulants for change.

■ FORCES FOR CHANGE

The following six forces are increasingly creating the need for change—the changing nature of the work force, technology, economic shocks, changing social trends, the new world politics, and the changing nature of competition.

Nature of the Work Force

The 1990s are a decade where organizations have to learn to manage diversity. The work force is changing, with a rapid increase in the percentage of women and minorities. Human resource policies and practices will have to change in order to attract and keep this more diverse work force.

It's easy to focus on the increasing educational levels of the work force. But there is a dark side that has important implications for organizations. A significant portion of new work force entrants do not have marketable skills. Many are high school dropouts. But a good number, and this is probably the most alarming, have high school and college degrees but can't adequately perform the basic reading, writing, and computational skills that organizations require. This is requiring organizations to introduce training programs to upgrade skills and, in some cases, deskill jobs so they can be adequately performed by employees.

Technology

Changes in technology change the nature of work. The adoption of new technologies such as computers, telecommunication systems, robotics, and flexible manufacturing operations have a profound impact on the organizations that adopt them.

For instance, IBM has built a system of modular work stations at a plant in Austin, Texas, that uses flexible manufacturing concepts to build personal computers. From receiving dock to exit dock, computers are assembled, tested, packed, and shipped without a human being so much as turning a screw. The entire operation is handled by 13 robots. Moreover, the entire manufacturing system was built with flexibility in mind. The plant is designed to be able to build *any* electronic product that is no bigger than 2 feet by 2 feet by 14 inches. So IBM's management can build printers, other types of computers, or even toasters in this plant.

Computers and sophisticated information systems, while only the tip of the technology iceberg, are having an enormous impact on organizations. They are stimulating widespread changes in the required skill levels of employees, the daily activities of managers, and the organization's ability to respond to the changing needs of customers. For instance, companies such as Motorola, General Electric, and AT&T can now develop, make, and distribute their products in a fraction of the time it took them a decade ago. And, as organizations have had to become more adaptable, so too have their employees. As we noted in our discussion of groups and organization design, many jobs are being reshaped. Individuals doing narrow, specialized, and routine jobs are being replaced by work teams whose members can perform multiple tasks and actively participate in team decisions.

Economic Shocks

We live in an "age of discontinuity." In the 1950s and 1960s, the past was a pretty good prologue to the future. Tomorrow was essentially an extended trend line from yesterday. That is no longer true. Beginning in the early 1970s, with the overnight quadrupling of world oil prices, economic shocks have continued to impose changes on organizations. In an indirect way, the changes we mention have affected all organizations. However, economic shocks typically hit some industries and firms much harder than others.

In the last 20 years, we've seen a number of major economic shocks in the United States. When the Organization of Exporting Countries raised the price of oil from under $3 to nearly $12 a barrel, companies like General Motors, Honda, Winnebago, and insulation manufacturer Johns-Mansville felt immediate repercussions. Skyrocking inflation in the mid-1970s drove interest rates through the roof and forced many home builders into bankruptcy. The stock market crash of October 1987 proved devastating to the financial services industry. Large layoffs on Wall Street immediately followed; and several major brokerage firms were forced to restructure or merge in order to survive. One of the latest shocks to the economy has been the massive defaults of savings and loans. This, in turn, has depressed real estate prices and resulted in large losses for real estate developers and others closely connected with the real estate industry.

During the remainder of the 1990s, we can forecast with almost complete certainty that there will be one or more shocks of similar magnitude to those of the past couple of decades. The only problem is that it is impossible to predict what those shocks will be and where they will come from. That is the irony of change in the age of discontinuity: We know almost for sure that tomorrow won't be like today, but we don't know how it will be different.

Social Trends

Take a look at social trends during the 1970s and 1980s. Employment opportunities greatly expanded for minorities and women. The proportion of high school graduates who went on to college nearly doubled. Young people delayed marriage. Consumer shopping patterns changed. On this last point, few retail businesses haven't been affected by the shift in consumer preferences for specialty stores. Large chains such as Sears, which try to be all things to all people, have suffered at the hands of discount and niche stores. Wal-Mart, Kmart, Circuit City, Toys "R" Us, Waldenbooks, Victoria's Secret, and Blockbuster Video are examples of firms that have responded to this trend. Many of the big retailers of yesterday—W.T. Grant, Gimbel's, F.W. Woolworth, Montgomery Ward, Macy's, Sears—are either dead or in extremely poor health.

World Politics

In Chapter 2 we argued strongly for the importance of seeing OB in a global context. Recent headlines reveal a very different world than existed just a few years ago. The fall of the Berlin Wall. Elections in Poland. Declarations of sovereignty by Soviet republics. The reunification of Germany. A massively destructive internal war in what was Yugoslavia.

What do the new world politics mean to students of management and organizational behavior? It's too soon to predict the full impact of these changes, yet some predictions seem relatively safe.

One certainty is that companies that have survived on defense contracts will be undergoing changes. Major defense contractors—like General Dynamics and McDonnell-Douglas—have begun comprehensive reorganization plans that include cutting tens of thousands of jobs.

Managers of most firms and a good portion of their employees will need to become attuned to cultural differences. They will increasingly be interacting with people in other countries and working alongside people raised in different cultures. So don't be surprised to find yourself working for a boss who was raised in a different land. It also may not be a bad idea to brush up or begin developing your foreign language skills—especially in Japanese and German.

Ownership of companies and property by people and organizations from other countries is likely to continue worldwide. As long as currencies fluctuate and some economies outperform others, assets will flow across borders. In the 1980s, Japanese money flowed into the United States. In the 1990s, it may well be United States, Canadian, and Japanese funds that flow into Eastern Europe. Where investment goes will fluctuate at different times, but in a true global economy resources will constantly seek out their best return, wherever in the world that might be. What this means, of course, is the realization that some businesses in some countries will fail because their products or services can be more efficiently produced in another country. Along these lines, it is no longer preposterous to conceive of a General Motors Corporation, headquartered in Detroit, that builds every one of its automobiles in plants outside the United States.

Competition

The last area we want to discuss is the changes that derive from increased competition. The global economy means that competitors are as likely to come from Japan, Mexico, or Germany as from the other side of town. But heightened competition also means that established organizations need to defend themselves against both traditional competitors who develop new products and services and small entrepreneurial firms with innovative offerings.

Successful organizations will be the ones that can change in response to the competition. They'll be fast on their feet, capable of developing new products rapidly, and getting them to market quickly. They'll rely on short production runs, short product cycles, and an ongoing stream of new products. In other words, they'll be flexible. They will require an equally flexible and responsive work force that can adapt to rapidly and even radically changing conditions.

■ MANAGING PLANNED CHANGE

A group of employees who work in a small retail women's clothing store confronted the owner: "The air pollution in this store from cigarette smoking has gotten awful," said their spokeswoman. "We won't continue to work here if you allow smoking in the store. We want you to post no smoking signs on the entrance doors and not allow any employee to smoke on the floor. If people have to smoke, they can go into the mall." The owner listened thoughtfully to the group's ultimatum and agreed to their request. The next day the owner posted the no smoking signs and advised all of her employees of the new rule.

A major automobile manufacturer spent several billion dollars to install state-of-the-art robotics. One area that would receive the new equipment was quality control. Sophisticated computer-controlled equipment would be put in place to significantly improve the company's ability to find and correct defects. Since the new equipment would dramatically change the jobs of the people working in the quality control area, and since management anticipated considerable employee resistance to the new equipment, executives were developing a program to help people become familiar with the equipment and to deal with any anxieties they might be feeling.

Both of the previous scenarios are examples of *change*. That is, both were concerned with making things different. However, only the second scenario described a planned change. In this section, we want to clarify what we mean by planned change, describe its goals, and consider who is responsible for bringing about *planned change* in an organization.

Many changes in organizations are like the one that occurred in the retail clothing store—they just happen. Some organizations treat all change as an accidental occurrence. However, we're concerned with change activities that are proactive and purposeful. In this chapter, we address change as an intentional, goal-oriented activity.

What are the goals of planned change? Essentially there are two. First, it seeks to improve the ability of the organization to adapt to changes in its environment. Second, it seeks to change employee behavior.

If an organization is to survive, it must respond to changes in its environment. When competitors introduce new products or services, government agencies enact new laws, important sources of supply go out of business, or similar environmental changes take place, the organization needs to adapt. Efforts to introduce work teams, decentralized decision making, and new organizational cultures are examples of planned change activities directed at responding to changes in the environment.

Since an organization's success or failure is essentially due to the things that employees do or fail to do, planned change also is concerned with changing the behavior of individuals and groups within the organization. Later in this chapter, we review a number of techniques that organizations can use to get people to behave differently in the tasks they perform and in their interaction with others.

Who in organizations is responsible for managing change activities? The answer is *change agents*. These change agents can be managers or nonmanagers, employees of the organization or outside consultants. For major change efforts, internal management often will hire the services of outside consultants to provide advice and assistance. Because they are from the outside, these individuals can offer an objective perspective often unavailable to insiders. However, outside consultants are disadvantaged because they usually have an inadequate understanding of the organization's history, culture, operating procedures, and personnel. Outside consultants also may be prone to initiating more drastic changes—which can be a benefit or a disadvantage—because they do not have to live with the repercussions after the change is implemented. In contrast, internal staff specialists or managers, when acting as change agents, may be more thoughtful (and possibly cautious) because they must live with the consequences of their actions.

■ TWO DIFFERENT VIEWS

"The organization is like a large ship traveling across the calm Mediterranean Sea to a specific port. The ship's captain has made this exact trip hundreds of times before with the same crew. Every once in a while, however, a storm will appear, and the crew has to respond. The captain will make the appropriate adjustment—that is, implement changes—and, having maneuvered through the storm, will return to calm waters. Implementing change in organizations should therefore be seen as a response to a break in the status quo and needed only in occasional situations."

"The organization is more akin to a forty-foot raft than to a large ship. Rather than sailing a calm sea, this raft must traverse a raging river made up of an uninterrupted flow of permanent white-water rapids. To make things worse, the raft is manned by ten people who have never worked together, none have traveled the river before, much of the trip is in the dark, the river is dotted by unexpected turns and obstacles, the exact destination of the raft is not clear, and at irregular frequencies the raft needs to pull to shore, where new crew members are added and others leave. Change is a natural state and managing change is a continual process."

These two metaphors present very different approaches to understanding and responding to change. Let's take a closer look at each one.[1]

The "Calm Waters" Metaphor

Until very recently, the "calm waters" metaphor dominated the thinking of practicing managers and academics. It is best illustrated in Kurt Lewin's three-step description of the change process[2] (see Exhibit 16–1).

---

[1] These metaphors were developed by Peter B. Vaill, *Managing as a Performing Art: New Ideas for a World of Chaotic Change* (San Francisco: Jossey-Bass, 1989).

[2] Kurt Lewin, "Group Decision and Social Change," in *Readings in Social Psychology*, 2nd ed., eds. G.E. Swanson, T.M. Newcome, and E.L. Hartley (New York: Holt, 1952), pp. 459–73.

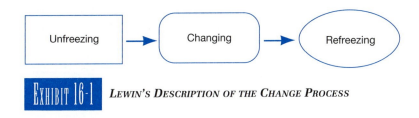

EXHIBIT 16-1 *LEWIN'S DESCRIPTION OF THE CHANGE PROCESS*

According to Lewin, successful change requires *unfreezing* the status quo, *changing* to a new state, and *refreezing* the new change to make it permanent. The status quo can be considered an equilibrium state. To move from this equilibrium, unfreezing is necessary. It can be achieved in one of three ways:

1. The *driving forces*, which direct behavior away from the status quo, can be increased.
2. The *restraining forces*, which hinder movement from the existing equilibrium, can be decreased.
3. The two approaches can be *combined*.

Once unfreezing has been accomplished, the change itself can be implemented. However, the mere introduction of change does not ensure it will take hold. The new situation therefore needs to be *refrozen* so it can be sustained over time. Unless this last step is attended to, there is a very strong chance the change will be short lived and employees will revert to the previous equilibrium state. The objective of refreezing, then, is to stabilize the new situation by balancing the driving and restraining forces.

Note how Lewin's three-step process treats change as a break in the organization's equilibrium state. The status quo has been disturbed, and change is necessary to establish a new equilibrium state. This view might have been appropriate to the relatively calm environment that most organizations faced in the 1950s, 1960s, and early 1970s. But one can argue that the "calm waters" metaphor no longer describes the kind of seas that current managers have to negotiate.

The "White-Water Rapids" Metaphor

The "white-water rapids" metaphor is consistent with our discussion of uncertain and dynamic environments in Chapter 13. It is also consistent with the dynamics associated with going from an industrial society to a world dominated by information and ideas.

To get a feeling for what managing change might be like when you have to continually maneuver in uninterrupted rapids, how would you like to attend a college that has the following curriculum? Courses vary in length. Unfortunately, when you sign up, you don't know how long a course will last. It might go for two weeks or thirty weeks. Furthermore, the instructor can end a course any time he or she wants, with no prior warning. If that wasn't bad enough, the length of the class changes each time it meets—sometimes it lasts twenty minutes, while other times it runs for three hours—and determination of when the next class meeting will take place is set by the instructor during the previous class. Oh yes, there's one more thing. The exams are all unannounced, so you have to be ready for a test at any time.

To succeed in this college, you would have to be incredibly flexible and able to respond quickly to every changing condition. Students who were over-structured or slow on their feet wouldn't survive.

A growing number of managers are coming to accept that their job is much like what a student would face in such a college. The stability and predictability of the "calm water" metaphor don't exist. Nor are disruptions in the status quo only occasional and temporary, followed by a return to calm waters. Many of today's managers never get out of the rapids. They face constant change, bordering on chaos. These managers are being forced to play a game they've never played before, governed by rules that are created as the game progresses.

Putting the Two Views in Perspective

Does *every* manager face a world of constant and chaotic change? No, but the set of managers who don't is dwindling rapidly.

Managers in businesses like women's high-fashion clothing and computer software have long confronted a world that looks like white-water rapids. They used to look with envy at their counterparts in industries such as auto manufacturing, oil exploration, banking, fast-food restaurants, office equipment, publishing, telecommunications, and air transportation because these managers historically faced a stable and predictable environment. That might have been true in the 1960s, but it's not true in the 1990s!

Few organizations today can treat change as the occasional disturbance in an otherwise peaceful world. Even these few do so at great risk. Too much is changing too fast for any organization or its managers to be complacent. Most competitive advantages last less than 18 months. A firm like People Express was described in business periodicals as the model "new look" firm, then went bankrupt a short time later. As Tom Peters has aptly noted, the old saw "If it ain't broke, don't fix it" no longer applies. In its place, he suggests "If it ain't broke, you just haven't looked hard enough. Fix it anyway."[3]

■ RESISTANCE TO CHANGE

One of the most well-documented findings from studies of individual and organizational behavior is that organizations and their members resist change. In a sense, this is positive. It provides a degree of stability and pre-

---

[3] Tom Peters, *Thriving on Chaos* (New York: Alfred A. Knopf, 1987), p. 3.

dictability to behavior. If there wasn't some resistance, organizational behavior would take on characteristics of chaotic randomness. Resistance to change can also be a source of functional conflict. For example, resistance to a reorganization plan or a change in a product line can stimulate a healthy debate over the merits of the idea and result in a better decision. But there is a definite downside to resistance to change. It hinders adaptation and progress.

Resistance to change doesn't necessarily surface in standardized ways. Resistance can be overt, implicit, immediate, or deferred. It is easiest for management to deal with resistance when it is overt and immediate. For instance, a change is proposed and employees quickly respond by voicing complaints, engaging in a work slowdown, threatening to go on strike, or the like. The greater challenge is managing resistance that is implicit or deferred. Implicit resistance efforts are more subtle—loss of loyalty to the organization, loss of motivation to work, increased errors or mistakes, increased absenteeism due to "sickness"—and hence more difficult to recognize. Similarly, deferred actions cloud the link between the source of the resistance and the reaction to it. A change may produce what appears to be only a minimal reaction at the time it is initiated but surfaces weeks, months, or even years later. Or a single change, in and of itself, has little impact. But it becomes the straw that breaks the camel's back. Reactions to change can build up and then explode in some response that seems totally out of proportion to the change action it follows. The resistance, of course, has merely been deferred and stockpiled. What surfaces is a response to an accumulation of previous changes.

Let's look at the sources of resistance. For analytical purposes, we've categorized them by individual and organizational sources. In the real world, the sources often overlap.

Individual Resistance

Individual sources of resistance to change reside in basic human characteristics such as perceptions, personalities, and needs. The following summarizes five reasons why individuals may resist change.

Habit. Every time you go out to eat do you try a different restaurant? Probably not. If you're like most people, you find a couple of places you like and return to them on a somewhat regular basis.

As human beings, we're creatures of habit. Life is complex enough; we don't need to consider the full range of options for the hundreds of decisions we have to make every day. To cope with this complexity, we all rely on habits or programmed responses. But when confronted with change, this tendency to respond in our accustomed ways becomes a source of resistance. So when your department is moved to a new office building across town, it means you're likely to have to change many habits: waking up ten minutes earlier, taking a new set of streets to work, finding a new parking place, adjusting to the new office layout, developing a new lunchtime routine, and so on.

Security. People who have a high need for security are likely to resist change because it threatens their feeling of safety. When General Dynamics announces personnel cutbacks or Ford introduces new robotic equipment, many employees at these firms may fear their jobs are in jeopardy.

Economic Factors. Another source of individual resistance is concern that changes will lower one's income. Changes in job tasks or established work routines also can arouse economic fears if people are concerned they won't be able to perform the new tasks or routines to their previous standards, especially when pay is closely tied to productivity.

Fear of the Unknown. Changes substitute ambiguity and uncertainty for the known. Regardless of how much you may dislike attending college, at least you know what is expected of you. But when you leave college and venture out into the world of full-time employment, regardless of how much you want to get out of college, you have to trade the known for the unknown.

Employees in organizations hold the same dislike for uncertainty. If, for example, the introduction by a book publisher of a desk-top publishing system means that editorial personnel will have to learn to do their entire jobs on computers, some of these people may fear they will be unable to learn the intricacies of the system. They may, therefore, develop a negative attitude toward working with desk-top publishing or behave dysfunctionally if required to use the system.

Selective Information Processing. As we learned in Chapter 3, individuals shape their world through their perceptions. Once they have created this world, it resists change. So individuals are guilty of selectively processing information in order to keep their perceptions intact. They hear what they want to hear. They ignore information that challenges the world they've created. To return to the book editor who are faced with the introduction of desk-top publishing, they may ignore the arguments that their bosses make in explaining why the new equipment has been purchased or the potential benefits the change will provide them.

Organizational Resistance

Organizations, by their very nature, are conservative. They actively resist change. You don't have to look far to see evidence of this phenomenon. Government agencies want to continue doing what they have been doing for years, whether the need for their service changes or remains the same. Organized religions are deeply entrenched in their history. Attempts to change church doctrine requires great persistence and patience. Educational institutions, which exist to open minds and challenge established doctrine, are themselves extremely resistant to change. Most school systems are using essentially the same teaching technologies today as they were 50 years ago. The majority of business firms, too, appear highly resistant to change.

Six major sources of organizational resistance have been identified.

Structural Inertia. Organizations have built-in mechanisms to produce stability. For example, the selection process systematically selects certain people in and certain people out. Training and other socialization techniques reinforce specific role requirements and skills. Formalization provides job descriptions, rules, and procedures for employees to follow.

The people who are hired into an organization are chosen for fit; they are then shaped and directed to behave in certain ways. When an organization is confronted with change, this structural inertia acts as a counterbalance to sustain stability.

Limited Focus of Change. Organizations are made up of a number of interdependent subsystems. You can't change one without affecting the others. For example, if management changes the technological processes without simultaneously modifying the organization's structure to match, the change in technology is not likely to be accepted. So limited changes in subsystems tend to get nullified by the larger system.

Group Inertia. Even if individuals want to change their behavior, group norms may act as a constraint. An individual union member, for instance, may be willing to accept changes in his job suggested by management. But if union norms dictate resisting any unilateral change made by management, he's likely to resist.

Threat to Expertise. Changes in organizational patterns may threaten the expertise of specialized groups. The introduction of decentralized personal computers, which allow managers to gain access to information directly from a company's mainframe, is an example of a change that was strongly resisted by many information systems departments in the early 1980s. Why? Because decentralized, end-user computing was a threat to the specialized skills held by those in the centralized information systems departments.

Threat to Established Power Relationships. Any redistribution of decision-making authority can threaten long established power relationships within the organization. Introduction of participative decision making or autonomous work teams are examples of changes that are often seen as threats to the power of supervisors and middle managers.

Threat to Established Resource Allocations. Those groups in the organization that control sizable resources often see change as a threat. They tend to be content with the way things are. Will the change, for instance, mean a reduction in their budgets or a cut in their staff size? Those who most benefit from the current allocation of resources are often threatened by changes that may affect future allocations.

Overcoming Resistance to Change

Six tactics have been suggested for use by change agents in dealing with resistance to change.[4] Let's review them briefly.

Education and Communication. Resistance can be reduced through communicating with employees to help them see the logic of a change. This tactic basically assumes that the source of resistance lies in misinformation or poor communication: If employees receive the full facts and get any misunderstandings cleared up, resistance will subside. This can be achieved through one-on-one discussions, memos, group presentations, or reports. Does it work? It does, provided that the source of resistance is inadequate communication and that management-employee relations are characterized by mutual trust and credibility. If these conditions do not exist, the change is unlikely to succeed. Additionally, the time and effort that this tactic involves must be considered against its advantages, particularly when the change affects a large number of people.

Participation. It's difficult for individuals to resist a change decision in which they participated. Prior to making a change, those opposed can be brought into the decision process. Assuming the participants have the expertise to make a meaningful contribution, their involvement can reduce resistance, obtain commitment, and increase the quality of the change decision. However, against these advantages are the negatives: potential for a poor solution and great time consumption.

Facilitation and Support. Change agents can offer a range of supportive efforts to reduce resistance. When employee fear and anxiety are high, employee counseling and therapy, new skills training, or a short paid leave of absence may facilitate adjustment. The drawback of this tactic is that, as with the others, it is time consuming. Additionally, it is expensive, and its implementation offers no assurance of success.

Negotiation. Another way for the change agent to deal with potential resistance to change is to exchange something of value for a lessening of the resistance. For instance, if the resistance is centered in a few powerful individuals, a specific reward package can be negotiated that will meet their individual needs. Negotiation, as a tactic, may be necessary when resistance comes from a powerful source. Yet one cannot ignore its potentially high costs. Additionally,

---

[4] John P. Kotter and Leonard A. Schlesinger, "Choosing Strategies for Change," *Harvard Business Review* (March-April 1979), pp. 106–14.

there is the risk that, once a change agent negotiates to avoid resistance, he or she is open to the possibility of being blackmailed by other individuals in positions of power.

Manipulation and Cooptation. Manipulation refers to covert influence attempts. Twisting and distorting facts to make them appear more attractive, withholding undesirable information, or creating false rumors to get employees to accept a change are all examples of manipulation. If corporate management threatens to close down a particular manufacturing plant if that plant's employees fail to accept an across-the-board pay cut, and if the threat is actually untrue, management is using manipulation. Cooptation, on the other hand, is a form of both manipulation and participation. It seeks to buy off the leaders of a resistance group by giving them a key role in the change decision. The leaders' advice is sought, not to seek a better decision, but to get their endorsement. Both manipulation and cooptation are relatively inexpensive and easy ways to gain the support of adversaries, but the tactics can backfire if the targets become aware they are being tricked or used. Once discovered, the change agent's credibility may drop to zero.

Coercion. Last on the list of tactics is coercion, that is, the application of direct threats or force on the resisters. If the corporate management mentioned in the previous discussion were really determined to close the manufacturing plant if employees did not acquiesce to a pay cut, then coercion would be the label attached to their change tactic. Other examples of coercion include threats of transfer, loss of promotions, negative performance evaluations, or a poor letter of recommendation. The advantages and drawbacks of coercion are approximately the same as those mentioned for manipulation and cooptation.

■ MANAGING CHANGE THROUGH ORGANIZATIONAL DEVELOPMENT

Organizational development refers to systematic, planned change. It's not an easily definable single concept. Rather, *organizational development (OD)* is a term used to encompass a collection of change techniques or interventions, from organization-wide changes in structure and systems to psychotherapeutic counseling sessions with groups and individuals, undertaken in response to changes in the external environment that seek to improve organizational effectiveness and employee well-being.

OD is built on humanistic-democratic values. In addition, OD characteristics that distinguish it from more traditional change approaches include (1) an emphasis on the work team as the key unit for learning more effective modes of organizational behavior, (2) an emphasis on participation and collaborative management, (3) an emphasis on changing the organization's culture, (4) the use of behavioral scientists as change agents; and (5) a view of the change effort as an ongoing process.[5]

What are some of the OD techniques and interventions for bringing about change? In this section, we review the more popular intervention techniques. We have categorized them under structural, task-technology, and people-focused interventions.

Structural Interventions

Structural OD interventions emphasize making organizations more organic and egalitarian. We can see this emphasis in OD programs that include major structural reorganization, introduction of new rewards systems, and efforts to change organizational cultures.

Structural Reorganization. Formal structures are not chiseled in stone. The structural configuration that was right for a firm in 1984 can put it at a competitive disadvantage in 1994. So structural reorganization may be necessary. Recent trends indicate that structures are becoming flatter, more decentralized, and more organic. Notice that these trends are all consistent with OD values.

OD change agents favor flatter organizations for at least three reasons. First, it provides economic benefits. By widening spans of control and cutting the number of vertical levels, the organization reduces administrative overhead costs because there are fewer managers. Second, fewer vertical levels improve communication. Third, wider spans of control typically result in employees having greater autonomy, since managers can't directly oversee their subordinates as closely.

Decentralized decision making is a popular intervention favored by OD change agents. Pushing authority downward creates power equalization. It allows people closest and most knowledgeable about an issue to make decisions regarding that issue. Decentralization also gives lower-level employees greater control over their work.

The trend in OD structural interventions has been toward making organizations more organic. Relating to Chapter 13, OD change agents are trying to make organizations less bureaucratic so they can respond more quickly to changes in the environment. Where bureaucratic structures are necessary to maintain competitive efficiency, OD change agents have often favored adding organic subunits to gain flexibility. IBM, for instance, developed its personal computer in a small organic unit located in Florida, far from the company's headquarters in New York. Once the PC was designed by the Florida group, responsibility for the product was subsumed by the company's large and efficient production and marketing bureaucracies.

---

[5] Adapted from Wendell L. French and C.H. Bell, Jr., *Organization Development: Behavioral Science Interventions for Organization Improvement*, 4th ed. (Englewood Cliffs, NJ: Prentice Hall, 1990), pp. 17–21.

Major structural reorganizations are typically quite disruptive and threatening to those people affected. As a result, OD change agents favor employees actively participating in the reorganization process.

New Reward Systems. OD change agents enthusiastically endorse operant conditioning's notion that behavior is a function of its consequences. This focuses attention on the organization's reward system.

Generally speaking, organizations did a poor job in the postwar era in linking rewards to employee performance. Production workers increasingly were paid by the hour rather than by output. Clerical and managerial personnel received a monthly salary that often had little direct relationship to productivity. In recent years, organizations have moved to enact "pay-for-performance" programs. OD change agents have been actively involved in helping to develop and implement these programs. While individual-based bonus plans are most popular, OD change agents typically favor plans that emphasize group and organizational performance in order to facilitate teamwork and cooperation.

Changing Organizational Culture. The challenges involved in changing an organization's culture were addressed in the previous chapter. Among those who argue that change is possible, it is still clear that it's a long-term process.

Regardless of the difficulty, many major corporations—for example, AT&T, Xerox, Scott Paper, and Ford Motor Company—have undertaken the task. Interestingly, consistent with OD values, the changes have been almost exclusively toward introducing new cultural values that support less management control, increased tolerance for risk and conflict, and opening up communication channels. Many large and historically successful organizations have learned the hard way that cultures can become obsolete and create serious impediments for responding to a changing environment. The emphasis has moved toward making organizational cultures more flexible, more responsive, and more focused on customer needs, service, and quality.

For those organizations taking on the task, what are they doing? They're reorganizing; replacing and reassigning people in key positions; changing their reward systems; creating new stories, symbols, and rituals; and modifying their selection and socialization processes to hire and support individuals who will espouse the new values.

Task-Technology Interventions

Task-technology interventions emphasize changing the actual jobs that people do and/or the technological processes and tools they use to perform these jobs. Included in this category are job redesign, sociotechnical systems, and quality-of-work life programs.

Job Redesign. We have discussed job redesign in Chapter 5. Examples of redesign interventions include job rotation, enlargement, enrichment, and autonomous work teams.

Job redesign is similar to structural reorganization except instead of focusing the change effort at the level of the organization, the focus is at the job level. As a result, in contrast to organization redesign, job redesign is more widely practiced and can be implemented by lower-level supervisors as well as by senior-level managers.

OD change agents have actively promoted the redesign of jobs along the lines suggested by the job characteristics model. That is, they have sought to take jobs and increase their skill variety, task identity and significance, autonomy, and feedback.

Successful job redesign interventions that follow the job characteristics model share several common qualities. They have cultures that support employee autonomy and participation, they have low formalization that allows flexibility in redesigning tasks, and they either are nonunionized organizations or have the support of the union.

Sociotechnical Systems. The accomplishment of any task requires a technology and a social system. The technology consists of the tools, techniques, procedures, skills, knowledge, and devices used by employees to do their jobs. The social system comprises the people who work in the organization and their interrelationships. Proponents of a *sociotechnical systems* approach to change argue that any successful work design must jointly optimize the social and the technological demands of the job.

When originally introduced in the 1950s, the sociotechnical systems perspective was one of the first to recognize that the needs of both the organization *and* the individual employee had to be considered in the design of work. Technology constrains the social system by shaping the behaviors required to operate it. However, if job designers ignore the personalities and attitudes of workers, their interaction patterns, their relationships with their supervisors, and the like, then the best designed technical system will fail to achieve its full potential.

For change agents who want to use sociotechnical systems as a guide in redesigning jobs, what should they do? Probably the best place to begin is to conceptualize work design as organizing *groups* of workers rather than *individuals* alone. Then the various technologies that are within the feasible set for achieving the group's objectives can be evaluated to find the proper match.

Quality of Work Life. As noted in Chapter 5, the term quality of work life (QWL) describes a process by which an organization responds to employee needs by developing mechanisms to allow them to share fully in making the decisions that design their lives at work. It may help to think of QWL as an umbrella concept that encompasses literally dozens of specific interventions that have a common goal of humanizing the workplace.

While QWL encompasses a large number of interventions, one author has divided them into eight specific categories:[6]

1. Adequate and fair compensation
2. A safe and healthy environment
3. Jobs that develop human capacities
4. A chance for personal growth and security
5. A social environment that provides personal identity, freedom from prejudice, a sense of community, and upward mobility
6. Rights of personal privacy, dissent, and due process
7. A work role that minimizes infringement on personal leisure and family needs
8. Socially responsible organizational actions

Any comprehensive list of QWL programs would encompass job redesign, participative management, and flextime, as well as programs that offer employees the opportunity to purchase equity in their firms, or programs that provide protection against arbitrary action by their supervisors.

People-Focused Interventions

The vast majority of OD intervention efforts have been directed at changing the attitudes and behaviors of organization members through the processes of communication, decision making, and problem solving. While this group of interventions could include corporate training programs and management development, OD has emphasized five specific people-focused interventions: sensitivity training, survey feedback, process consultation, team building, and intergroup development.

Sensitivity Training. It can go by a variety of names—laboratory training, *sensitivity training*, encounter groups, or T-groups (training groups)—but all refer to a method of changing behavior through unstructured group interaction. Members are brought together in a free and open environment in which participants discuss themselves and their interactive processes, loosely directed by a professional behavioral scientist. The group is process oriented, which means that individuals learn through observing and participating rather than being told. The professional creates the opportunity for participants to express their ideas, beliefs, and attitudes. He or she does not accept—in fact, overtly rejects—any leadership role.

The objectives of the T-groups are to provide the subjects with increased awareness of their own behavior and how others perceive them, greater sensitivity to the behavior of others, and increased understanding of group processes. Specific results sought include increased ability to empathize with others,

---

6 Richard E. Walton, "Improving the Quality of Work Life," *Harvard Business Review* (May-June 1974), p. 12.

improved listening skills, greater openness, increased tolerance of individual differences, and improved conflict resolution skills.

If individuals lack awareness of how others perceive them, then the successful T-group can effect more realistic self-perceptions, greater group cohesiveness, and a reduction in dysfunctional interpersonal conflicts. Further, it will ideally result in a better integration between the individual and the organization.

Survey Feedback. One tool for assessing attitudes held by organizational members, identifying discrepancies among member perceptions, and solving these differences is the *survey feedback* approach.

Everyone in an organization can participate in survey feedback, but of key importance is the organizational family—the manager of any given unit and those employees who report directly to him or her. A questionnaire is usually completed by all members in the organization or unit. Organization members may be asked to suggest questions or may be interviewed to determine what issues are relevant. The questionnaire typically asks members for their perceptions and attitudes on a broad range of topics, including decision-making practices; communication effectiveness; coordination between units; and satisfaction with the organization, job, peers, and their immediate supervisor.

The data from this questionnaire are tabulated with data pertaining to an individual's specific "family" and to the entire organization and distributed to employees. These data then become the springboard for identifying problems and clarifying issues that may be creating difficulties for people. In some cases, the manager may be counseled by an external change agent about the meaning of the responses to the questionnaire and may even be given suggested guidelines for leading the organizational family in group discussion of the results. Particular attention is given to the importance of encouraging discussion and ensuring that discussions focus on issues and ideas and not on attacking individuals.

Finally, group discussion in the survey feedback approach should result in members identifying possible implications of the questionnaire's findings. Are people listening? Are new ideas being generated? Can decision making, interpersonal relations, or job assignments be improved? Answers to questions like these, it is hoped, will result in the group agreeing on commitments to various actions which will remedy the problems that are identified.

Process Consultation. No organization operates perfectly. Managers often sense that their unit's performance can be improved, but they are unable to identify what can be improved and how it can be improved. The purpose of *process consultation* is for an outside consultant to assist a client, usually a manager, to perceive, understand, and act on process events with which he or she must deal. These might include work flow, informal relationships among unit members, and formal communication channels.

Process consultation (PC) is similar to sensitivity training in its assumption that organizational effectiveness can be improved by dealing with interpersonal problems, and in its emphasis on involvement. But PC is more task directed than sensitivity training.

Consultants in PC are there to give the clients insight into what is going on around them, within them, and between them and other people. They do not solve the organization's problems. Rather, the consultant is a guide or coach who advises on the process to help the clients solve their own problems.

The consultant works with the client in *jointly* diagnosing what processes need improvement. The emphasis is on jointly, because the client develops a skill at analyzing processes within his or her unit that can be continually called on long after the consultant is gone. Additionally, by having the client actively participate in both the diagnosis and the development of alternatives, there will be greater understanding of the process and the remedy and less resistance to the action plan chosen.

Importantly, the process consultant need not be an expert in solving the particular problem that is identified. The consultant's expertise lies in diagnosis and developing a helping relationship. If the specific problem uncovered requires technical knowledge outside the client and consultant's expertise, the consultant helps the client to locate such an expert and then instructs the client in how to get the most out of this expert resource.

Team Building. Organizations are made up of people working together to achieve a common end. Since people are frequently required to work in groups, considerable attention has been focused in OD on *team building*.

Team building can be applied within groups or at the intergroup level where activities are interdependent. For our discussion, we emphasize the intragroup level and leave intergroup development to the next section. As a result, our interest concerns applications to organizational families (command groups), as well as committees, project teams, and task groups.

The activities that form team building can typically include goal setting, development of interpersonal relations among team members, role analysis to clarify each member's role and responsibilities, and team process analysis. Of course, team building may emphasize or exclude certain activities, depending on the purpose of the development effort and the specific problems with which the team is confronted. Basically, however, team building attempts to use high interaction among group members to increase trust and openness.

It may be beneficial to begin by having members attempt to define the goals and priorities of the group. This will bring to the surface different perceptions of what the group's purpose may be. Following this, members can evaluate the group's performance—how effective are they in structuring priorities and achieving their goals? This should identify potential problem areas. This self-critique of means and ends can be done with the total group present or, where large size impinges on a free interchange of views, may initially take place in smaller groups followed up by the sharing of their findings with the total group.

Team building can also address itself to the clarification of each member's role in the group. Previous ambiguities can be brought to the surface. For some individuals, it may offer one of the few opportunities they have had to think through what their job is all about and what specific tasks they are expected to carry out if the group is to optimize its effectiveness.

Still another team building activity can be similar to that performed by the process consultant, that is, to analyze key processes that go on within the team to identify the way work is performed and how these processes might be improved to make the team more effective.

Intergroup Development. A major area of concern in OD is the dysfunctional conflict that exists between groups. As a result, change efforts have been directed toward improving intergroup relations.

Intergroup development seeks to change the attitudes, stereotypes, and perceptions that groups have of each other. For example, in one company the engineers saw the accounting department as composed of shy and conservative types, and the human resources department as having a bunch of "smiley-types who sit around and plan company picnics." Such stereotypes can have an obvious negative impact on the coordinative efforts between the departments.

Although there are a number of approaches for improving intergroup relations, a popular method emphasizes problem solving. In this method, members of each group meet independently to develop lists of their perception of themselves, the other group, and how they believe the other group perceives them. The groups then share their lists, after which similarities and differences are discussed. Differences are clearly articulated, and the groups look for the causes of the disparities.

Are the groups' goals at odds? Were perceptions distorted? On what basis were stereotypes formulated? Have some differences been caused by misunderstandings of intentions? Have words and concepts been defined differently by each group? Answers to questions like these clarify the exact nature of the conflict. Once the causes of the difficulty have been identified, the groups can move to the integration phase and work to develop solutions that will improve relations between the groups.

Subgroups, with members from each of the conflicting groups, can now be created for further diagnosis and to begin to formulate possible alternative actions that will improve relations.

■ CONTEMPORARY ISSUES IN ORGANIZATIONAL CHANGE

For many employees, change creates stress. As a result, many managers are asking, *How do I reduce stress among my work staff?* One of the most popular phrases managers are currently using to describe their change objectives is "to empower our employees." *How do managers empower their people?*

"Innovate or die" is another popular phrase in management circles. *What can managers do to help their organizations becomes more innovative*? In the following pages, we address these three questions.

Work Stress

Stress is a dynamic condition in which an individual is confronted with an opportunity, constraint, or demand related to what he or she desires and for which the outcome is perceived to be both uncertain and important.

Stress is not necessarily bad in and of itself. While stress is often discussed in a negative context, it also has a positive value, particularly when it offers a potential gain. For example, it often helps athletes or stage performers achieve a superior performance in a critical situation. However, stress is more often associated with constraints and demands. A constraint prevents you from doing what you desire; demands refer to the loss of something desired. When you take a test at school or you undergo your annual performance review at work, you feel stress because you confront opportunity, constraints, and demands. A good performance review may lead to a promotion, greater responsibilities, and a higher salary. But a poor review may prevent you from getting the promotion. An extremely poor review might cause you to be fired.

Symptoms of Stress. What signs indicate that an employee's stress level might be too high? Stress shows itself in a number of ways. For instance, an employee who is experiencing a high level of stress may develop high blood pressure, ulcers, irritability, difficulty in making routine decisions, loss of appetite, accident proneness, and the like. These symptoms can be subsumed under three general categories: physiological, psychological, and behavioral.

Most of the early concern with stress was directed at physiological symptoms. This was predominantly because the topic was researched by specialists in the health and medical sciences. This research led to the conclusion that stress could create changes in metabolism, increase heart and breathing rates, increase blood pressure, bring on headaches, and induce heart attacks.

The link between stress and particular physiological symptoms is not clear. There are few, if any, consistent relationships. This is attributed to the complexity of the symptoms and the difficulty in measuring them objectively. But physiological symptoms have the least direct relevance to managers.

Of greater importance are the psychological symptoms. Stress can cause dissatisfaction. Job-related stress can cause job-related dissatisfaction. Job dissatisfaction, in fact, is the simplest and most obvious psychological effect of stress. But stress shows itself in other psychological states—for instance, tension, anxiety, irritability, boredom, and procrastination. Behaviorally related stress symptoms include changes in productivity, absence, and turnover, as well as changes in eating habits, increased smoking or consumption of alcohol, rapid speech, fidgeting, and sleep disorders.

Reducing Stress. Not all stress is dysfunctional. Moreover, realistically, stress can never be totally eliminated from a person's life, either off the job or on. As we review stress reduction techniques, keep in mind that our concern is with reducing the part of stress which is dysfunctional.

In terms of organizational factors, any attempt to lower stress levels has to begin with employee *selection*. Management needs to make sure that an employee's abilities match the requirements of the job. When employees are in over their heads, their stress levels will typically be high. An objective job preview during the selection process will also lessen stress by reducing ambiguity. Improved organizational communications will keep ambiguity-induced stress to a minimum. Similarly, a goal-setting program will clarify job responsibilities and provide clear performance objectives. Job redesign is also a way to reduce stress. If stress can be traced directly to boredom or work overload, jobs should be redesigned to increase challenge or reduce the work load. Redesigns that increase opportunities for employees to participate in decisions and to gain social support have also been found to lessen stress.

Stress that arises from an employee's personal life creates two problems. First, it is more difficult for the manager to directly control. Second, there are ethical considerations. Specifically, does the manager have any right to intrude—even in the most subtle ways—in the employee's personal life? If a manager believes it is ethical and the employee is receptive, there are a few approaches the manager can consider. Employee *counseling* can provide stress relief. Employees often want to talk to someone about their problems; and the organization—through its managers, in-house personnel counselors, or free or low-cost outside professional help—can meet that need. For employees whose personal lives suffer from a lack of planning and organization that, in turn, creates stress, the offering of a *time management program* may prove beneficial in helping them to sort out their priorities. Still another approach is organizationally sponsored *physical activity programs*. Some large corporations employ physical fitness specialists who provide employees with exercise advice, teach relaxation techniques, and show individual employees physical activities they can use to keep their stress levels down.

Empowerment

We empower people by putting them in charge of what they do. But how does a manager specifically empower his or her employees? How does he or she enact changes to give employees more control? Actually, there are a number of actions that lead to empowering employees. In aggregate, the following will empower your people.

1. *Use participative decision making.* By including employees in the decision process, managers share their power.
2. *Delegate authority.* Delegation is more empowering than participation because delegation requires giving up authority and distributing it to employees.

3. *Create autonomous work teams.* By allowing employees to select and train new group members, allocate activities and schedule work, set production levels, and solve operating problems, they take ownership of their work.

4. *Install upward performance appraisals.* By using subordinates' ratings of how well their bosses manage, the organization becomes less hierarchical and the power of supervisors is lessened.

5. *Lessen formalization.* Employees have greater autonomy when rules and regulations are reduced.

6. *Encourage goal setting.* Help people set goals, then let them select the means for reaching those goals.

7. *Train employees.* Train workers so they have the skills to take charge of their work and make appropriate decisions. This includes things like scheduling, reading blueprints, negotiating with suppliers, and writing up purchasing specifications.

8. *Reeducate managers.* Empowerment requires managers to let go. For many, this is very hard. So managers need to undergo training to learn how to stop being the "boss" and how to become a "coach" and "facilitator."

Stimulating Innovation

3M Company has set the standard for guiding managers in how to make their organizations more innovative. 3M has developed a reputation for being able to stimulate innovation over a long period of time. It has a stated objective that 25 percent of each division's profits are to come from products developed in the prior five years. In 1990 alone, 3M launched more than two hundred new products and better than 30 percent of its $13 billion in revenues came from products introduced since 1986.

What's the secret of 3M's success? What can other organizations do to clone 3M's track record for innovation? While there is no guaranteed formula, certain characteristics surface again and again when researchers study innovative organizations. We group them into structural, cultural, and human resource categories. Our message to change agents is that they should consider introducing these characteristics into their organization if they want to create an innovative climate.

Structural Variables. Structural variables have been the most studied potential source of innovation. Findings on the structure-innovation relationship lead to the following conclusions: First, organic structures positively influence innovation. Because they're lower in vertical differentiation, formalization, and centralization, organic organizations facilitate the flexibility, adaptation, and cross-fertilization that make the adoption of innovations easier. Second, long tenure in management is associated with innovation. Managerial tenure apparently provides legitimacy and knowledge of how to accomplish tasks and obtain desired outcomes. Third, innovation is nurtured where there are slack resources. Having an abundance of resources allows an organization to afford to purchase innovations, bear the cost of instituting innovations, and absorb failures. Finally, interunit communication is high in innovative organizations. These organizations are high users of committees, task forces, and other mechanisms that facilitate interaction across departmental lines.

Cultural Variables. Innovative organizations tend to have similar cultures. They encourage experimentation. They reward both successes and failures. They celebrate mistakes. Unfortunately, in too many organizations, people are rewarded for the *absence* of failures rather than for the *presence* of successes. Such cultures extinguish risk taking and innovation. People will suggest and try new ideas only where they feel such behaviors exact no penalties.

Human Resource Variables. We find that innovative organizations actively promote the training and development of their members so that they keep current, offer high job security so employees don't fear getting fired for making mistakes, and encourage individuals to become champions of change. Once a new idea is developed, champions of change actively and enthusiastically promote the idea, build support, overcome resistance, and ensure that the innovation is implemented.

Summary. Given the status of 3M as a premier product innovator, we would expect it to have most or all of the properties we've identified. And it does. The company is so highly decentralized that it has many of the characteristics of small organic organizations. All of 3M's scientists and managers are challenged to keep current. Idea champions are created and encouraged by allowing scientists and engineers to spend up to 15 percent of their time on projects of their own choosing. The company encourages its employees to take risks— and rewards the failures as well as the successes. And very importantly, 3M doesn't hire and fire with the business cycle. During the 1991–1992 recession, while almost all major companies cut costs by firing employees, 3M initiated no layoffs.

■ IMPLICATIONS FOR MANAGERS

The need for change has been implied throughout this book. It encompasses almost all of the concepts within organizational behavior. Think about attitudes, perceptions, teams, leadership, motivation, organization design, and the like. It is impossible to think about these concepts without inquiring about change.

If environments were perfectly static, if employees' skills and abilities were always up-to-date and incapable of deteriorating, and if tomorrow was always exactly the same as today, organizational change would have little or no relevance to managers. But the real world is turbulent, requiring organizations and their members to undergo dynamic change if they are to perform at competitive levels.

In the past, managers could treat change as an occasional disturbance in their otherwise peaceful and predictable world. Such a world no longer exists for most managers. Today's managers are increasingly finding that their world is one of constant and chaotic change. In this world, managers must be continually acting as change agents.

$\mathcal{S}$UGGESTIONS FOR FURTHER READING

BURKE, W. WARNER, AND GEORGE H. LITWIN, "A Causal Model of Organizational Performance and Change," *Journal of Management*, September 1992, pp. 523–45.

GOODSTEIN, LEONARD D., AND W. WARNER BURKE, "Creating Successful Organization Change," *Organizational Dynamics*, Spring 1991, pp. 5–17.

KAHN, ROBERT L., AND PHILIPPE BYOSIERE, "Stress in Organizations," in M.D. Dunnette and L.M. Hough, eds., *Handbook of Industrial & Organizational Psychology*, 2nd ed., Vol. 3 (Palo Alto, CA: Consulting Psychologists Press, 1992).

KANTER, ROSABETH M., "Transcending Business Boundaries: 12,000 World Managers View Change," *Harvard Business Review*, May-June 1991, pp. 151–64.

MONGE, PETER R., MICHAEL D. COZZENS, AND NOSHIR S. CONTRACTOR, "Communication and Motivational Predictors of the Dynamics of Organizational Innovation," *Organization Science*, May 1992, pp. 250–74.

PORRAS, JERRY I., AND PETER J. ROBERTSON, "Organizational Development: Theory, Practice, and Research," in M.D. Dunnette and L.M. Hough, eds., *Handbook of Industrial & Organizational Psychology*, 2nd ed., Vol. 3 (Palo Alto, CA: Consulting Psychologists Press, 1992).

SULLIVAN, SHERRY E., AND RABI S. BHAGAT, "Organizational Stress, Job Satisfaction and Job Performance: Where Do We Go from Here?" *Journal of Management*, June 1992, pp. 353–74.

WOODMAN, RICHARD W., JOHN E. SAWYER, AND RICKY W. GRIFFIN, "Toward a Theory of Organizational Creativity," *Academy of Management Review*, April 1993, pp. 293–321.

EPILOGUE

The end of a book typically has the same meaning to an author that it has to the reader: It generates feelings of both accomplishment and relief. As both of us rejoice at having completed our tour of the essential concepts in organizational behavior, this is a good time to examine where we have been and what it all means.

The underlying theme of this book has been that the behavior of people at work is *not* a random phenomenon. While employees are complex entities, their attitudes and behavior can nevertheless be explained and predicted with a reasonable degree of accuracy. Our approach has been to look at organizational behavior at three levels: the individual, the group, and the organization system.

We started with the individual and reviewed the major psychological contributions to understanding why individuals act as they do. We found that there are individual differences among employees. However, many of these differences can be systematically labeled and categorized, which allows for generalizations. For example, we know that individuals with a conventional type of personality are better matched to jobs in corporate management than are people with investigative personalities. So placing people into jobs that are compatible with their personality types should result in higher-performing and more satisfied employees.

Next, our analysis moved to the group level. We argued that the understanding of group behavior is more complex than merely multiplying what we know about individuals by the number of members in the group. Since people act differently when in a group than when alone, we demonstrated how roles, norms, leadership styles, power relationships, and other similar group factors impacted on the behavior of employees.

Finally, we overlaid system-wide variables on our knowledge of individual and group behavior to further improve our understanding of organizational behavior. Major emphasis was given to showing how an organization's structure, performance appraisal and reward systems, and culture affect both the attitudes and behavior of employees.

Looking back on this book's 16 chapters, it may be tempting to criticize the stress placed on theoretical concepts. But as a noted social psychologist once said, "There is nothing so practical as a good theory." Of course, it is also true that there is nothing so *impractical* as a good theory that leads nowhere. To avoid presenting theories that led nowhere, this book included a wealth of examples and illustrations. Additionally, we regularly stopped to inquire about the implications of theory for the practice of management. The result has been the presentation of numerous concepts that, individually, offer some insights into behavior, but which, when taken together, provide a complex system to help you explain, predict, and control organizational behavior.

INDEX